NO ONE'S
DEAD

NO ONE'S DEAD

THE JESUS MESSAGES

JONATHAN BEECHER

WHITE CROW

www.whitecrowbooks.com

He who fears death either fears the loss of all sensation, or fears a different kind of sensation. But if you will have no sensation, you will feel nothing, and if you acquire a different kind, you will be a different sort of living being and will not cease to live.

— Marcus Aurelius
Meditations

ACKNOWLEDGMENTS

My heartfelt thanks go to Astrid, Dougie, Jane, Martin, Mike, and Velin for your counsel, support, and help in bringing this book to fruition. Thanks also to Tom Whitmore at the Course in Miracles Society, Karl Jackson Barnes at the Leslie Flint Trust, and Sue Farrow at the Spiritual Truth Foundation for permissions.

CONTENTS

ACKNOWLEDGMENTS   vii

YOU GOT HERE!   5

WELCOME TO LEVEL ZERO   7

PART ONE: EVIDENCE FOR A GREATER REALITY   11

1. WHO'S CALLING?   13

2. WHY JESUS?   29

3. JESUS HERE, JESUS THERE: *Jesus, Jesus, Everywhere*   37

4. UNUSUAL PEOPLE   49

5. PSYCHIC STIGMA: *1542-2014*   67

6. THE ARCHBISHOP AND THE SPIRITUALISTS   79

7. ESP: *Real or Imagined?*   87

8. SPIRIT COMMUNICATION: *A Tricky Business*   95

9. WHY PADGETT?   111

10. RIDDLE   119

11. BELIEF: *Does it Matter?*   125

12. THREE BODIES: *Physical, Spirit, Soul*   133

PART TWO: I AM NOT GOD: 143

13. THE BIBLE: *Built on Shaky Foundations?*   145

    The Trinity   151

    The Original Jews for Jesus: Heretics or Truth Tellers?   152

Messiah	154
Original Sin: A Mocking Damnable Lie	157
Vicarious Atonement	160
In Christ	162
The Sonship	164
Baptism	165
Free Will	166
The Rapture: Vanities of Vanities	168
The Resurrection	169
Hell	172
14. PAST LIVES OR OTHER LIVES?	177
15. SENECA AND THE CRUCIFIXION	185
PART THREE: THE WIDE GATE: *The Road to Nowhere*	**193**
16. WAR: *Not in God's Name*	195
17. THE DIVINE RIGHT: *A Reckoning?*	209
18. EVERY DAY IS JUDGMENT DAY	217
19. SUICIDE: *Poor Perry Sees the Light*	225
PART FOUR: THE NARROW GATE: *The Road Ahead*	**233**
20. CROSSING OVER	235
21. PRAYER: *Meet Me Halfway*	243
22. THE NUMBERED LEVELS	253
23. IMMORTALITY: *The Great Gift*	261
EPILOGUE: *The Protagonist*	273
A Bit About Me	277
BIBLIOGRAPHY	281
REFERENCES	285
INDEX	293

THIS IS A POLEMIC AGAINST MATERIALIST PHILOSOPHY.

ITS PURPOSE IS TO GLEAN HIGHER TRUTHS.
HIGHER TRUTHS ARE THOSE THAT BECOME APPARENT WHEN
YOU'VE LEFT THE PHYSICAL WORLD.

WHEN YOU'RE DEAD.
EXCEPT YOU'RE NOT DEAD.

ACCORDING TO THE COMMUNICATORS IN THIS BOOK:

YOU ARE MORE THAN YOUR PHYSICAL BODY.
YOU CONTINUE AFTER DEATH IN WHAT IS KNOWN AS A SPIRIT
BODY.

DEATH IS AN ILLUSION.
YOU CANNOT DIE (FOR NOW).

EVERY HUMAN WHO HAS EVER LIVED BUT IS NO LONGER WITH US
STILL EXISTS IN WORLDS BEYOND THIS ONE. THE COMMUNICATORS
CALL THEM LEVELS, PLANES, AND SPHERES.

HIGHER LEVELS DO NOT INDICATE GEOGRAPHICAL LOCATIONS
OR SUPERIORITY OVER OTHERS.
JUST A DEEPER UNDERSTANDING OF REALITY.

ALL DATA/MEMORIES ARE STORED.
A SPIRITUAL CREDIT SCORE IS OPERATING.

THE FIRST JUDGMENT IS WHEN YOU DISCOVER WHAT YOUR
SCORE IS.
AFTER YOU HAVE LEFT THE PHYSICAL WORLD.

THE SYSTEM IS FULLY AUTOMATED.
YOUR CONSCIENCE IS THE JUDGE.

YOU ARE YOUR OWN ARCHITECT.
YOU ARE CREATING YOUR POST-PHYSICAL ENVIRONMENT RIGHT
NOW.

THERE IS NO HELL AS CHRISTIANITY TEACHES.
IT'S NOT A PERMANENT STATE.
ALTHOUGH WE MIGHT EXPERIENCE HELLISH ENVIRONMENTS
UNTIL OUR SCORE IS SETTLED.

THE PURPOSE OF SOUL INCARNATION IS INDIVIDUALIZATION.
THE PURPOSE OF SOUL INDIVIDUALIZATION IS TO OBTAIN DIVINE
LOVE.

THE PURPOSE OF DIVINE LOVE IS TO ACHIEVE IMMORTALITY.
IMMORTALITY MEANS TO NO LONGER BE BOUND TO THE
LIMITATIONS OF THE NUMBERED LEVELS.

IT'S AN ACCESS-ALL-AREAS PASS.
IMMORTALITY IS OPT-IN. IT'S A GIFT NOT AN OBLIGATION.

IT'S A PERFECT SYSTEM.

BASED ON LOVE

Some of the names of those still living in the physical world have been omitted for the sake of privacy or because they're not important to the story. Names of the dead have been included as reported. Saints from the gospels such as St. Paul and St. John are recorded as Paul and John. Yeshua is recorded as Jesus.

YOU GOT HERE!

You are truly privileged to be on this little planet, which some call the only planet of choice. Here, anything goes. You might be at the end of your life or just getting started. You might be getting married, filing for divorce, in a war zone, languishing in prison, terminally ill, in the depths of depression, feeling suicidal, or leading a happy life. You might be a movie star, a president, a queen, or a king. You might be doing menial tasks to scratch out a living. The important thing is you got here!

According to the communicators in this book, you have already achieved your aim, which as a soul of the human variety, is to individualize, and the only way for a soul to individualize and begin the journey home, is to attach itself to a fetus. As far as we know, the only place where this happens is here—the physical world—the starting point for the individualized soul.

WELCOME TO LEVEL ZERO

In 2021, Robert Bigelow, a Las Vegas entrepreneur, launched a competition to find the best evidence for survival after bodily death.[1] The first prize was $500,000, with total prize money amounting to almost $2 million.

Bigelow has had personal experiences and is somewhat familiar with the enormous body of literature demonstrating evidence for survival—evidence that could be argued goes beyond a reasonable doubt, beyond chance, and can't be attributed to coincidence, fraud, delusion, or wishful thinking by those reporting the events. And this doesn't include the metaphysical and religious literature that has been passed down to us over the past few thousand years.

He says he doesn't personally need more evidence but wants to encourage debate. He's a truth seeker, and there aren't too many of those around, at least not many who are willing and able to invest large amounts of money in an attempt to find an answer to what could be argued is one of the most important questions.

It's actually a two-part question: (a) do we survive death? And (b) if we do, do our thoughts and actions here have consequences after death?

Bigelow is familiar with the evidence for phenomena suggesting we are more than our physical bodies, and that under certain conditions we can receive information and experience connectivity with others, alive and dead, and have knowledge of past and future events not accessible using our physical senses. This happens to many people in many ways, including a near-death experience (NDE); out-of-body experience (OBE); remote viewing (a form of clairvoyance); clairvoyance; electronic voice phenomena; mediumship; deathbed visions; precognition; telepathy; distant healing; psychokinesis; experience of other lives; shared

7

dreams—the list goes on. This is important evidence because, logically, to exist after our physical body is no longer functioning, we need to be more than a physical body.

Not just anyone could participate in the competition; the applicants had to have extensive experience or exposure to research suggesting that our consciousness survives death. More than 1,300 people applied, and 205 were invited to submit essays. No essay could exceed 25,000 words, so potentially 5 million words could have been submitted.

Of course, there would have been some duplication, but that's a lot of evidence for something that materialist philosophy—the foundation of our academic institutions—denies the existence of. At one end of the spectrum, materialists insist they are the arbiters of truth, while at the other, religious fundamentalists have faith that they have the answers. Meanwhile, in the middle lies a vast body of evidence which suggests both propositions might be incorrect.

Most, if not all, of us "free-thinking" atheists don't contemplate the question of surviving death and satisfy ourselves with the idea that religions are manmade organizations designed to control the masses—and there's plenty of evidence to make that case. But many religious organizations do great work—altruistic work, helping those in need—and they rely on the good will of people who desire or are willing to help others. Fortunately, there are billions of those people around the world.

When I say "us" I'm including my former self in that atheist cohort. By atheist, I really mean materialist. Buddhists don't believe the soul or God exists, but they do believe in some sort of afterlife, so they could be considered atheists if we define atheism solely as "The belief that no god or gods exist."

The materialist model of reality proposes that the physical universe is all that exists, with everything in it arising through non-conscious physical and chemical processes. According to this worldview, life has no inherent meaning beyond what contributes to survival and reproduction. All experienced phenomena are ultimately reducible to matter, and the existence of spiritual entities—such as the soul, spirit, or God—is rejected.

A typical response to the question of survival is, "No one has ever come back after death, so there's no proof." But time and time again, in different parts of the world as far back as we have records, there is evidence that someone or something is communicating from beyond the grave.

The communicators tell us they are not bound by space and time. They are what some scientists call nonlocal, meaning they can influence something instantly, even where there is what we would perceive as a physical separation. They send messages in various ways, such as through a medium, a dream, electrical equipment, or a vision. Some communicators claim to be nonhuman (and in some instances, animals), but in this book we are only concerned with humans.

Religions, particularly the Judeo-Christian denominations, are all based on ancient texts which have been copied, edited, translated, interpreted, misinterpreted, and altered over thousands of years. What they all have in common is the idea that our beliefs and actions here determine our existence after death.

The communicators tell us no one's dead. Every person is still alive—whether it be a fetus, a stillborn child, or someone who lived to be a hundred. When they say everyone, assuming they are talking about Homo sapiens, by some estimates, the total number of people who have been born since 190,000 BCE is 117 billion.[2] Minus the 8 billion currently living here, that means potentially 109 billion people, give or take a few billion, are still living their lives in levels beyond this one.

In today's world where virtual reality gaming is prevalent, futurists, physicists, and cosmologists ponder other dimensions and multiverses. At a time when tech companies are creating metaverses, "level" seems an appropriate term, and it could be said we are in level zero: the physical world.

The Game

Imagine you are playing a fully immersive multiplayer role-playing game (RPG) with many dimensions of time, levels, and worlds. At the start of the game, you are assigned a name and given a body to navigate the various worlds. You have 100 units of life force, represented as "natural love." The objective of the game is to progress to higher levels by dispensing love while ensuring your 100 units remain fully charged. With every unit you dispense, say by giving love to another, you receive another unit, so you'll always maintain your 100 units. If you inflict pain on others, your life force goes dark, and as you dispense darkness, you receive darkness in return. Once you reach the end of each level, your 100 units of life force determine the next level you enter. One hundred percent of natural love takes you to level two or higher, while too much darkness leads to level one.

At level zero, you can play any game you like within the parameters of the system. You might do Christlike things without even realizing it and engage in evil pursuits, knowing you will get away with it. However, when you leave this level, after an adjustment period, there's an accounting, and you will be attracted to whatever level is appropriate based on your beliefs and memories, which remain intact. Your baseline is fixed at that point; there's no regression, but to move to the next level, you must (a) accept that there is another level and (b) work through the memories of your experience.

Each level above zero is a consensus reality in which appearance and surroundings mirror the player's internal state. Players sending out negative, hateful thoughts manifest as repulsive, poverty-stricken beings in dark, foggy, hostile environments, while loving thoughts propel players to lighter, more beautiful worlds where they appear as beautiful beings. Incorrect, rigid belief systems create worlds within worlds in which, without a change of thought process, progress to the next level can be challenging. As a player's thoughts and beliefs align with the system, their environment and appearance change. Help from more advanced players is always available.

When all players have completed the journey, the game ends.

PART ONE

EVIDENCE FOR A GREATER REALITY

1

WHO'S CALLING?

A man from Pretoria, South Africa, currently living in the USA, builds rockets and is planning an ambitious mission to Mars.[1] Because of the time and vast distances involved, it is accepted that those who make the voyage won't return to earth. A number of people have already volunteered to go, fully aware they may not survive the journey, and even if they do, their short-term life expectancy will be precarious.

Imagine for a moment one of your friends or loved ones is part of the crew. If they made it, I'm sure some would be desperate to get a message back to earth, while others might be happy to have left home and couldn't care less about making contact.

Now imagine one of them communicates with you via computer, either in writing or by voice message. With the advent of artificial intelligence (AI), in that situation it would be hard if not impossible to be certain that the communicator was who they said they were. Obviously, you would try to ensure someone wasn't trying to trick you but how would you know the communication was genuine? You might never know for sure, but if you received information of a personal nature, however trivial, that's unknown to anyone else on Mars or here, you might be open to it. Ultimately, if you wanted to discover whether there were people living on Mars, you would probably have to consider messages from people who claim to be there. So it is between this world and the spirit world.

When a person appears to receive a message from someone who has died, it can be bewildering, inexplicable, confusing, joyful, stressful, or revelatory, depending on the person's worldview, their state of mind at the time, and the quality of the information. Some will put it out of their mind and later question whether it actually happened.

A person might be devastated from the loss of a loved one and in that situation it's natural to think they might look for signs—however opaque—that their loved one survived in some shape or form. Another—and I include myself in this group—might not be grieving or searching for answers, but, when faced with evidence they can't explain by normal means, dig deeper into the subject. This is not to say grieving people are less objective. My experience has been that once the door has been opened and a glimmer of light shines through, when it comes to evidence the bar is raised and the seeker often demands more specific information than the casual enquirer.

∞

The first time I visited a medium was in 2003. I wasn't bereft or grieving, but it had been a year since my friend B.J., who died in my house in 1988, had seemingly sent a message to me through a medium to a woman unknown to me.

In 2002, I was writing a journal one evening and B.J. popped into my mind. That prompted me to write about the circumstances of his death (a brain hemorrhage from a fall) and ask the question, had I made a different decision that day, such as taking him to a hospital, could his death have been avoided? While I was writing I took a break to make some toast, and when I turned the toaster on the kitchen electrics fused.

Later that week, a schoolfriend of my sister, whom I didn't know other than by name, rang her one evening to say his wife had a message for me. His wife, M.L., who didn't know me, had been to see a medium. During the sitting, she received a message for someone called John who, she was told, was connected to her. Her husband's name was John, and even though she didn't understand the content, when she arrived home she gave him the information thinking it might be for him.

I presume he knew about B.J.'s death in my home years earlier through my sister (although it could have been from the local paper), and he knew my name was Jon. He recognized that the message might be for me and called her. She then called me and asked me to call his wife, which I did, though at the time I didn't know her and had no idea why I was calling her.

M.L explained that her grandfather had died and she was feeling low. "One of my friends suggested I see someone," she said.

"Do you mean a therapist?" I asked.

"No, a medium."

At the time, I knew nothing about mediums, and momentarily I wondered if my sister was playing a trick on me, even though she hadn't before, nor since.

M.L. gave me information such as what B.J. did for a living, and described his personality accurately, all of which was information she could have obtained from elsewhere, even though she didn't know him or me, and had no other reason to contact me.

During our conversation, she said he had a message for me. "He said you've been thinking about him recently,"—which I had. He had been dead for fourteen years and I didn't think about him often, but that week he had popped into my mind, and for the first time, I had written about the circumstances of his death and asked whether I could have done anything about it.

She said, "He told me (via the medium) there was nothing you could have done. It was his time to go." Then added, "He said there's a problem with your kitchen electrics. We've had ours checked and they're fine."

The message meant nothing to her, her husband, my sister, or the medium, but for me it was highly evidential. Indeed, my electrics had fused while I was writing about him, which was interesting, but it was the answer to a specific question I was writing about that stopped me in my tracks. Neither she nor anyone else could have known about that and I couldn't explain it by normal means. I was at a loss as to how that communication occurred and wanted to understand more.

I began reading Arthur Findlay's books and other life after death literature, and became aware of the Arthur Findlay College,[2] his former home, a nineteenth-century mansion in Essex, England, which he bequeathed to the Spiritualists' National Union upon his death in 1964.

Findlay, born in Scotland in 1883, was a successful stockbroker, accountant, and magistrate. In 1918, he had a life-changing experience in Glasgow involving a medium named John Campbell Sloan. That encounter set him on a path to demonstrate that life after death was a fact, a mission to which he devoted the rest of his life.

The college still attracts aspiring mediums from all over the world and runs courses on Spiritualist philosophy and mediumship. On their website I found a medium named B.L., a Spiritualist minister and tutor at the college who appeared to be well thought of. B.L. didn't advertise any services so I wrote to her asking if she could recommend a medium and she agreed to see me.

I went to the sitting with an open-mind and with no expectations as to who might communicate, if anyone. I wasn't in my usual skeptical mindset but neither did I think I was being gullible or experiencing wishful thinking. On the way there I told myself to *keep my mind open and my mouth shut.*

Whenever I have sat with a medium, if they've asked if I'm trying to get in touch with anyone in particular, I have always said no, but I'm happy to hear from anyone if it might be helpful to me or others. I have never asked to communicate with anyone and always tried to be as neutral as possible with the idea that being calm and open-minded makes for a better sitting. Of course, it's natural to ask questions, particularly if you've lost a loved one, but generally, I've found the less they know about me, the better the evidence.

Before that first visit, I wrote a list of all the people I knew who had died. It was a long list, and while there was no one I particularly expected to hear from, I would have been more than happy to connect with any of them. B.L. knew nothing about me other than my name was Jon—I think I even called myself John because it's a more common spelling.

She asked for a modest fee and added that if I wasn't satisfied in the first ten minutes there would be no charge.

During the first few minutes of the sitting she said, "I have your father here." My father died two years before, that was correct. A two-to-one chance if she was guessing. Then she said, "You never lived with him."

The first time I remember meeting my father was when I was twenty-seven years old, so her second statement was also correct. Better than two-to-one odds.

She went on to describe his mannerisms and what he liked to do, which meant nothing to me. Then there was a pause—"He wants to show you something so you'll know it's him."

She held out her hand and said, "He's put a pigeon in my hand."

Shortly before my father's death in 2001, I received a call from his brother whom I'd never met, informing me he was dying. A few weeks later, I was at his funeral with my son, surrounded by his family and friends who were mostly unknown to us. It was a strange day.

After the service, I was talking to one of his brothers who I had just met, and I said, "The only memory I have of my father is pigeons. Why do I have a memory of pigeons?" He replied that they used to race pigeons and the loft was in dad's garden. "I still have a pigeon," he said. "It's called Eric!" He was still very involved with the pigeon-racing fraternity and later sent me a picture of my dad holding a pigeon.

Two years later, I was sitting with a medium who was telling me my dad was there and showing me a pigeon so I'd know it was him. I couldn't calculate the odds of that happening by chance or guessing.

∞

My mother's twin brother, John, died in the late eighties at the age of fifty-four. They were very close. A few weeks before his death, I was on my way to Heathrow airport to catch a flight to Miami when mom called to say he was in hospital, although she didn't know why. She was going on vacation and asked if I would visit him in her absence. I said I'd be back in a week and would head straight to the hospital if he was still there. Uncle John had been a continual presence in my life and we were close. A few months before, he'd told me he planned to retire at fifty-five, move to Portugal, and buy a fishing boat. He didn't have long to go.

After I returned to London, I called the hospital and was told he was having treatment. I drove straight there and arrived just as he had been informed by the doctor he had three months to live, maybe less. He was a big drinker and his liver had had enough. I broke the news to my mother and he died a few weeks later. Since that time, whenever his name was mentioned or when she looked at his photograph she would cry. It was sad to see.

After that first sitting with B.L., whenever I visited my parents, if I saw her getting upset, I'd say, "Don't worry about Uncle John, Mom. He's doing fine. He's around." She didn't know what to make of those statements, and they made dad (my stepfather) visibly uncomfortable.

Prior to my visit to B.L., we had never had conversations about life after death or anything like that. One day she said, "I know you haven't gone crazy and you're not lying to me, so I want you to organize for me to see the medium." Then dad piped up, "Me too." I was surprised he wanted to go but he insisted.

I called B.L. and made an appointment. I only gave their first names and didn't mention they were my parents. She probably would have guessed who they were but didn't ask and I wanted her to have as little information as possible.

On the way to the sitting I gave them a cassette each and suggested they record the sessions because it's easy to forget or embellish what happens after an event like that. Dad said he was worried about mom getting emotional. I said I thought she would probably have an evidential sitting because she was open-minded and in good spirits, whereas he might not because he didn't want to believe it was real. At the time I had this idea that as sitters, we can block things out. Parapsychologists studying extra-sensory perception (ESP) call it the experimenter effect: the idea that the motivation of the experimenter can affect the result of an experiment. Whether that's true or not I don't know, but anecdotally, it seems to be the case.

When we arrived at B.L.'s home, her husband made us a cup of tea. B.L. came in and said, "Who wants to go first?" Dad stood up. "I'll go first." He was usually quite a gentleman and it was unusual for him to put himself before my mother. I put it down to nerves. Dad and B.L. went to the other room while mom and I drank our tea.

Two minutes later they returned, and B.L. said to my mother, "Sometimes this happens. I think this is for you, not him. I'm getting a twin brother. Do you have a twin brother in Spirit?" Mom smiled and nodded, yes.

"He's here!"

And with that, she waved mom into the other room.

Dad sat down beside me and finished his tea. I said, "Did you tell her mom had a dead twin brother?"

"No, of course not! I never said a word." I thought the twin brother in spirit was a good start. There was no easy way for B.L. to have known that.

After her sitting, my mother told me about the evidence she received that her brother John had come through. For me, the most interesting part was the discussion about a photo.

B.L. said, "Your brother says you carry a picture of the two of you." Mom confirmed she usually did but didn't have it with her.

A few minutes later she said, "He's saying that you do have it with you."

Mum rummaged through her handbag but there was no sign of the picture. There was a pause and B.L. said, "He's being quite pedantic. He insists you have it with you."

She emptied the contents of her bag on the table. It was one of those big square leather bags, full of stuff she rarely needed. Then she pulled out her credit cards and receipts from her purse, and sure enough there was a small photo of the two of them tucked in the back.

B.L. also said her brother was there with her other brother. Mom had two brothers, John, deceased, and Dennis who was still alive.

"That's wrong," mom replied. "My brother is still alive."

"He's not talking about him. He says you have another brother in spirit."

Then she remembered her parents' first child was called Derek. He was born in Jersey, Channel Islands, which had limited medical facilities during the late 1920s. Derek died when he was three weeks old, before mom was born, which prompted her parents to move to London. Until that day, I hadn't been aware of Derek's existence.

Around thirty minutes later, dad came back into the room looking sheepish. We said goodbye to B.L., and I drove them home.

On the journey back, I said, "how did you get on, Dad?"

"Oh, nothing really," he replied.

"Nothing? You must've got something. Give me the tape and let's play it." But he wouldn't. For some reason, he didn't want us to hear what was on it. I asked him again what she'd said.

"Well," he replied, "she said I was a navy man, and there are a lot of women in my life with the initial 'V.'"

That was correct. Dad was in the navy during World War II, but most men of his age would have done national service in the army, navy, or air force, so if she was guessing, it would have been a one in three chance.

It's funny how the mind works; he was convinced there was nothing. He didn't even comment on mom's experience. We were joking about it.

"Hmm, let's see," I said. "A lot of women in your life with the initial V. Who could that possibly be?" Then I reminded him, "Your ex-wife's name is Vera, your daughter, Vanessa, your daughter-in-law, Victoria, and your granddaughter, Victoria. How many V's do you want!"

After that day, I never saw my mother get upset when her twin brother was mentioned. For me, that alone made it all worthwhile.

The following year, people were talking about Facebook, the new online network that had just launched. Dad, being an early adopter of technology, had signed up. On his profile, the lifelong atheist listed himself as "agnostic."

Since that time, I have received messages via mediums from communicators claiming to be my grandmother, her sister and brother, my father, stepmother, step-grandmother, two uncles, a business partner, three friends, an aborted baby girl presenting as a seven-year-old, and others. What all these messages had in common was, the mediums in question could not have known about my relationship with the communicators by normal means. In some cases, I was given information that even I didn't know, such as the names of my grandparents whom I never met, and the week of my father's birthday, which I wasn't aware of at the time. I found that information out later. In many of those cases, the communicators purported to be from my biological father's family.

My mother married my stepfather when I was four years old, and I grew up without any real knowledge or contact with my father or his side of the family, so it would have been highly unlikely or impossible for the mediums, whom in some cases I had just met, to have known about them, and even if they'd somehow done some background checks on me, they wouldn't have found their identities easily because I have a different family name than my father.

On one occasion, I was sitting outside a pub in London with a woman who had mediumistic abilities, whom I'll call I.D. I wasn't there for a reading and I hadn't paid her any money. She was visiting London and we had arranged to meet for lunch. While we were chatting, she suddenly said, "I have your mother's mother here. She's with her sister, Louise, and Bill. They're concerned about your mother. They say she's feeling very down at the moment, very low, and not telling you or the family about a problem she has. They say she must get the eye test."

After the message, I explained that my mother was a very positive person and not prone to getting depressed, and that as far as I knew she didn't have any eye problems. "I only tell you what they tell me," she replied, in a nonchalant sort of way.

Later that day, I called my mother and told her I'd had lunch with a medium, and that someone claiming to be her mother had come through and that her sister, Louise, and Bill were with her. She confirmed Louise and Bill were her mother's siblings. I remember some of my grandmother's relatives, and I asked her why I didn't recognize the name, Louise. She replied that when I was a child I called her Auntie Luli (pronounced Loolee).

"They told me you must go and have an eye test," I said. I could hear her coughing and spluttering at the end of the phone.

"Oh my God!" she replied. "It's all true. My eyesight has been deteriorating for months. I went to see the doctor and he told me I have cataracts, but before I have the operation I have to go for an eye test. I'm scared and haven't done anything about it. I haven't told anyone, not even your father, and it's been getting me down." I suggested she make the appointment and that I would take her, and since her deceased mother had advised her to get the test it would probably be fine, which it was.

I first met I.D. in 2008. We were sitting in a restaurant when she first told me she had someone there for me. On that occasion, she said it was a girl named Jackie who had died at a young age. Jackie said she was happy to be able to get through and wanted to thank me for visiting her just before she died.

When I was in my late teens, my then girlfriend, whom I later married, had a best friend named Jackie. Jackie was dating A.B. when she was diagnosed with terminal cancer. By then she was in her early twenties. Jackie wanted to get married before she died and A.B. being an honorable man, agreed. My wife and I went to their wedding and she passed away shortly after.

Twenty-five years had passed, and I had rarely thought about Jackie, yet ostensibly, here she was thanking me for visiting her just before her death. These are just a few personal examples and there are plenty of others that I don't have space for here.

Some philosophers and scientists who acknowledge the reality of ESP hypothesize an alternative to the spirit communicator explanation, which they call living agent psi (LAP).[3] The idea is that the medium can somehow tap into a cosmic reservoir of memories and access information without any deceased person being involved. However, this hypothesis doesn't adequately explain how "accessed information" could give specific advice to a living person, as in the case of my mother and her eye problem.

The LAP hypothesis suggests that information is not coming from deceased individuals, but instead from the living—perhaps through telepathy or another form of ESP—tapping into the memories of the sender and receiver. While this is one possible explanation, in some instances, the LAP hypothesis seems more far-fetched than the age-old spirit communicator explanation.

∞

In the New Testament we are told: "Dear friends, do not believe every spirit, but test the spirits to see whether they are from God, because many false prophets have gone out into the world. This is how you can recognize the Spirit of God: Every spirit that acknowledges that Jesus Christ has come in the flesh is from God, but every spirit that does not acknowledge Jesus is not from God. This is the spirit of the antichrist, which you have heard is coming and even now is already in the world (1 John 4:1–3)."

Before the arrival of Jesus, the Old Testament commanded: "A man or woman who is a medium or spiritist among you must be put to death. You are to stone them; their blood will be on their own heads" (Lev. 20:27).

Despite John's verse, many Christians ignore Jesus and instead defer to Leviticus. They may have stopped stoning mediums to death, but they reject any form of communication from beyond—even when the communicator acknowledges that Jesus is from God, or claims to be Jesus himself.

Paul wrote: "This is what we speak, not in words taught us by human wisdom but in words taught by the Spirit, explaining spiritual realities with Spirit-taught words (1 Cor. 2:13).

The stories of prophets in the Bible, the resurrection appearances, and angelic messages could all be seen as forms of spirit communication that seem very similar to what modern people might think of as mediumistic.

Jesus and Paul seemed to be implying that the world beyond this physical level can be as uncertain as this one. They weren't saying "don't accept spirit communication"; they were saying "be careful out there—you never know whom you might encounter."

We are bombarded on a daily basis with stories that politicians, bankers, doctors, scientists, spiritualists, priests, gurus, teachers, and others have scammed and misled people. Why would we expect them to be any different after death? Then there's the assumption that they become all-knowing. People ask, "Why can't they cure cancer? Why can't they give us winning lottery numbers?" The communicators tell us that the idea that they suddenly gain knowledge, wisdom, can tell the future, and are omniscient is not correct.

Like many who enquire into this subject, I'm skeptical by nature. I spent the first forty-three years of my life as an atheist, having grown up with my stepfather, who before meeting my mother was married to Vera, a German Jew, whom he met at the end of World War II. He was in his seventies when I finally got round to asking him why he was an atheist. He said that if there is a god, he couldn't believe he would have let the Holocaust happen. It didn't sound like a good answer.

There was no religion in our home when I was growing up, and when I asked my mother why she'd had me Christened, she said, "Because everyone did it in those days." That didn't sound like a good answer either.

In hindsight, I consider myself fortunate because, although I had followed his lead for so many years, it was because I hadn't given it much thought, and not believing in anything was so much easier than being attached to a particular doctrine. In contrast to someone who has grown up with religion and has faith in God—which I guess you could call a top-down approach—I started from the bottom, not believing in anything beyond this life, and I came to *know* that there is. I say *know* because what is knowing but a feeling? I appreciate I might be wrong, after all, there are many people in the world who think they know things that aren't correct, and I realize I might be one of them.

In my case, that knowing didn't come from visiting mediums or reading the literature—although it has validated it. It was the result of an accident I had in 2000. My wife was woken up by a bang in the early hours of the morning. She discovered I wasn't in bed and found me lying on the bedroom floor, having sustained a head injury from falling on my face.

I've written about it elsewhere so won't write too much here, but suffice to say, it was a Damascene moment. I went to sleep that night having rarely thought about, discussed, or contemplated religion, spirituality, or the paranormal. I had no interest in supernatural horror movies, the occult, haunted houses—nothing like that. It just wasn't on my radar.

That accident—apart from the inconvenience of the physical injury— seemed inconsequential at the time, but it turned out to be life changing. I now had an awareness—a *knowing* that there is no death other than the physical body—that this isn't home, and we are just passing through; that God *is*, although I didn't then, and still don't know what God is. The fear of death was absent, not that I really thought about it at that age. Now, it was more of an embracing of death—not in any morbid sense—but the idea that it's a release from the physical shell rather than the end of life. Since that time, that *knowing* has never diminished.

Before that accident, these ideas were completely alien to me. Some might call it a spiritually transformative experience, a near-death experience, or an epiphany. I don't know what it was but it was certainly transformative. I didn't meet a beautiful being or go through a tunnel or meet dead relatives—I just woke up feeling like I'd had a software update but not understanding how or why. I wasn't even aware of the term "near-death experience" in this context. At the time I would have thought it was a close shave or a lucky escape from death.

After that, all kinds of odd things started happening—precognitive dreams, synchronicities—thinking about people and then finding out they had died. Prior to the accident, I had no memory of dreaming since childhood—although science shows that we all dream every night, whether we remember it or not.

One morning, while I was sitting up in bed, eight beings appeared on the other side of the room. They looked like human-sized skittles made of light. I looked at them, blinked a few times thinking it was a trick of the light, but they were still there for a few seconds, and then they were gone. In case you're wondering, I hadn't been drinking or taken drugs, and I wasn't feeling ill or on any medication other than an inhaler for asthma. I had no fear of them. They were just there and then they weren't. It all seemed perfectly normal, whereas it was anything but.

∞

In 2013, one morning I woke up and my partner told me that during the night, I had sat bolt upright and said, "This is George," and then promptly gone back to sleep. I laughed and said I had no memory of it and didn't know anyone called George, but that he would probably show up in the next couple of days. I don't know what prompted me to say that, but two days later I received an email from a man called George.

In the early 1990s, George Moss, a retired scientist specializing in chemistry, joined a trance-channeling circle with his son. After twenty years of communication—allegedly with deceased human and nonhuman entities—he wrote a book about it. The group had been sitting quietly on a weekly basis for more than forty years. No money changed hands; they were doing it to obtain wisdom, guidance, and to be of service to others who had died and appeared to be struggling on the other side, sometimes unaware they were dead.

Anecdotally, some people in the earth planes of the spirit world can be helped by the living more easily than those in the higher levels because they remain attached to their earthly memories.

A week later, George and I met and he invited me to a session with a group. On that day, there were six or seven others present. I was the only guest. Besides the main deep trance medium, other sitters had mediumistic abilities. Some had been in the group for decades, and it was kind of them to invite me because rapport is everything, and when someone new arrives, harmony can be disrupted.

During the session, the medium said to me, "There's someone here for you. He's talking about your mother and a recent falling out she's had with someone close to her. He's saying it shouldn't have happened. I think he's your grandfather. All our mothers have gone, so it must be for you."

It was a fairly general statement, but at that time, after an argument, my mother and my Auntie Shirley, her sister-in-law, had become estranged. They were both in their eighties and had been in each other's lives since childhood. In an effort to mediate, I spoke to both of them, but neither would tell me what the argument was about and they were adamant they wouldn't be making up.

Something else happened at that meeting. We were asked to quiet our minds and ask the question, "Why are we here?" I didn't know whether he meant the global *we* or just me, but a voice or a thought, I'm not sure which, but something that felt external appeared clearly in my mind and said, *To evolve spiritually and Jesus is the benchmark.* It's not a statement that had ever occurred to me before and it wasn't what I would call evidential, but on a personal level it has stayed with me ever since.

One year later, on Christmas Eve, my partner and I were walking along a beach in Brighton. We had relatives coming for Christmas and decided to walk to the city center to buy last-minute provisions. It was a sunny morning; the beach was empty and I was feeling healthy.

As we walked along, I noticed a fishing net had washed up close to the sea; it had an anchor sticking out of it and I walked over to it and lifted my foot to see if I could move it. At that moment, the tide came in and I stepped back thinking I was going to get my feet wet. Then I heard a click in my mind and thought I had sprained my ankle—I was waiting for the pain and I passed out.

During the next fifteen minutes, apparently, I woke up, vomited, and passed out again three times. My partner didn't have her phone with her and she asked a woman out walking her dog if she could borrow hers. She called an ambulance while the woman stayed with me.

While unconscious, I found myself in a blissful, peaceful environment surrounded by thousands of loving beings. Everything was neon blue. Blissful doesn't adequately explain it, intense love might get a little closer but it's hard to describe.

When I woke up, the woman was kneeling next to me, her dog looking on. I asked her where everyone was. "There's only me and the dog, love," she replied. Then I realized I was still on a beach in Brighton. I was disappointed. It felt as if I had been with the beings for an undetermined amount of time, a sort of no time.

An ambulance arrived and two paramedics put me in the back. They took my blood pressure which was dropping. One shone a light in my eye and said, "Right eye, no dilation." I was in a daze—a hypnopompic state—as if coming out of a dream. I felt very calm—serene might be a better word.

I asked the paramedic what "no dilation" meant; he said it was an indication of a brain injury. They told me they didn't think I'd had a seizure. They kept me in the ambulance doing various tests for what seemed like more than an hour before taking me to the hospital where I spent the rest of the day being monitored.

All I could think about was the unconscious experience; it was unlike any dream I've ever had and the blissful feeling was unlike anything I had experienced before or since. I never got the chance to thank the woman on the beach, so wherever you are, thank you. These events have given me a *knowing* that this is only one small part of our reality.

Even for those who accept that life continues after death, what happens after we leave this world remains largely a mystery. The occasional visits to a medium provided me with evidence that deceased people were making contact, but that's about it. If they are living, where are they living? How are they living? Are they in heaven, hell, or purgatory, as Catholicism claims, or the Buddhist bardo—the intermediate state between this life and the next—or in an environment much like our own? And what do they look like? We live in a world where our appearance changes as "time goes on." But if time isn't going on as it is here, does their appearance change—if so—how and why?

In the late nineteenth and early twentieth centuries, a small number of dedicated American and European scientists conducted extensive experiments with mediums on both sides of the Atlantic, and while they undoubtedly uncovered instances of fraud, many of their findings haven't been debunked or explained using physicalist explanations. Nevertheless, they have been ignored by the wider scientific community, perhaps due to their departure from the current materialistic worldview.

Today, it's challenging for universities to fund research into paranormal phenomena unless they receive a donation or legacy. Historically, research has been conducted by independent organizations or individuals who can afford to fund their own research, and while small groups exist, in my limited experience they operate privately and have little interest in convincing professional skeptics or subjecting themselves to endless tests.

A huge number of books and papers have been published during the past 170 years or so, detailing reported communication from deceased people. As one might expect, there are differences of opinion between communicators. Imagine if an extraterrestrial came to earth and communicated with a South African Sans elder, a Wall Street stockbroker, a London taxi driver, and a software engineer in China, they would get a diverse range of worldviews, but eventually they might scratch the surface of what goes on here.

As we might expect, communicators report what they experience, what they see around them, and how they interact with their environment. Some say they are suffering, some are okay, while others report joy, happiness and peace beyond anything we can imagine. They describe living in breathtaking countryside settings with lakeside homes, futuristic crystal cities, and dark, misty environments. Some appear to be worldly wise, while others don't appear to know they are dead. So, if we want to explore evidence for what lies ahead, whom should we listen to?

2

WHY JESUS?

What do Saul—aka St. Paul, a tentmaker from Tarsus, Turkey; Emanuel Swedenborg, a scientist from Stockholm; James E. Padgett,[1] an attorney from Washington, D.C., and Helen Schucman, a psychologist from New York City, have in common? They all claimed to have been contacted by Jesus after his death and instructed to get his message on the nature of our ultimate reality to the wider world.

This book focuses on two twentieth-century works in which a spirit communicator claimed to be Jesus. Why Jesus? Because he is still one of the most influential and revered people in the world for Christians and non-Christians alike. He's what some have called the high watermark of humanity—and for those who are prepared to accept communication between the spirit world and physical world occurs—why not from someone who claims to be Jesus?

The two works are the automatic writing of James E. Padgett, an attorney who lived and worked in Washington, D.C., and the widely read text: *A Course in Miracles.*[2]

∞

Padgett was married to Helen, the daughter of a Methodist minister. They had three children. In 1910, the couple separated and in February 1914, Helen passed away, aged fifty-one. Padgett was distraught and visited Spiritualist meetings hoping to hear from her.

During one meeting, a medium claimed Helen was there and described her more or less accurately. The medium told Padgett that he possessed an ability to perform automatic writing, and that if he sat quietly holding a pencil over paper, eventually Helen would be able to communicate directly without the need for an intermediary. He was skeptical but at the same time very motivated to connect with her.

After a while and with practice, he wrote scribbles on paper which he described as fishhooks and hangers. Then one day, without any conscious effort on his part, he wrote a message ostensibly from Helen that said she was close to him. He was still skeptical, believing the words were from his subconscious, a trick of the mind, but it prompted him to start reading literature on life after death which was abundant at that time—and still is—and with perseverance he began to get more lengthy messages from Helen detailing events which convinced him she was communicating.

Helen told him she was in the second sphere, and now being familiar with the "spheres" that communicators sometimes report being in, and having a high opinion of her, he thought she should be in a more advanced state of existence. He suggested she try to connect with his grandmother Ann Rollins, who had passed away years earlier, which she did. It turned out that Ann was—and presumably still is—residing in the celestial spheres, beyond the levels of the spirit world.

Ann Rollins is described as a high spirit—someone In Christ. "High" doesn't imply a hierarchical power over others but a deeper awareness of reality. She is portrayed as a radiant spirit, more beautiful than we can imagine, and according to their definition: an angel. An angel in this context is someone who has reached the celestial world—the kingdom. .

During the next few months, messages came through purporting to be Padgett's family members, including his mother, Ann, and father, John. Padgett's confidence in the authenticity of the communicators grew, and his conversations became a nightly occurrence.

Automatic writing has been reported around the world for centuries. It's as if a deceased human or nonhuman entity—a sender—tunes into a receiver's brain, which acts as a filter, similar to a TV or radio, allowing the sender to transmit information to the receiver.

During the process, a person writes without being aware of the content being written. The receiver of the information is sometimes in a meditative or trance state, allowing their hand to write down words, phrases, and images without any conscious effort.

WHY JESUS?

In Chinese folk religion and some Daoist schools, it's known as spirit writing. In Mandarin, "笔仙" (bǐxiān) means "pen fairy" or "pen immortal."

In the case of Padgett, he would mentally ask a question and the answer would come back through his hand. As a result, the messages don't include his questions, so in some cases because they are obvious, I've assumed the question to avoid repetitive phrasing.

In early September 1914, another message came through, this one attributed to Jesus. Padgett didn't know what to make of it; he certainly didn't believe it was from Jesus and threw it away. The messages kept on coming, and later in September others came through from Jesus, which he kept.

Since Padgett was an attorney, one might infer that he liked evidence— evidence beyond a reasonable doubt—as close to proof as one can get. But it's hard to imagine how a deceased communicator could convince Padgett he was Jesus, possibly the most famous person on the planet, and that he wanted to write through him. It wasn't a unique event; people claiming to be historic figures occasionally drop in during séances and meetings of like-minded people who are trying to connect with the departed.

Famous communicators aren't that interesting from an evidential point of view. Unless they are known to the sitter, they are unlikely to give personal evidence which can be verified, or tell us anything that's not in the public domain. Nevertheless, what they say about their experiences after death—what their opinions, regrets, and hopes are—can be revealing.

For Padgett it must have been a big event and probably a confusing one. Having just gotten used to his deceased family and friends interacting with him and accepting them as genuine, he now had to decide whether to accept that Jesus was who he said he was. That didn't happen right away. Family members came through who appeared to be as surprised as he was, but insisted it was Jesus communicating and encouraged him to accept the messages as genuine.

Like anyone who reads these messages, I don't know if the communicators were who they said they were. But what we do know is that Padgett—a very accomplished man with a busy professional life—came to accept that the messages from deceased friends, family, and business acquaintances were genuine. They, in turn, insisted that Jesus and the other communicators were who they claimed to be.

Importantly, they said this was all happening because Jesus had identified Padgett as someone who could help set the record straight about the Bible—particularly the New Testament—and how it's been interpreted and misinterpreted. As far as Padgett was concerned, he had been handed an important task, and he spent the last nine years of his life devoted to it.

Leslie R. Stone

An important character in the Padgett story is Leslie R. Stone. It was Stone's first time at a Spiritualist meeting when a communicator who identified as his father came through. Having recently arrived in Toronto, Stone had seen the séance advertised on a notice board and was curious.

"Your father, who says he is William Stone, is here and is glad that he is able to greet you," said the medium, pointing at Leslie. His father was indeed called William Stone and had passed away twenty years earlier in England when Leslie was seven years old, and receiving that message was a pivotal moment because no one present, least of all the medium, could have known that his father's name was William Stone and that he had died.

Stone emigrated to Canada in 1903 when he was twenty-seven years old. He was born in Aldershot, a small town in Southeast England, coincidently, just a few miles from B.L., the medium mentioned in the previous chapter. He worked in his father's saddlery shop and later in London, but making a living was not easy at that time, and the New World beckoned for adventurous souls. He asked his mother what she thought about his emigrating to Canada. She prayed and the answer came back: he should go to Canada.

Like many people who experience a communication ostensibly from a deceased person, particularly a loved one, he wanted to know more and began reading Spiritualist literature. He moved to Detroit, where cars were becoming popular, although demand for his saddlery skills was in decline. He continued to attend séances, where he received spiritual guidance, which led him to Buffalo, New York, where he worked in a hospital for seven years and trained as a graduate nurse, which sparked an interest in healing. Subsequently, he qualified as a chiropractor.

At a Spiritualist meeting in Buffalo, more evidence came through that convinced him of the reality of the spirit world. In his book, *The True Gospel Revealed Anew by Jesus: Vol.1*, he wrote, "I was seated next to a woman who happened to be a medium. She suddenly turned to me and said, 'Your mother is here with you.' I replied, 'You must be mistaken, Madam. I had a letter from my mother quite recently, and she is in good health.'

"The medium shrugged and replied, 'Your mother never lived in this country. She tells me she lived in England and died a short time ago.' She went on to report what my mother presumably had died of, described the funeral, and mentioned the names of those present. She told me that I had a sister, Edith, from whom I would receive a letter confirming what she said. The letter arrived just as the woman had predicted, and corroborating her statements. If I ever had doubts then as to the truth of spirit communication, I lost them at that point."

Stone started sitting alone, and with practice claimed he could achieve a trance or out-of-body state and enter the spirit world, where he met his mother, sister Kate, and brother Willie, who had passed away in 1908. "I knew I was in my spirit body and had left my mortal frame," he wrote, "and indeed, I had no desire to return to it, but my mother and sister insisted that I had a spiritual work to accomplish in the earth plane and that I could not come permanently into the spirit world until I had accomplished that task."

Eleven years after arriving in the New World, Stone opened an office in Washington, D.C. to do his chiropractic work. It was in Washington in September 1914, that he was introduced to Padgett and his colleague Eugene Morgan, and witnessed Padgett's automatic writing.

Having experienced personal communication from deceased family members via mediums and during his own OBEs, he concluded that Padgett was an honest man and an authentic medium, and like Padgett and Morgan, he came to accept the messages as genuine. This was important because in the years after Padgett's death it became Stone's task to transcribe the thousands of hand-written messages and bring them to the wider world.

By the 1940s, four books had been published in the *True Gospel Revealed Anew by Jesus* series, which contained many of the messages, and in 1958 a church known as the "Foundation Church of the New Birth" was incorporated in Washington. D.C.

The trio, Padgett, Stone, and Morgan, became a communication hub for the seemingly endless number of people queuing up on the other side wanting to correspond with the living. During those nine years, approximately 2,500 messages came through Padgett's hand from deceased family members, friends, business associates, and historic figures, of which more than a hundred purported to come from Jesus himself. Key figures include his grandmother Ann Rollins, his boss, Albert Riddle, who died in 1902, and Joseph H. Salyards, his college professor who passed away in 1885.

The overriding message from Jesus and other communicators is that many of the "truths" in the Bible attributed to them are not correct and that it's important they are corrected if we are to be guided back to the right path.

∞

One of the most famous contemporary works purporting to be from Jesus is *A Course in Miracles* (ACIM), a 480,000-word channeled text that came through Helen Schucman between 1965 and 1972. First published in 1976, the book has sold millions of copies worldwide and has been translated into all the major world languages, including Spanish, French, German, Chinese, Arabic, and Hebrew

Schucman was a clinical psychologist at the College of Physicians and Surgeons, Columbia-Presbyterian Medical Center in New York. She had been religious as a child. Her parents were Jewish—her mother was Baptist—father an atheist. As an adult, she rejected religion, and at the time of her revelation was agnostic leaning toward atheism—not an obvious person to suddenly start uttering what some might call "spiritual truths" that would change the course of her life. But that's what happened.

On October 21, 1965, an inner voice, as she described it, dictated, "This is A Course in Miracles. Please take notes." Prior to that day, she and her colleague William Thetford had been questioning their work; they were feeling dissatisfied and philosophizing that there must be a better way. She had been having vivid dreams for months leading up to October 21, in which someone whom she identified as Jesus communicated with her.

When the communication began, she told Thetford about the inner voice and was surprised that he was supportive. It doesn't seem as if she had any affiliation with the information she was receiving. It was in complete opposition to her beliefs, and she found the content troubling.

Schucman was no New Age guru or religious devotee, and the teachings appear to have been outside of her conscious knowledge. Nor did she like the idea of it being a psychic experience. But despite being a "reluctant secretary," as she called it, she took the inner dictation down in shorthand, which she often used for her psychology work, and

Thetford transferred it to longhand. She said the voice appeared in her mind but not in an auditory way speaking English—no hearing was involved. The "voice" dictated quickly, but unlike Padgett's automatic writing, in which he had to keep writing or lose the connection, she was able to pause it at any time, like starting and stopping a digital voice note or tape recorder, which was essential because she had a busy life.

As annoying and baffling as she said she found the experience, she took the task seriously and made a point of not editing it in any way. If a mistake or assumption about a word or phrase occurred, the voice would instruct her to rewrite. She was impressed with the consistency and coherence of the text, and when she talked about it in interviews, it's as if she were reviewing someone else's work.

Given that she was an atheist with no interest in the subject, it's remarkable that the book exists. She could have just stopped the process at any time and carried on with her life; after all, she had no idea what it would become. But she didn't. She saw it through to the end.

The revelation—if that's the appropriate word—took seven years to come through. It's a large tome consisting of three books: "The Text," "The Manual for Students," and "The Manual for Teachers." Schucman was an educator so it's reasonable to think that the style of the text was influenced by her—turning a revelation into a course is something an educator might do in the twentieth century.

There is no way of knowing whether Jesus communicated with Padgett and Schucman, but for the purposes of this book, I'm assuming that Jesus—and the other communicators—were who they said they were. I haven't prefaced names with "allegedly" or "claimed to be." When I use terms like "dead," "death," "passed away," or "deceased," I don't mean dead as in "annihilation"; I simply mean no longer in the physical body.

These messages can be viewed in several ways: as fiction, as messages from impostors, or as genuine. Depending on the reader's worldview, they can be ignored or taken as guidance from people who have gone before us—and used as a roadmap of the levels beyond death.

If all religions, scriptures, churches, mosques, and temples disappeared today, it would not alter the nature of our ultimate reality. The aim here is not to advocate for any particular religion, doctrine, or philosophy, but to explore the truth about what happens after death— what the consequences of our lives are—and whether the claims made by communicators, especially those who say they are Jesus, hold up in light of the evidence available in the twenty-first century.

There are thousands of religious denominations, each with its own version of what it believes is the truth. Even within Christianity alone, there are countless interpretations, all claiming to represent the true message on how to live our lives. But when it comes to the nature of reality—God, heaven, hell, the afterlife, and so on—there can be only one truth. This book is another contribution to that ongoing search.

Martin Luther is often credited with saying, "Every man must do two things alone: he must do his own believing and his own dying." That didn't work out too well for Luther—but more on him later.

3

JESUS HERE, JESUS THERE

Jesus, Jesus, Everywhere

One afternoon, I was invited to have tea at the home of a friend of a friend in Hounslow, Southwest London. The host was a medium, and during the visit, while I was tucking into their chocolate cake and coffee, he smiled and said, "Jesus is behind you." I must admit I wasn't expecting Jesus to be in Hounslow on a weekday afternoon.

I grinned and said, "Did he say anything?"

"No," he replied. "He's just present."

With a hint of sarcasm I asked if he had dropped in before. He said he hadn't. I didn't think for a second that Jesus was looking in on me. There were two other options: he was talking nonsense or hallucinating. In all other respects he appeared to be lucid. He wasn't trying to sell me anything and had welcomed me into his home. He didn't offer to give me a reading and I didn't ask, and with no disrespect, I decided he was talking nonsense. It wasn't the idea of Jesus or a proxy communicating— after all, that's the subject of this book. It was the suggestion that Jesus *appeared* that I didn't accept.

Having said that, imagine you are Jesus and you're hard at work in the spirit world and beyond, and you hear from new arrivals that back on earth you're still the most famous person on the planet despite having been gone for two thousand years, and you are continually being misquoted and misrepresented. You might want to try to set the record straight occasionally when the opportunity presents itself. But to me? In Hounslow? It seemed unlikely.

Aside from Padgett and Schucman, reports of Jesus' communicating occur around the world from time to time. During a near-death experience, people sometimes report meeting a "beautiful being" whom they identify as Jesus or God. Hindus occasionally report meeting Hindu gods, which one might expect.

Documented NDEs among Muslims are scarce but they do exist. Some researchers hypothesize that Muslims, having a strong belief in an afterlife and God, may be less likely to need the experience as a form of confirmation, while others suggest that their strong devotion might make them more likely to have such experiences.

There doesn't appear to be a consensus on why some people have NDEs while others don't. This holds true regardless of gender, religious beliefs, or moral character. Notably, while belief doesn't seem to be a factor in who has one, it might influence *what* they experience. One person will report meeting a beautiful being who had brown eyes; another will notice his "piercing blue eyes." Both are convinced it was Jesus, yet both describe a physically different Jesus. It's a small but significant detail, which suggests that Jesus is either a shapeshifter who likes to change his eye color, or that those having the experience are being "presented" with someone they can relate to.

Personally, I find it more interesting when a person who has momentarily died, or come close to death, or suffered a traumatic event resulting in an out-of-body experience, reports meeting someone they didn't know had existed, such as a sibling who died at birth whom their parents hadn't told them about, that's later verified—what's known as a Peak-in-Darien experience—because that's evidence that's hard to discount using materialist explanations.

Cardiologists who survey cardiac arrest survivors report that around 18 percent report an "other-worldly" experience while anesthetized, therefore they should be devoid of any conscious experience. In the United States, in excess of 356,000 people experience cardiac arrest each year and approximately 10 percent survive.[1] So, the number of people who have an NDE might be small but significant.

Throughout the years, there have been reports that Jesus and other biblical figures have come through to impart wisdom. In the 1920s and '30s, an Australian deep-trance medium named Stan Walsh held sittings where biblical figures came through and shared their understanding of what lies ahead. One of Walsh's circle, L. C. Landy, wrote in his book The Certainty of Eternity: "Many of Christ's disciples and followers visited us—Mary Magdalene; John the Baptist;

Matthew; Peter; Mark; John, the most beloved; Paul; Stephen, the first martyr; and many others."

In New Zealand during the 1970s, Anglican priest Michael Cocks and a small group held a seven-year dialogue with a communicator who identified himself as Stephen the Martyr, a biblical figure. "Stephen" spoke through a trance medium, sometimes in Greek, and on one occasion a language that was later identified as a virtually unknown ancient Greek dialect. However, the medium, in his normal waking state, didn't speak Greek. It's a phenomenon known as "xenoglossy," and for Michael, it was good evidence that something otherworldly was going on. In 2011, his book *The Afterlife Teachings of Stephen the Martyr* was published in which he documented the communications.

In 2012, a medium in the United States claimed she contacted Jesus and was told he didn't die on the cross but moved to France, had subsequently reincarnated a number of times, and was living as a woman in India.[2] At the time of writing, a channeler[3] in California claims "Yeshua" is communicating through her, and A-list Hollywood celebrities pay her handsomely to hear what he has to say.

Due to space constraints, we can only scratch the surface of *A Course in Miracles* and the Padgett messages, but if the author is one and the same, it would be logical to think there shouldn't be contradictions. Both mention the Atonement, the Trinity, reincarnation, and immortality, but the Course is written as if it's intended for a completely different audience. Jesus in ACIM doesn't appear to dwell on the things that occupy our lives, such as wealth, poverty, war, peace, marriage, gender, violence, and things of that nature. It's as if he's an advanced being at a level beyond the physical and spirit world—like a psychiatrist explaining to a patient who's hallucinating—he's telling us, "None of this is real. It's all in your mind," and trying to get us to snap out of our delusion.

At the beginning of the book there's a sentence that sums up the whole work: "Nothing real can be threatened, nothing unreal exists. Herein lies the peace of God."

A little later Jesus says, "Only eternity is real." Still later we are told repeatedly: "You are as God created you. You are His Son eternally." My understanding of those statements is that we are part of eternity. We are *real* and cannot be *threatened*, whereas our physical bodies, our planet, our world, are *not*.

He is asking us to understand that we exist beyond time and space. We are participating in an experience which is not our ultimate reality. The "Miracle" is when we change our thought process from wrong thinking to right thinking, from perception to knowledge, and understand who and what we are: "38 55 A miracle is a correction factor introduced into false thinking by me. It acts as a catalyst, shaking up erroneous perception and reorganizing it properly. This places man under the Atonement principle, where his perception is healed. Until this has occurred, revelation of the divine order is impossible" (1.I:38).

In the Padgett messages, Jesus is relatively straightforward and easy to understand. We might not agree with him or believe what he's saying, or accept that it's Jesus communicating—that's down to the individual—but we can grasp the concepts. But if Jesus had dictated *A Course in Miracles* in the early twentieth century, the Padgett era, with its emphasis on oneness, the interconnectedness of all things, and the illusion of time, space, and separation, people might have found it too mystical, particularly in the West. Yet two decades later, in 1935, Einstein and other physicists fueled ideas about quantum entanglement, nonlocality, and the potential non-fundamentality of spacetime.

Augustine, one of the most influential Church Fathers, reasoned that God created the universe "with" time, not "in" time. Therefore, God is outside of time and space. In his *Confessions*, to God, written towards the end of the fifth century, he wrote: "In the eternal, nothing is transient, but the whole is present. Yet no time is entirely present; thus You created time itself. And all time is subject to You, since before time You were not in time; time could not pass and You be. But You are the same, and all things of tomorrow and beyond, and all that was yesterday and before, You make present today."

Today, many scientists agree that time and space came into being when the universe began—the Big Bang. While the Big Bang theory is widely accepted, the question of whether the universe was created out of nothing is unknown, but if the universe had a beginning, it's reasonable to think what caused it might be outside of time and space.

Currently, theoretical physicists explore the idea that space and time emerge rather than being fundamental and consider dimensions beyond our own where space and time may be absent.

Our perception of reality is shaped by our brains, which interpret energy and matter through our senses. While the physical world exists, our experience of it is a constructed interpretation, a concept that echoes the ancient Hindu notion of Maya—the illusion of perceived reality.

Viewers of the movie *The Matrix* will remember Cypher, the bad guy, the Judas in the story, who realizes he's living in a simulation but wants to stay in it. In one scene, while sitting in a restaurant, he remarks, "I know this steak doesn't exist. I know that when I put it in my mouth, the Matrix is telling my brain that it is juicy and delicious."

Life on earth is a deeply immersive experience, and to contemplate the idea that it's not our ultimate reality is counterintuitive, yet this is what the *Course* is asking us to do.

As with any form of orthodoxy there are those who believe in Bible infallibility, despite the apparent inconsistencies and contradictions that scholars continue to point out, and they will defend that orthodoxy at all costs. When it comes to faith, it's one thing to have faith in God and Jesus, but it's quite another to put our faith in human infallibility and biblical literacy for the past two thousand years, and deny later revelations purportedly coming from the very people whom Christians put their faith in.

Both the Padgett and ACIM texts have been called heretical by some Christian commentators, despite both Padgett and Schucman "testing the spirits" and being told they were from God. It's understandable: I can't imagine the Church conceding, "We were wrong about the Bible. There's something you need to know." But Jesus and the other writers are telling us that their words and writings have been misinterpreted, misunderstood, and misused by accident and design, and they are accusing the Church and its representatives of misleading their followers.

One of the first recorded messages Jesus wrote to Padgett was on September 12, 1914. it reads: "I am here, Jesus. God is love and they that worship Him in spirit and love will not be forsaken.

"I came to tell you that you are very near the kingdom; only believe and pray to the Father and you will soon know the truth, and the truth will make you free. You were hard hearted and sinful, but now that you are seeking the light I will come to you and help you; only believe and you will soon see the truth of my teachings. Go not in the way of the wicked for their end is punishment and long suffering. Let your love for God and your fellow man increase. You are not in condition for further writing. I will come to you again when you are stronger.

"Yes, it is Jesus and I want the world to follow the teachings of my words.

"Goodbye and may the Holy Spirit bless you as I do."

∞

The New Testament includes thirteen letters (epistles) attributed to Paul, though scholars debate the authorship of some. Paul's teachings and ministry stem from his conversion experience on the road to Damascus—estimated to have occurred between four and seven years after Jesus's death—during which he saw a bright light and heard the voice of Jesus instructing him to stop persecuting his followers. It could be argued that without that event, his subsequent visions, and his interpretations of Old Testament prophecies, Christianity as we know it today would not exist.

One might reasonably ask: Why accept these communicators as genuine? It's a fair question, to which I don't have a definitive answer—other than, "By their fruits you shall know them." One could just as easily ask: Why accept Paul? He is no sacred cow. He could have misinterpreted his visions or the Hebrew prophecies. His writings could have been mistranslated over the centuries, or later writers might have used his name for political or ideological reasons—or all of the above.

Paul reportedly said: "I want you to know, brothers and sisters, that the gospel I preached is not of human origin. I did not receive it from any man, nor was I taught it; rather, I received it by revelation from Jesus Christ" (Gal. 1:11–12).

If Paul could be an instrument of Jesus, why not others since that time?

As far as we know, both Schucman and Padgett never attempted to get in touch with Jesus or anyone else (Padgett's wife aside). Neither were fundamentalists or ideological nor motivated by financial reward. Fame doesn't appear to have been a factor. Padgett kept his communications secret to all but his close friends and continued to receive and document messages until he died in 1923, while Schucman ensured that Jesus wasn't publicly identified as the author of *A Course in Miracles* until after her death in 1981.

Like Paul, Padgett and Schucman were transformed by their encounters with Jesus. They took the authorship seriously and felt that the information had to be shared with the world.

Jesus: Fact or fiction?

If we are relying on historic texts other than the New Testament and the Quran, there is historic evidence that Jesus existed. However, there are scholars who believe he didn't, and propagate the Christ Myth Theory[4] which claims that Jesus was a fictional character created by the early Christian Church.

Flavius Josephus, a first-century Jewish historian, is considered to be a primary non-Christian source for the historical Jesus. He was born in 37 CE, around the same time that Paul had his conversion experience on the road to Damascus.

Josephus's book, *Antiquities of the Jews,* described the execution of James, the brother of Jesus: "Albinus was but upon the road; so he assembled the Sanhedrin of judges, and brought before them the brother of Jesus, who was called Christ, whose name was James, and some others, [or, some of his companions]; and when he had formed an accusation against them as breakers of the law, he delivered them to be stoned." It's thought James was martyred sometime between 62 and 69 CE.

In Book 18 of *Antiquities,* there's a section that reads: "Now there was about this time Jesus, a wise man, if it be lawful to call him a man. For he was a doer of wonderful works; a teacher of such men as receive the truth with pleasure. He drew over to him both many of the Jews and many of the Gentiles. He was [the] Christ. And when Pilate, at the suggestion of the principal men among us, had condemned him to the cross, those that loved him at the first did not forsake him. For he appeared to them alive again, the third day; as the divine prophets had foretold these and ten thousand other wonderful things concerning him. And the tribe of Christians, so named from him, are not extinct at this day."

Today, some scholars suggest that the section in Book 18 is either a forgery inserted at a later date or that Josephus wrote about Jesus and his words were later embellished to fit the Christian story. There is no evidence that Josephus converted to Christianity or that he believed that Jesus was the Messiah.

The Padgett messages include a few from Josephus. On August 8, 1915, he wrote, "He [Jesus] lived just before I wrote, but I had heard of him many times, and I know that he was a real existing being. In my history of the Jews, I mentioned him, and when the learned say that what is there said is interpolated, they say what is not true; for he did live and taught in Palestine as the New Testament claims.

"I never met him, but the wonders of his works were circulated all over the country and caused much agitation on the part of the leaders of the Jews. I never wrote much about him, because we all looked upon him as a mere agitator and destroyer of our religion, and to such we never gave much notoriety in our writings. But this same Jesus of Nazareth lived as a man and was crucified by the Romans at the clamor of the Jews. I want to tell you this, because it is claimed that he never lived on earth.

"I am a follower of him, and believe in his teachings and have received the New Birth that he taught. I live in the celestial heavens where only his followers live."

Tacitus, a Roman senator and historian, writing about Nero in his *Annals* in the early second century, reported:

"Christus, the founder of the name, had undergone the death penalty in the reign of Tiberius, by sentence of the procurator Pontius Pilatus, 29 and the pernicious superstition was checked for a moment, only to break out once more, not merely in Judaea, the home of the disease, but in the capital itself, where all things horrible or shameful in the world collect and find a vogue. First, then, the confessed members of the sect were arrested; next, on their disclosures, vast numbers 30 were convicted, not so much on the count of arson as for hatred of the human race."

In first- and second-century Rome, superstition (*superstitio*) meant excessive or exaggerated religious practices, and the new Christians were seen as a cult of stubborn extremists who had the potential to disrupt society. In contrast, while life was difficult under Roman rule, Jews who followed the Torah and prayed to their God were not viewed as superstitious outliers by the authorities and had legal rights that Christians didn't.

Around 112 CE, Pliny the Younger, governor of Bithynia in Asia Minor, wrote a letter to Emperor Trajan seeking guidance on how to handle Christians accused of crimes. Notably, aside from being guilty of simply being a Christian, Pliny didn't specify what laws might have been broken. He devised a scheme whereby, when questioning someone suspected of being a Christian, if they denied it, he asked them to pray to the gods, offer wine, and curse Christ. If they refused, they were executed. If they admitted to being a Christian, they were given the opportunity to recant. If they refused, they were asked a second time and threatened with death. If they refused three times, they were executed.

Trajan instructed Pliny not to actively hunt Christians down, but if anyone was found guilty of being a Christian, they had to be punished. If they denied it and showed proof by worshiping the gods, they should be released.

Nag Hammadi

In 1945, in the aftermath of World War II, a man digging in the Egyptian desert in a place called Nag Hammadi, stumbled across some clay jars in a cave. The contents included thirteen books (or codices). The leather-bound papyrus books date back to the third and fourth centuries CE, and scholars estimate the scripts themselves were composed in the second and third centuries CE. Some of the scripts are described as Gnostic; they include titles such as The Dialogue of the Savior; The Gospel of Mary; The Gospel of Philip; The Secret Book of John; The Gospel of Thomas; and Hypostasis of the Archons (Reality of the Rulers).

That event was one of the most important historic findings from the early Christian period. The scripts had been known about since the early days of Christianity, principally, because the early Church fathers mentioned them in their writings, referring to them as abominable, diabolical, and heretical. Since that time, it was thought the texts had been systematically rooted out and destroyed, so to find them buried in a cave almost two thousand years later is remarkable.

Some scholars suggest that certain texts may have been secret teachings given to the disciples rather than to the masses. In Mark, Jesus tells his disciples: "The secret of the kingdom of God has been given to you. But to those on the outside everything is said in parables" (Mark 4:11).

There are competing ideas about the origins of Gnosticism. The movement existed as part of early Christianity during the first and second centuries CE, although the word "Gnostic" is a modern word. Gnostics considered themselves to be the "true Christians," believing they possessed a deeper knowledge (*gnosis*) of the divine. Gnostics believed Jesus was not God but a teacher sent by God to reveal our true origins and guide us back to our spiritual home: to salvation.

The concept of a supreme God who created the spiritual realms is central to Gnosticism. The God of the Old Testament is seen as a lesser creator: a demiurge, mistakenly believing himself to be the true God. The Gnostic demiurge is sometimes portrayed as a flawed and malevolent figure and earth as a prison. This concept differs from the benevolent creator-demiurge described by Plato in his work *Timaeus*, who is seen as a half-creator, a creator of the physical world, but not God, the creator of all.

According to Gnosticism, the demiurge created the material world and humanity. Humans possessed a soul but lacked the divine spark, a fragment of the supreme God. The supreme God infused humans with this spark which allows us to escape the control of the Archons: malevolent beings who rule the material world from the spirit realms. The Archons themselves lack the divine spark (*pneuma*, meaning breath or spirit) and cannot harm our essence, but they can influence our thoughts, keeping us blind to our true potential, to reunite with the divine.

The word *Archon* is not found in traditional Bible translations. In the New Testament, Ephesians warns that dark forces—rulers and authorities—are trying to influence us from the spirit world: "For our struggle is not against flesh and blood, but against the rulers, against the authorities, against the powers of this dark world, and against the spiritual forces of evil in the heavenly realms. Therefore, put on the full armor of God, so that when the day of evil comes, you may be able to stand your ground, and after you have done everything, to stand" (Eph. 6:12–13).

In a 2017 translation of the New Testament by the scholar David Bentley Hart, "Rulers and Authorities" is translated as Archons:

> Because we are wrestling not against blood and flesh, but against the Archons, against the Powers, against the Cosmic Rulers of this darkness, and against the spiritual forces of wickedness in the Celestial Places. Therefore, take up God's panoply, so that on the evil day you might be able to resist and, having accomplished all things, take your stand (Eph. 6:12–13 Hart, D. B.).

The Padgett communicators would argue that there are no "spiritual forces of wickedness in the Celestial Places"—the celestial realms being a world beyond the reach of wickedness.

One of the more interesting texts with respect to Jesus found at Nag Hammadi is, The Gospel of Thomas. It is sometimes referred to as a Gnostic Gospel, although it could be argued that it's neither Gnostic nor a gospel. There is no mention of the demiurge, the pleroma, or the evil god associated with Gnosticism, and unlike the narrative structure of the canonical gospels, it's a collection of 114 sayings attributed to Jesus, more than half of which appear in the New Testament. Written in Coptic, it's believed to have been translated from Greek. Estimates place its composition in the second century, possibly with additions over time.

The text begins: "These are the secret words which the living Jesus spoke, and Didymus Judas Thomas wrote them down."

The first saying reads: "And he said, He who shall find the interpretation of the words shall not taste of death" (Gospel of Thomas 1). The third saying describes the coming of the Kingdom of Heaven:

Jesus said, "If your leaders say to you, 'Look, the (Father's) kingdom is in the sky,' then the birds of the sky will precede you. If they say to you, 'It is in the sea,' then the fish will precede you. Rather, the (Father's) kingdom is within you and it is outside you.

"When you know yourselves, then you will be known, and you will understand that you are children of the living Father. But if you do not know yourselves, then you live in poverty, and you are the poverty (Gospel of Thomas 3).

This corresponds with the idea that the celestial spheres—the kingdom—is both an environment and a state of being. The state of being can be achieved during physical life but the environment is beyond physical death. Jesus famously said, "In my Father's house are many mansions: if it were not so, I would have told you. I go to prepare a place for you" (John 14:2 NKJV). Mansion is a translation of the Greek word $\mu o\nu\acute{\eta}$ (monē), which means "a place to live" or "residence." Reportedly, the kingdom is where the upscale neighborhoods are.

Conversely, it suggests the lowest level of the earth planes are not so pleasant, and poverty is both an environment and a state of being. "You live in poverty, and you are the poverty."

The early Church fathers clearly didn't like the idea that the kingdom could be reached with gnosis without the Church hierarchy acting as intermediaries. Ignatius of Antioch, a leading Church father in the early second century, wrote a letter, "Ignatius to the Smyrnaeans," which reads: "You must all follow the lead of the bishop, as Jesus Christ followed that of the Father; follow the presbytery as you would the Apostles; reverence the deacons as you would God's commandment. Let no one do anything touching the Church, apart from the bishop."

Jesus is mentioned on scores of occasions in the Nag Hammadi texts, which suggests that despite claims that he didn't exist, the writers, Christian or otherwise, were certain he did.

The existence of some first- and second-century Christian communities is well-documented, despite their being disparate groups with differing beliefs about Jesus's status. During that time, there was no centralized Church or codified doctrine, which would come later with the arrival of the Roman Emperor Constantine.

The historical Roman accounts, the New Testament, and the Nag Hammadi scripts indicate that Jesus was no mere myth.

Of course, it's easy to scoff at the suggestion that Jesus has communicated during the past few hundred years and to disregard the many after-death communicators who have validated his status. If you don't accept spirit communication or the idea that life continues after death, that's a reasonable assumption. But if you are open to afterlife sources, there's good reason to believe that Jesus existed and exists—and is the most spiritually advanced human we can contemplate. If we are following in his footsteps and taking the same journey, he's probably worth listening to.

If you believe that Jesus lived and died two thousand years ago—whether you're a Christian who believes he is God, a Muslim who believes he was a prophet, a Jew who believes he was a rabbi and a Messiah, or someone who believes he was a spiritual teacher—if his teachings have been distorted or just misunderstood, the question isn't why would he communicate? The question is, *why wouldn't he?*

4

UNUSUAL PEOPLE

Kim

Geniuses, savants, and people with rare skills are often unknown to most of us.

Kim Peek,[1] the subject of the 1988 Oscar-winning movie *Rain Man*, was known as a mega-savant. Born with a brain abnormality, he had difficulty with day-to-day tasks such as dressing, shaving, and brushing his teeth, and for most of his life was cared for primarily by his father. Despite his disability, he could memorize anything he read, read two pages at once, and know the day of a historic date without calculating. He could recall entire map books and give directions to cities he had never visited. He memorized phone books, historic data, and by the age of six could recite the Bible.

Although a brain abnormality was thought to be the cause of his disability, there is no scientific consensus on how that abnormality could account for his mental superpowers.

A possible explanation might be, if our data—our memories—are never lost and stored on something akin to a cosmic data server, Kim's brain abnormality might have allowed him to tap into those memories. Scientific materialism rejects the idea that mind and memory extend beyond the brain, and his abilities remain unexplained.

If it hadn't been for *Rain Man*, Kim's name might well have faded into obscurity by now and accounts of his abilities dismissed by many as a myth. Similarly, in the world of spirit communication there are people who have rare abilities, or gifts, depending on your perspective, gifts which, unless experienced or witnessed, many of us wouldn't believe exist.

Chico

Chico Xavier[2] was a remarkable man. He was one of Brazil's most renowned automatic writing mediums. In a country where belief in life after death is widespread, Chico was revered as a spiritual teacher, healer, and humanitarian.

During his life, he penned more than four hundred books and thousands of letters on spiritual and philosophical themes, all reportedly channeled from deceased friends, family, poets, novelists, and philosophers who allegedly wrote through his hand. Many of the books were best sellers, yet he never claimed authorship of the writings, and royalties from tens of millions of copies sold were and still are used for charitable causes in Brazil.

In 1981, Chico was nominated for a Nobel Peace Prize, and in 2012, a TV series: *O Maior Brasileiro de Todos os Tempos* (The Greatest Brazilian of All Time) held a poll to determine who was the greatest Brazilian. More than a million votes were recorded and Chico was voted the winner beating cultural icon Pele, who is regarded as one of the world's all-time great professional soccer players, and Ayrton Senna, the world champion Formula One racing driver, both Brazilian heroes.

Movies and documentaries have been made about Chico and he's appeared on postage stamps in Brazil, yet he is virtually unknown outside his native country—although that is changing.

Throughout his life, he lived modestly and worked tirelessly in the service of God and his neighbors. He said of Jesus: "Let us remember that Jesus is the path, the truth, and the life, and that no one will reach the higher realms without passing through his teachings of love, fraternity, and forgiveness."

According to family and friends, Chico told them he had asked God to "take him on a day Brazilians were happy and celebrating." He passed away on June 30, 2002, at the age of ninety-two, just hours after Brazil beat Germany in the World Cup Final.

Emily

Emily Sofia McCoy French[3] was a woman with the rare gift of direct-voice mediumship. Direct-voice or independent-voice is a phenomenon where a medium sits in a darkened room, and in their presence, voices of deceased communicators manifest independently. Voices have been known to speak in multiple languages, in some cases at the same time, far beyond the capabilities of the medium and sitters.

Born into the wealthy Pierpont family in Buffalo, upstate New York, she later married Lieutenant James H. French from Rochester, New York. James died during the War of the Rebellion at the age of forty, and her son died when he was twenty-two years old. We don't know when Emily discovered her ability, but it's possible, as appears to be the case sometimes, that the deaths in the family caused her to look to the heavens for guidance.

Twenty-five years after James' death, Emily, then in her sixties, came to the attention of Edward C. Randall, a Buffalo attorney. Like many at that time, Randall became interested in the subject of life after death after attending a séance, and subsequently he and his wife started their own home circle with a group of friends that included Judge Dean Stuart of Rochester.

Judge Stuart had previously participated in séances with Emily, and on one occasion a skeptical journalist suggested to Stuart that fraud was a rational explanation, to which he replied: "If there is fraud in Mrs. French's circles I would like to know it, because my time is too precious to waste by attending these séances. I have been sitting with Mrs. French from time to time for the past five years and tested her in every possible way that my mind could suggest, but I have never discovered the slightest trace of fraud. My friend, you will, if you continue your investigations, be compelled to acknowledge that Mrs. French's voices are occasioned by a power beyond the material, and the only conclusion you can arrive at is that they are as they claim to be: Spiritual."

At first, Randall was skeptical of direct-voice. At that time, frauds posing as mediums were jumping on the Spiritualist bandwagon because fame and money beckoned, but Randall felt that if Emily were a fraud he would certainly unmask her. He invited her to his home and after ruling out ventriloquism, accomplices, hypnosis of the sitters, and other possible deceptions, he accepted the genuineness of the phenomenon.

In her later years, despite her increasing deafness and frailty, whenever she was accused of deception, she was happy to go to an accuser's home where sleight of hand could be ruled out. Like all communication of this kind, the acceptance for many experiencing the phenomenon comes from personal evidence, and that was the case with Randall. He received messages purporting to come from his deceased parents that satisfied him they were communicating. But he was interested in exploring more profound questions such as "What happens after death?" and "Where is the afterlife?"

During one sitting a communicator responded:

"There are innumerable spheres in the spirit world. If it were not so, progression would be a myth. Some tell you that there are only seven. That is because they have no knowledge beyond that sphere. I do not mean a place fixed by boundaries, for the spheres or degrees in spirit life are only conditions and are not confined to a limited space; as a soul develops, it naturally arises above its surroundings and consequently experiences a change in its spheres or conditions."

This concurs with what communicators were telling Padgett a few years later. Aside from the physical world, they reported there are seven "spirit spheres," which we are confined to until we become "In Christ." After reaching the celestial levels the demarcations cease and progress appears to be unlimited.

For the next two decades, Emily participated in Randall's home circle on more than seven hundred occasions, and never charged a cent for her time, seeing her gift as a service to others. During those years, thousands of spirits communicated and shared their after-death experiences, as they perceived them from their respective levels. Emily passed away in 1912; Randall in 1935.

If the cases in this book are anything to go by, attorneys and judges appear to have taken a keen interest in this subject. It could be due to their expertise in distinguishing fact from fiction, constructing logical arguments and judging evidence. That said, magicians and illusionists will tell you that lawyers can be deceived like anyone else. But when it comes to detailed personal information unknown to the medium and sitters, however trivial, that argument doesn't always stand up to scrutiny.

William

"Chief Steady, you crossee big pond one time more before you shuttee eye one time more!" said Grayfeather to William Stead,[4] during a sitting of "Julia's Circle" in 1911 at Cambridge House, Stead's home in Wimbledon, Southwest London. Grayfeather was one of the spirit team, and the control of J.B. Johnson, a medium from Toledo, Ohio, who frequented sittings at Cambridge house.

The following year, at the invitation of U.S. President, William Howard Taft, Stead headed to New York to take part in a peace congress at Carnegie Hall. He was travelling on RMS *Titanic* and perished along with some 1,500 passengers and crew, when in the early hours of the morning of April 15, the ship sank after hitting an iceberg in the Atlantic Ocean.

Grayfeather's intriguing comment had come to pass.

William Thomas Stead is known today as one of the pioneers of investigative journalism. He edited two London periodicals: the *Review of Reviews* and the *Pall Mall Gazette*. He was controversial in his methods, but effective.

In 1885, his series of articles exposing the scale of child prostitution and trafficking in the UK were published in the *Gazette* under the title "The Maiden Tribute of Modern Babylon." In a bid to expose the practice, part of his investigation involved procuring a five-year-old child named Eliza Armstrong. The high profile case resulted in the government of the day raising the legal age of consent from thirteen to sixteen in what became known as the "Stead Act," and Stead was sentenced to three months in prison.

Stead was a well-loved, larger-than-life figure. His friend of thirty years, Lord Fisher, aka "Jacky," British Admiral of the Fleet and the driving force behind HMS *Dreadnaught*, the first modern British battleship, said of Stead, "First and foremost, he feared God, and he feared none else. He was, indeed, a human Dreadnought. And next, he had an impregnable belief that Right is Might, and not the other way round!"

Stead referred to God as the "Senior Partner." His view was that it was no use sitting down and expecting Providence to do a man's work for him. "We must first seek earnestly for 'signposts,' and having found them we must 'go ahead' with all our might, asking God to be our Senior Partner and realizing that He will expect us to carry out our full share of the undertaking," recalled his personal assistant, Edith K. Harper, in her book, Stead: *The Man*.

"I have gone doubles or quits on the Senior Partner all my days," he said. "He has never failed me, and I don't think He ever will."

It was on March 14, 1893, during a speech in London when Stead "came out" and shared his conviction that communication with the dead was a fact. It was there that he spoke of his ability to write automatically and receive messages through his hand from both living and deceased people.

During that speech, he announced the formation of "Julia's Bureau," an organization whose mission was to enable the living to communicate with deceased loved ones in a controlled setting and without payment—the greater mission being to show humans they had nothing to fear from the *sting of death.*

Julia A. Ames[5] was a journalist from Odell, Illinois. She was active in the thriving Temperance Union, a social movement that advocated healthy living, feminism, and the abstinence of alcohol. She was a Methodist and reportedly very devout. She had a deep friendship with Helen Hood, whom she met through the movement. The two were close and for a time lived together.

Julia worked for the Woman's Christian Temperance Union newspaper, the *Union Signal*, in Boston. In 1890, on a trip to London she met Stead at Mowbray House, Embankment, his London office of the "Review of Reviews." She impressed him and he invited her to Cambridge House where she met members of his family before returning to Boston.

The following year, at the age of thirty, she died of pneumonia.

In 1892, Hood visited the UK to help with Temperance reform. She stayed at Eastnor Castle in Herefordshire with Lady Henry Somerset, who had been elected president of the British Women's Temperance Association. Lady Henry met Julia when she visited the USA two years earlier and the two became friends. It was there that Lady Henry was introduced to Frances Willard, the worldwide president of the association, who put her forward for the British post.

A few weeks after Julia passed away, Hood woke up one night and "Julia" appeared by her bedside "looking radiantly happy, with a bright light all around her." Naturally, she was distressed by her friend's death and questioned what she was seeing. Soon after, another visitation occurred and she became convinced it was no mere hallucination. She felt that Julia was trying to communicate, and while at Eastnor Castle asked one of Lady Henry's inner circle if they could recommend a medium. Stead happened to be staying at the castle and the two were introduced.

It's not clear whether Hood was aware that Stead had met Julia previously, but he saw their meeting as a meaningful coincidence—a synchronicity—although it would be sixty years before psychologist Carl Jung coined the term.

During Hood's stay, Stead suggested he try to connect with Julia using automatic writing to see if he could get anything that would be evidential for her. She agreed. In *W. Stead: My Father*, authored by Stead's daughter, Estelle Stead Wilson, Stead reported:

"The following Sunday morning I was alone in my bedroom. I sat before the window, with the pencil in my hand and said, 'Now Miss Ames, if you are about and care to use my hand, it is at your disposal if you have anything to say to Miss E' (a pseudonym for Hood).

"Almost immediately my hand began to write, not in my accustomed handwriting, and not in the handwriting of either Mrs. D. or Henry L. The handwriting was clear and distinct. It ran thus: 'Julia Ames tell Miss E. not to worry so much about Lady Henry Somerset. We will take care of Lady Henry.'

"This was written slowly and deliberately, and I watched every word as it was being written. Then I said, 'that is all very well, but how do I know that this is not merely the unconscious action of my own subliminal consciousness? How do I know it is you? Can you give me a test?'

"My hand wrote, 'Yes; ask her if she remembers what I said to her when last we came to mine,' then the writing got straggly, and looked like 'ura.'

"I said, 'this is nonsense.' Then my hand wrote, 'You have got it wrong.'

"I said, 'Then write the letters in capitals,' and my hand wrote MINERVA.

"When I saw it was *Minerva* I felt sure there must be some mistake. Then it occurred to me that Minerva might be the name of some American town, and I asked, 'Is Minerva a place?'

"My hand wrote, 'No.'

"'Is it a person? Do you mean Minerva the heathen goddess?'

"'Yes.'

"'But,' I said, 'this is nonsense. How could you and Miss E. come to Minerva?'

"Then my hand wrote, 'Never mind; give that message to Miss E.; she will understand.'"

Stead, fearing that the message was nonsense, was reluctant to give it to Hood, but she insisted. The message read, "Ask Miss E. if she remembers what I said to her the last time we came to Minerva?"

"To my surprise Miss E. looked very grave and said, 'I remember it quite distinctly.'

"'Remember what?' I said, 'there is no sense in that.'

"'Yes,' said Miss E., 'she then said just the same about Lady Henry as your hand has written this morning.'

"'But,' I said, 'how could you come to Minerva. This is nonsense.'

"Then Miss E. smiled. 'Of course, I forgot, you do not know anything about Minerva. This is how it came about. Miss Ames said, before she died: "The Woman's Christian Temperance Union has come into existence as a great power in America. It is like the Minerva who sprang full grown from the temples of Jupiter," 'and she suggested we should call Miss Willard, Minerva. She bought a Cameo brooch of Minerva and gave it to Miss Willard and always called her "Minerva," till the day she died.'

"'Really?' said I.

"'Yes,' said Miss E., 'and the last time we saw Minerva together was the day before Julia died. Miss Willard came to the hospital to bid her good-bye, and it was then Julia spoke to me about not worrying about Lady Henry.'

"I felt utterly taken aback. The very thing that seemed to me the most utterly absurd thus seemed to prove the identity of the communicating intelligence."

Like many who experience communication purporting to come from a deceased person, what appears to be a trivial message is often the most evidential for those concerned. Stead and Hood were looking for evidence that Julia was communicating through his hand, and MINERVA was a trivial yet evidential word for both of them.

This was the beginning of ten years of communication with Julia, which Stead recorded in his book, *After Death: Letters from Julia*, in which she reported her experiences of life on the other side. Stead was enthusiastic about the book's potential and declared, "*Julia's Letters* will be the Thomas à Kempis *Imitation* of the new century." Later, when asked what the most important moment in his life was, he replied, "The most important moment in my life was when Julia first wrote with my hand!"

Stead's eldest son, Willie, died in December 1907. When given a friendly warning by an eminent statesman at the possible loss of prestige by openly professing his belief in life after death, he responded, "That is nothing! I have my son Willie's messages telling me he is alive and well in the Beyond."

After Stead's passing, Julia's bureau continued for a time. On occasions, communication was buoyed by Etta Wriedt,[6] a direct-voice medium from Detroit, who gave many evidential sittings to scientists and researchers on both sides of the Atlantic during the late nineteenth and early twentieth centuries.

"Mrs. Wriedt's visit was a marked feature in the history of Julia's Bureau," Harper wrote in *Stead: The Man*: "It cannot be too often repeated, however, that the great number of sitters who have related their personal experiences were neither visionaries nor mystics giving utterance to the revelations of the "contemplative life," but practical men and women of the most widely differing types: professional men, clergymen, soldiers, sailors, society dames, literary men, scientists and others; and of these, many represented different nationalities, but all were in agreement on one fundamental point, namely, that they had held conversations with departed friends, who had spoken to them in the "direct voice," and of whose continued life and activity in the next state of consciousness they had received convincing proof. ...

"Conversations in foreign languages, and in sundry dialects, frequently took place, and many of Mrs. Wriedt's sitters have on different occasions heard French, German, Danish, Norwegian, Serbian, Italian, Spanish, Arabic, Hindustani, and even Croatian, uttered in the séance-room. Two and even three voices have often been heard speaking at one time to different persons. I have even heard as many as four and five speaking simultaneously, Mrs. Wriedt herself often joining in the conversation."

Leslie

Leslie Flint[7] was a direct-voice medium. Born in London on January 21, 1911, he experienced communication with "dead people" from a young age and went on to hold private and public sittings for more than fifty years.

George Woods met Flint in 1945 after being introduced by Charles Drayton Thomas, a Methodist minister, who took a keen interest in psychical research. In 1953, Woods took Betty Greene to a sitting and both agreed that taping the sittings could preserve valuable evidence, and for the next twenty years they recorded hundreds of sessions, often with just the two of them in the room with Flint.

A.R. met Flint after his son passed away in 1978. He was given a tape recording of a sitting from 1962, in which Lord Birkett, a British politician who had achieved the rank of Lord High Chancellor of Great Britain and died in 1930, had come through.

On the tape, Birkett discussed the foolishness of the death penalty, having been a staunch supporter of it while he was alive. At the time, A.R. was a prominent London lawyer. He was intrigued by the recording and was introduced to Flint. He attended sittings where he received personal evidence from deceased relatives and the two became friends.

As with other mediums who operate over a long period, famous people occasionally came through during the Flint sessions. Reportedly, the spirit team on the other side encouraged and guided people to communicate if they thought there would be a benefit. Sometimes, they were helping someone stuck in the lower levels. Other times, they encouraged famous people to say a few words in the hope of spreading the good news of continued existence to a wider audience.

Some people comment that certain individuals sound different than when they were alive. I imagine some sitters were open-minded as to whether someone they didn't know was who they claimed to be, while others were skeptical. When it came to the voices, there were so many: upper class, working class, Scottish—not like Flint at all—and some of them spoke at the same time as Flint. Additionally, there were women who sounded like ... well, women.

A.R. attended sittings with Flint for sixteen years and witnessed the voices time after time until Flint's death in 1994. I have been fortunate to spend some time with A.R., and I consider him to be a reliable witness. Since direct-voice is as rare today as it was in the past, witnesses are few and far between.

In recent years, the Leslie Flint Trust has digitized many of the recordings, and they are well worth listening to for anyone interested in the subject.

Barbie

Maurice Barbanell[8]—or "Barbie" as he was affectionately known— was the son of Polish parents who emigrated to London in 1899. Born in 1902 in London's East End, he was one of five children. His mother was devoutly religious—his father an atheist. He adopted his father's atheism, reasoning that he seemed to win the arguments when it came to religion.

At a young age, he volunteered as a secretary at a local literary club, where he booked speakers and acted as the house critic to challenge and encourage debate. Having once been taken to a fake séance by his friends, he had an aversion to Spiritualism. However, during a debate at the club, he was challenged by a Spiritualist speaker who said that before he dismissed the topic out of hand, he should spend six months investigating it himself. Barbie decided the man had a point and arranged to visit some séances, though he didn't for a minute believe they were real.

During one sitting, he fell asleep, and afterward, he was told that he had been in a trance, and that a North American Indian named "Big Jump" had spoken through him. He was embarrassed and apologized, saying he remembered nothing. That event, however, would change the direction of his life. He started his own home circle, and Big Jump spoke through him, sharing spiritual philosophy.

By the mid-1920s, Barbie had caught the attention of Hannen Swaffer[9], a renowned journalist and drama critic who worked for the newspaper magnate Alfred Harmsworth, more commonly known as Lord Northcliffe,[10] who passed away in 1922.

Swaffer was one of the original gossip columnists, writing for the *Daily Mail*, the *Daily Sketch*, and other Northcliffe periodicals. Respected and feared in the world of media and theater, novelist H. G. Wells called him "The most dangerous man in London." Lord Beaverbrook, the press baron, and influential politician, said he was "The greatest personality that has walked down Fleet Street in our time."

Like many, Swaffer was curious about séances, which had become a popular pastime. On October 7, 1924, he and Northcliffe's secretary, Louise Owen, were guests of H. Dennis Bradley and his wife, who held regular séances with visiting mediums at their home in Kingston, Southwest London. In Bradley's book, *Wisdom of the Gods*, he reported that during the sitting, a communicator announced himself as "The Chief"—Northcliffe's moniker during his career. The voice said excitedly, "I am so glad to see you, Swaff," and a conversation between Owen, Swaffer, and "Northcliffe" followed."

On October 12, Swaffer's favorable account of the séance was published in the British national paper, the *Sunday People*.

Bradley had previously been invited to a forthcoming sitting with Mrs. Gladys Osborne Leonard at her home in Hertfordshire. Leonard had become known for her sittings with the physicist Sir Oliver Lodge, which he documented in his book, *Raymond or, Life and Death*. At the last minute, Bradley invited Swaffer but didn't forewarn Leonard. She hadn't met Swaffer before and at that séance Northcliffe came through again. A long conversation ensued, in which Northcliffe advised

Swaffer on some personal and work-related issues, which convinced him his old boss was communicating. This was the advent of a series of communications between Swaffer and Northcliffe, which resulted in his writing a book about his experiences.

During one séance, Swaffer, having finished writing the book, asked Northcliffe, "Have you got a title for me, Chief?" To which the reply came, "Call it *Northcliffe's Return*." The book was published under that title the following year.

Swaffer invited Barbie to join his home circle and the two became friends. The sittings usually involved six people, and a stenographer transcribing the communications. Barbie decided to change "Big Jump's" name to Silver Birch, after receiving a postcard with a picture of a birch tree on it.

Swaffer introduced him to his accountant who suggested he publish a newspaper in which he could share Silver Birch's philosophical teachings, and in 1932, the first issue of *Psychic News* rolled off the press. Barbie kept his identity as the medium secret, not wanting to be thought of as promoting himself through the paper.

During one sitting, Silver Birch explained that he was part of a larger group trying to share spiritual truths, as they understood them:

"We have sought to reveal the Nazarene as a great exemplar," he said. "And many have seen the reason that lies in our teaching. Great work has been done, but a greater work still has to be done. There is war in your world of matter, war that need not be, for if your world knew these truths and lived them, men would not kill. ... I am only the mouthpiece of those who sent me, and I seek no glory for myself and no reward. I have no desire to aggrandize myself or my personality. I rejoice to be a vehicle for expressing these truths, lost for many centuries, and now restored to the world of matter, stamped with the seal of divine truth."

Barbie and Swaffer gave lectures across the UK spreading Silver Birch's teachings that life continued beyond death, and during a three-year period they reportedly spoke in front of 250,000 people.

In the 1970s, Barbie and Paul Beard,[11] one of his peers, made a pact that whoever died first would attempt to come through to the other and report back on his findings.

In 1982, a year after Barbie's passing, he came through to a medium named Marie Cherrie who worked at the College of Psychic Studies in London. Beard, the president of the college at the time, was the sitter.

The communication between Barbie and Beard, via Cherrie, lasted four years. Barbie proposed that his account should be published so the information could reach a wider audience. He got his wish and in 1987 a book was published titled *The Barbanell Report.*

Barbie had been a leading light in the Spiritualist movement for decades and possessed significant knowledge of the subject; therefore it was assumed—although maybe not by him—he would be well placed when he arrived on the other side. But as he explained to Beard, it wasn't that simple.

Having entered the spirit world, Barbie discovered that his long relationship with his guide, which had defined much of his adult life, had fundamentally changed. Like a parent, sending a child off into the wider world, Silver Birch[12] left him largely to fend for himself.

In the early stages, Barbie observed that there were two types of people among his deceased peers, friends, and family: those like him who were trying to understand the nature of their reality and asking questions, and those who were content to continue with life as they had before. Because he remained a questioner ever seeking answers, he was finding life far more complex than he had envisaged. For many, it seemed ignorance was bliss—at least for a while.

He told Beard, "It's much more exciting than I expected; the possibilities are endless and quite daunting. Still some confusion with realities, so much depends on what you want to see. Difficult to keep readjusting."

He described meeting his mother who appeared to be on a different level and experiencing a different reality than his.

"Mother's reality is not my reality. ... When I am with her [I] have to accept her reality."

"Because she would not be able to accept yours quite so readily?" said Beard.

"Wouldn't understand it, confuse her.

"Understand the experience of seeing through their eyes. Like speaking to people with different points of view, only the points of view are reflected around them. And so they have reality. Can be confusing. I am groping towards my own reality; can't be sure if I have achieved it yet. I know how easy it is to see what you expect to see. Must be careful to stay away from this trap. Comfortable trap but still a trap. Guide says I'm on my own now. Get a little bit of help but not a lot. Tremendous sense of well-being; feel you could move mountains. Probably could if you knew how! Hear people's thoughts as if they are speaking.

"I continue to find difficulty in controlling my thoughts. I would have said of myself that I was disciplined in this way when I was in this world."

"I would have said so too," said Beard.

"But compared with over here I realize I was only a beginner. I can sustain it for periods and these periods are getting longer but there are also periods when I cannot remember what I have done or where I have been."

"Do you mean on earth or over there?"

"Over here. One could almost call them blackouts."

"Can they be recovered later on?"

"So I have been told. I have been told by others that my time sense and awareness will get better but I was never a patient man. I have been told that I am trying to learn things too quickly. ... At times it seems very dream-like. It seems to need an effort of will to concentrate on. These periods when I speak to you encourage this."

"Are they tiresome to you in a way?"

"They start off that way, then I become interested."

"I see."

"And of course there are still ties of love where I remain interested in the well-being of those close to me. I have tried to analyze this. It is possible that because I have such an enquiring mind, I have pulled more away from the bonds than the average person whose sole interests were family and friends. This is a possibility. But we spend so much of our time on this level speculating on the nature of things and what could be learned, to us this is a great adventure to be explored as much as possible. This may be why we did not hear so much from the brilliant minds of previous centuries, for by the very nature of their thinking they would have been drawn further away from the level they had left."

"Yes, understood."

"This may also explain why the average person has less trouble contacting relatives, again and again, for they merely continue to do what they did on earth. One thing you become aware of over here is that although there can be some help and guidance given by others, most of the progress is done by you. There is a sense of *Déja Vu* about the whole thing. One is constantly coming up against an inner knowledge, an inner knowing that recognizes and understands what is taking place."

"So this is both old memories and a condition to which you will restore yourself?"

"Yes. One of my first recollections when I passed over was to rid myself of a dream-like feeling. I can see now why it would be so easy for people to exist in this state and find it difficult to come out of it. Unless one were aware of this and prepared for it, one could exist in this state for some time. Being prepared for it, I was on my guard and was not seduced by it. We were right, however: transition is easy. I suppose I had to prove it for myself. It is all very well to be told this but to experience it gives you personal proof."

Barbie explained the problem he was having in convincing those on earth who knew him that he was who he said he was.

"Know the group is still not totally convinced I'm communicating. Some are, some are not, but then I would be the same in their place. It will all have to be individual."

"I see and if they won't come to the water it's a difficult thing isn't it?" said Beard.

"You know, I know, that what convinces you will not convince them and vice versa. Although they treat this in a scientific way there will still be that need for personal evidence, something that will be relative between myself and them.

"Have spent some time travelling."

"Up or down?" Beard asked.

"Wish I could go up! Little bit down, not much, more across."

"Is it more different than you expected?"

"In some ways it's familiar to me, like an echo."

"After all, you've done it before."

"But in other ways different. Think it's because I'm more aware this time. Maybe awareness makes the difference. Amazing the number of people who live in their own worlds, can't reach them."

Throughout the sessions, Barbie talked about his relationship with time, and how as he progressed, he was losing track of it.

"The difficulty which I still experience, which I am still experiencing, regarding time when I try to relate it to your world."

"A common problem," said Beard.

"So our meeting now is in the future of the first one ahead of it," Barbie explained. "If I had not the knowledge that we had spoken on this subject previously, I would have had difficulty perceiving which was the past and which the future. I do not know if I am explaining this very well."

"Well, the very fact is hard for us to take up isn't it?"

"Yes, because for me it does seem we are carrying on a conversation that has not had much of a break between. Yet the time sense I have learned in this level has made me realize that time has passed. Whether this time sense will stay with me much longer I do not know, for I am beginning to realize that I can be in two times at once."

"Two times?"

"Not just two places, and so you can see my difficulty."

"How much division of consciousness does this bring about?"

"Not as much as I would have expected. The difficulties were at first, when I began to become aware of what I was doing. Then there was a confusing period."

"Is this what you meant by feeling not adjusted?"

"Yes. As you know, you and I both realized that there would be the ability to be in two places at once but we did not realize this could also tie in with time also. As I speak to you now, I have already done it."

"That's a puzzler to me obviously."

"But I am also doing it," said Barbie. "Words are so clumsy. I have tried to think of ways to explain it to you. The nearest I can come to explaining it is by speaking of those people who can go to sleep at night and witness events happening on ahead, maybe months or weeks later. In the past I, and I suspect you, have always thought of the spirit travelling on in time."

"Yes, odd not to."

"Leaving the shell in the other time sense but not the spirit."

"I'll have to think about that one."

"However, I now am beginning to understand that the spirit can inhabit both these time phases simultaneously and so the dreamer is not empty while the spirit travels on but merely inhabiting two time levels with more consciousness of the future time level."

"So that's how precognition comes about is it?"

"Yes."

Being in two times at once sounds like science fiction but it might be a hint of what's happening during a premonition.

Barbie discovered that in the spirit world logic and intellect didn't help as much as he had previously thought, and in some ways were a hindrance. Maybe it's not surprising. Imagine a person with a high IQ and a PhD in computer science going into the Amazon rainforest with a hunter-gatherer tribe without any preparation. Or consider a member of the tribe trying to make sense of a science lab for the first time. They are different realities just as the world Barbie described is a different reality.

Barbie said it was "amazing the number of people who live in their own worlds" whom *he couldn't reach,* which seems to be a common theme. Those in the spirit world may say the same about us.

As we experience time, he had been in the spirit world for a year when the Beard communications began, and was still trying to get to grips with his reality. If he's correct, it seems that no matter how prepared we think we might be when the day comes, the journey has only just begun and there's much to learn and discover.

Life on the other side sounds complex, although if it's a perfect system—and let's assume if God created it, whatever God is, it's perfect—then it has to be accessible for everyone, whether they be a hunter-gatherer or a computer scientist.

5

PSYCHIC STIGMA

1542-2014

Witches:
A danger to Shipping

In 1542, the English Parliament passed the first Witchcraft Act, making witchcraft, sorcery, and conjuring, along with other demon-related activity, punishable by death. Five years later, the act was repealed, only to be reinstated in 1563 with even harsher provisions. The new Act formally criminalized witchcraft and imposed the death penalty on those convicted of using magic to cause harm or death.

In 1589, the seeming obsession with witches escalated when King James VI of Scotland was married by proxy to Anne of Denmark. While sailing to Scotland to meet her future husband, Anne's ship was caught in violent storms and forced to anchor on an island off the coast of Norway.

Anne wrote to James and informed him that her crew had made a number of attempts to set sail but each time they were thwarted by the weather. With winter setting in, she said they wouldn't be attempting to make the trip again until the spring.

It was decided that the bad weather was due to witchcraft. Dark forces were at work in Denmark and they had steered the fleet to Norway.

The king, no doubt feeling put out by the thought of his nuptials being delayed and wanting to meet his bride, ordered the Royal Fleet to make ready, and on October 22, 1589, he set sail to Norway with six ships. Due to the weather conditions, the trip took three weeks, but eventually they reached Oslo where the happy couple were married.

On the return voyage, the king's fleet was battered by severe storms resulting in the loss of one of the ships. James believed witches had struck again—this time it was Scottish witches.

The following year, witch trials were held at a small Scottish town called North Berwick. People—usually women—who were thought to be witches were arrested, tortured, and in some cases, garroted and burned at the stake.

The king, possibly still smarting from the Norway experience, wrote a book titled *Daemonologie*, which was published in 1597 in Scotland. The book warned that witchcraft, demonic possession, and sorcery were real and present dangers, and that even In Christian Scotland, practitioners should be hunted down and, in certain cases, executed for the benefit of all.

In 1603, Queen Elizabeth I died childless, and James—the son of Mary, Queen of Scots and Elizabeth's first cousin once removed— became King James I of England (he was already James VI of Scotland), uniting the English and Scottish kingdoms.

By this time, the Protestant Reformation was well underway—and skepticism about witchcraft was growing—particularly among some intellectuals. Nevertheless, James remained committed to stamping out the practice, and that year *Daemonologie* was published in England.

In 1604, England passed a new Witchcraft Act, broadening the legal definition of witchcraft and making it a capital offense under secular courts, which were often harsher than the ecclesiastical courts that previously handled such cases.

In 1727, Janet Horne became the last known person to be executed for witchcraft in the British Isles. According to folklore, she was covered in tar and burned at the stake. She was elderly, possibly suffering from dementia, and probably no danger to anyone.

By the early eighteenth century, belief in witchcraft had declined significantly. In 1735, Parliament passed a new Witchcraft Act, which shifted the legal focus from prosecuting witches to penalizing fraud. Instead of treating witchcraft as a genuine supernatural crime, the law made it illegal to falsely claim magical powers, such as fortune telling and necromancy. While this effectively decriminalized the practice of witchcraft itself, offenders could still face up to a year in prison for fraudulent claims.

All was quiet for a while. Then in the mid-1800s, a series of unexplained taps, knocks, and rappings were reported in the USA, France, and Great Britain. Seemingly out of nowhere, the dead appeared eager to make contact. Perhaps it was because people had stopped killing witches. Within a few years, home circles were springing up in the UK and both the working class and aristocracy had their favored mediums.

In 1871, London was the most populated city in the world and home to 3.3 million people. Queen Victoria opened the Royal Albert Hall, and Charles Darwin's second book *The Descent of Man* was published. Many of the educated classes were basking in Darwin's glory. The materialists were happy with the certainty that humans were merely sophisticated apes and could rest assured there was no going to heaven or hell—no torturous eternity, no monotonous harp playing while gazing at the creator. God was out—evolution was in. Science had the answer and they worshiped at its altar in the belief it could explain everything. Having decided there was no longer a need for God, it was the survival of the fittest, and those who had the most educated minds, were at the top of the evolutionary tree. They were intellectual apex predators— or so they thought.

Meanwhile, Christians who took the Abrahamic timeline literally, tried to explain what dinosaur remains, demonstrably older than Adam and Eve, were doing in England.

Neither the Christians nor the materialists liked the idea of some kind of "other place" inhabited by real-living beings communicating with people on earth. It threatened both their worldviews. The materialists were certain that after death they were just bones in the ground, which in the meantime left them to do just as they pleased without being judged by a higher authority, while many Christians thought the dead were asleep, tucked up in their graves waiting for the trumpet to sound, and if something was communicating, it must be demonic. Spirit communication from deceased loved ones, reassuring the living they were alive and well, was just too inconvenient.

But some scientists were courageous and ever curious. They were open-minded and followed the evidence wherever it led them.

The Medium and the Physicist

"Robert Chambers is here," uttered Home. "I feel him."

D. D. Home's arms and legs shook violently, as if he were having a seizure.

Robert Chambers had died seven weeks earlier on March 17, 1871, in St. Andrews, Scotland. He was the co-founder of the W. and R. Chambers publishing house and had written the introduction to medium Daniel Dunglas Home's autobiography, *Incidents in my Life*, which was first published in 1863.

The sitting took place on May 9, 1871, in the drawing room of the home of Miss Douglas at 81 South Audley Street, Mayfair, London. Along with the medium, Daniel Dunglas Home,[1] six sitters were present: Miss Douglas; the esteemed physicist and chemist, Sir William Crookes;[2] Mr. O. R.; and three others.

Douglas was reading extracts from Chambers' introduction, and prior to Daniel's utterance, three loud raps were heard from the small sofa table behind her, which was about two feet away. The table levitated and slowly glided to within five inches of Douglas and Home, seemingly announcing Chambers' presence.

The room was furnished with a loo table with the traditional center pillar; it weighed thirty-two pounds, was three feet in diameter, and covered with a tablecloth, which was occasionally turned up to give light from the open fire.

"It was a wood fire, somewhat dull in the grate. Temperature very comfortable all the evening," Crookes reported in *Notes on Séances with D.D. Home.* "The table tilted several times in four or five directions at an angle of about 25 degrees, and kept inclined sufficiently long for those who wished to look under [it] with a candle and examine how the hands of Mr. Home and the others present were touching it. Sometimes it stood on two legs, and sometimes it was balanced on one."

In Home's presence, tables reportedly levitated, hands materialized, an accordion played when he touched it or was nearby, and on more than one occasion he was said to have been levitated in full view of the sitters.

Crookes wanted to test the force being used to levitate or "tip" the table to ascertain whether it was the result of "psychic force," a term he coined, or whether Home or one or more of the sitters were consciously or unconsciously manipulating the table.

"I, who had brought a spring balance in my pocket, was now invited by Mr. Home to try an experiment in the alteration of weight ... the balance was hooked under one edge of the table, and the force required to tilt it measured." Experiment 1: "Be light. An upward pull of 2lbs required to lift one of the feet off the ground, all hands lightly touching the top of the table," Crookes observed. In the second experiment the instruction was to be heavy. "The table creaked, shuddered, and appeared to settle itself firmly into the floor. The effect was as if the power of a gigantic electro-magnet had been suddenly turned on, the table constituting the armature." A pull of thirty-six pounds, significantly more than before, was now needed to lift it. Crookes verified that everyone's hands remained light to touch and Home's feet were tucked under his chair.

There were five experiments in all. In the fifth, again, the instruction was to be heavy. "The index of the balance rose steadily without the table moving in the least until it pointed to 46lb. At this point the table rose an inch, when the hook of the balance slipped off, and the table returned to its place with a crash. The iron hook had bent out sufficiently to prevent it holding the table firmly any longer, so the experiments were obliged to be discontinued."

After the table weighing experiment, Home went to the fire and stirred the coal with his bare hand. He took out a red-hot piece as big as an orange. Showing it to Crookes, he cupped it in his hand and blew on it until it became white hot. Then he fell to his knees as if to pray and said, "Is not God good? Are not His laws wonderful?"

At the end of the sitting, five raps indicated a call for the alphabet, as was tradition. The following message spelled out: "It is a glorious truth. It was the solace of my earth life and the triumph over the change called death."—Robert Chambers

∞

Two months later, Alfred Russel Wallace[3] attended a séance at 81 South Audley Street in which he experienced the same phenomena. Wallace was a naturalist, biologist, anthropologist, and explorer who proposed a theory of natural selection. In June 1858, Charles Darwin received a letter from Wallace outlining his competing theory. This shocked Darwin who had been working on his own theory for decades, and prompted him to finish his paper. Later that month, their respective papers were presented together to the Linnean Society in London.

Having witnessed psychic phenomena, Wallace had different ideas than those of Darwin about the mind, consciousness, and survival of death. In *Alfred Russel Wallace: Writings on Evolution 1843-1912* edited by Charles H. Smith, Wallace said, "On the spiritual theory, man consists essentially of a spiritual nature or mind intimately associated with a spiritual body or soul, both of which are developed in and by means of a material organism."

In 1871, Crookes invited George Stokes and William Sharpey, both secretaries at the Royal Society, to his house to participate in a sitting with Home. Both declined his invitation. Later that year, when he submitted a paper to the society it was rejected. However, not everyone dismissed Crookes's experiments. Darwin's half-cousin Francis Galton[4] was also on Home's trail.

Known today as the father of eugenics, Galton advocated selected breeding to weed out the weak. He described eugenics as "the science which deals with all influences that improve the inborn qualities of a race, also with those that develop them to the utmost advantage."

In 1869, following the publication of his book, *Hereditary Genius*, Galton wrote a letter to Darwin seeking his validation:

> I always think of you in the same way as converts from barbarism think of the teacher who first relieved them from the intolerable burden of their superstition. I used to be wretched under the weight of the old fashioned 'arguments from design', of which I felt though I was unable to prove to myself, the worthlessness. Consequently the appearance of your *Origin of Species* formed a real crisis in my life; your book drove away the constraint of my old superstition as if it had been a nightmare and was the first to give me freedom of thought.

Galton might have been feeling unchained from his old superstitions about design, but by 1872 he was attending séances with the celebrated medium who was confounding Darwin's peers.

On June 4, Lady Derby, described as a political hostess and part of the Victorian elite, wrote to Darwin asking if he would ask Galton to arrange for her son Lord Sackville Cecil, to attend one of Home's séances.

A few days later, Galton replied:

42 Rutland Gate SW.
June 7/72.

My dear Darwin[5]

I did not reply yesterday about the Spiritualists as I expected that day & this to have heard from Mr. Home & Crookes is out of town.

It will give me great pleasure to do what I can for Lord Sackville Cecil, but rather doubt whether I shall have [the] power to do much. I can't myself get to these séances as often as I like—indeed I have had no opportunity for a long time past. The fact is, that first class mediums are very few in number & are always ailing—Also that Crookes & others are working their very best at the subject and entertain a full belief that they will be able to establish something important and lastly what, I see, is a real difficulty with them, the introduction of a stranger always disturbs the séances. I say all this to excuse me in your eyes, if I don't fulfill your wishes as you wd. [sic] like, but I will do my best & write—whenever I have anything to say, to Ld. S. Cecil as you propose.

The person most likely to help would, I think, be Lord Lindsay.

I wonder if I have offended Home by my last letter to him—he has never replied & I hear incidentally there is to be an important séance this very night! Alas for me.

Ever yours sincerely,
Francis Galton

Darwin identified as an agnostic in his later years and was skeptical of Spiritualism. There is evidence that he attended one physical séance at the home of his brother George, who had hired a medium for the afternoon; however, he left before any phenomena occurred.
In a letter to J.D. Hooker[6] on January 18, 1874, he wrote:

It was in the dark, but George & Hensleigh Wedgwood held the medium's hands & feet on both sides all the time. I found it so hot & tiring that I went away before all these astounding miracles or jugglery took place. How the man could possibly do what was done, passes my understanding. I came down stairs & saw all the chairs &c &c on the

Table which had been lifted over the heads of those sitting round it.—
The Lord have mercy on us all, if we have to believe in such rubbish.
F. Galton was there & says it was a good séance.

Nullius in Verba

As is often the case with anyone attempting to unearth the nature of
reality that differs with the orthodoxy of the time, Crookes was ridiculed
by his peers. Despite his being an accomplished scientist, many didn't
believe what he reported. Some attempted to discredit him, accusing
him of somehow losing his otherwise sound mental faculties, even
though they hadn't witnessed what he was reporting. They claimed
Home must have been tricking or manipulating him, to which Crookes
replied, "The answer to this as to all other like objections is, prove it to
be an error by showing where the error lies, or, if a trick, by showing
how the trick is performed. Try the experiment fully and fairly. If then
fraud be found, expose it; if it be a truth, proclaim it. This is the only
scientific procedure, and this it is that I purpose steadily to pursue."

In 1913, forty-two years after the sitting at Audley Street, Crookes
was elected president of the Royal Society. Responding to accusations
of credulity, he famously said, "I never said it was possible, I only said
it was true."

When the Royal Society was founded in 1660, its motto was *Nullius
in verba* ("Take nobody's word for it," or "On the word of no one").
Crookes was suggesting to his peers, "Don't take my word for it, come
and see for yourself."

Darkness and Ectoplasm

An understandable criticism from some of those who witness physical
mediumship is sitting still in the dark for two hours and wondering if
what is happening is some sort of conjuring trick. That was my experience.
However, I witnessed phenomena such as musical instruments
illuminated with fluorescent tape flying around the room—while
playing—between and above the heads of the sitters at high speed, which
seemed inexplicable by normal means. But it was hearing a voice in the
room, which didn't come from any of the sitters, answer a question in
Russian that was compelling. The only other person in the room who

could have spoken was the English medium who was in trance with a gag tied round his mouth. That left me open to the possibility that the communicator was who he purported to be—my partner's deceased Russian grandfather.

The purpose of moving objects doesn't seem to be anything other than an attempt from someone or something in the higher levels to get our attention. Why does it have to be dark? Reportedly, for anything to materialize, whether it be a body part, a person, or a voice independent of anyone present, physical material has to be gathered from a physical body, invariably the medium's, which can be reassembled to create a materialization.

Charles Richet,[7] a French physiologist who was awarded a Nobel Prize in 1913 for his work in anaphylaxis, took an interest in psychical research. He experimented with a number of mediums who were known to produce physical phenomena in which he witnessed a substance that exuded from the medium's orifices that resembled "sticky muslin." It was a biological substance, which he termed *ectoplasm*. Others referred to it as teleplasm or adopted Crookes's term, psychic force.

Impersonators trying to recreate the substance use cheese cloth, and would-be debunkers claim it must have always been cheese cloth and insist ectoplasm doesn't exist. Yet, according to Richet, what he analyzed wasn't any kind of cloth. He described it as a "gelatinous protoplasm, amorphous at first," and went on to say that it "crawls like an animal, rises from the ground, grows tentacles like an amoeba. It is not attached to the body of the medium during the whole time, but more often it emanates from, and is connected to it."

Richet wasn't ready to accept spirit communication publicly, but he did satisfy himself that the existence of psychic phenomena was a tried and tested fact. In a letter to Sir Oliver Lodge,[8] he wrote, "I will publish a book entitled *La Grande Espérance* [The Great Hope]. And, without being resolutely spiritist in the sense of Conan Doyle and Allan Kardec, I gradually get closer to your ideas. I say to you, which is absolutely true, that your deep and scientific conviction had great influence, a very great influence."

Lodge, a pioneering physicist in electromagnetism and wireless telegraphy, demonstrated one of the first public radio transmissions in 1894 in Oxford, England.

He took a keen interest in psychical research and considered the evidence for life after death to be scientifically demonstrated. In his 1902 book *Proofs of Life After Death*, he wrote: "Basing my conclusions on experience, I am absolutely convinced not only of survival but of demonstrated survival—demonstrated by occasional interaction with matter in such a way as to produce physical results."

That same year, Lodge was knighted by King Edward VII and went on to receive further honors for his scientific work. Like Crookes, once Lodge began to investigate life after death, members of the scientific community attempted to discredit him.

Richet almost certainly received the same treatment. When questioned on the possibility of fraud, which he was fully aware of, he said, "When I think of the precautions that we have taken, twenty times, a hundred times, a thousand times, it is unacceptable that we were all twenty times, a hundred times, a thousand times misled."

Reportedly, light is destructive to ectoplasm, and if introduced suddenly, it causes the substance to snap back into the medium's body, resulting in harm. In his autobiography Voices in the Dark, direct-voice medium Leslie Flint recounted an incident from World War II when, as a non-combatant private, he was giving a séance in a dormitory. "One of the sergeants suddenly hammered on the door of our hut and then barged in, putting on the light as he did so, and our séance ended very abruptly. This caused the ectoplasm, which the other side had taken from me to form the artificial larynx through which the voices speak, to rush back into my body, and I felt as though I had been kicked in the solar plexus."

Like all skills, mediumistic ability comes in varying degrees. Mental mediumship can occur in both light and darkness, whereas physical phenomena—the movement of objects, voices, or materializations— seem to require darkness. Some mediums cope better with light than others. Flint, for example, experienced severe pain. Red light appears less destructive than white light. An analogy might be the process of developing photographs, which happens only in darkness. Although physical manifestations have occasionally been reported in daylight, they generally only occur in darkness—the darker, the better. Perhaps that's where the saying "things that go bump in the night" comes from.

In the 1800s and early 1900s, before electricity was in every home and on every street, natural darkness was the norm. D. D. Home reportedly never produced full materializations. He would sometimes ask a sitter to dampen the fire or turn down the gaslight to see if they could get better physical phenomena, and candles were used.

Of course, magicians challenged the mediums, calling it all sleight of hand, and still do, but they never reproduce all the phenomena.

Magician, entertainer, and self-proclaimed exposer of charlatans, James Randi,[9] famously marketed his million-dollar challenge to anyone who could demonstrate psychic ability, but it had to be under his conditions and he decided who could enter, which ensured that he never had to pay out.

Less well known is Victor Zammit,[10] a human rights lawyer in Sydney, Australia, who with his wife, Wendy, has had hundreds of sittings with mental and physical mediums in their own home and elsewhere. In the early 2000s, Zammit ran a million-dollar counterchallenge to Randi and any magician who could replicate the phenomenon, which the mediums produced under the same conditions. During that time, he and Randi communicated yet no one took up the challenge.

The last person to be prosecuted in the UK under the Witchcraft Act was Helen Duncan, who was imprisoned for nine months in 1944.

In 1951, the Fraudulent Mediums Act made it illegal for mediums or psychics to claim to communicate with the dead for payment if they were found to be acting fraudulently. The Act was repealed in 2008 and replaced by consumer protection laws. Today, mediums are treated like any other tradesperson and can face fines or imprisonment if they knowingly mislead customers. While being a medium itself is not illegal, you could face legal action if you charge clients for contacting "Uncle Bob" and knowingly deceive them.

In 2014, a petition was posted on the UK parliament website to make it illegal for a psychic or medium to charge in a public or private setting, until it has been scientifically proven, and until that time it should be considered fraud. In order for a petition to be debated in parliament it has to have 100,000 signatures. This one had sixty-one.[11]

Psychic stigma still exists, but genuine mediums can breathe a sigh of relief—for now.

6

THE ARCHBISHOP AND THE SPIRITUALISTS

The July 18, 1940, edition of the British periodical *Light* published a letter by the Swedish politician and minister Baron Erik Palmstierna, titled "Suppression of the Report Foreseen."[1] Palmstierna served as Minister for Naval Affairs during World War I, and was influential in maintaining Swedish neutrality at that time. He blamed Germany and Russia for the outbreak of the war in what he called "The Madhouse of Europe." Having been influenced by his mother's Christian beliefs, he appears to have taken a keen interest in psychical research and religion, as is evidenced by his books: *Horizons of Immortality: A Quest for Reality* (1937), and *The World's Crisis and Faiths* (1942).

His letter read: "Sir,—At a meeting on June 25th, 1938, we had discussed the report of the Archbishop's Committee on Spiritualism, which I was informed had been finally drafted and was to be submitted to Lambeth Palace. Then the following uncalled-for message arrived: 'The Church will not have the courage to reveal to the world what they really feel and think about communications with us. Many of them have visions, but lack courage and are filled with self-consciousness.'

"We answered that a valuable report on such a vital subject could not be suppressed, after all; but another message intimated that it was doubtful that the Church authorities would be willing to make it public."

The report Palmstierna referred to was a report on Spiritualism[2] commissioned in 1937 by Cosmo Lang, the Archbishop of Canterbury.

In the wake of World War I, which two decades earlier had claimed almost 900,000 British lives, and with another global war looming, death was at the forefront of people's minds. For tens of thousands of families grieving lost loved ones, the assurances of church leaders and clergy to have faith wasn't enough. People wanted evidence that life continued after death, and for some, Spiritualism provided that evidence. Home circles were becoming popular. By one estimate, there were 20,000 across the country. Meanwhile, church attendance was in decline.

In 1936, Francis Underhill, the Dean of Rochester, asked Lang to commission a report to look into Spiritualism. Lang was aware of its growing popularity and had previously commented that Christian clergy and lay people alike were "dabbling in Spiritualism." Underhill had been researching the subject and confessed in a letter to Lang that he had attended "sittings with several mediums in which the late Archbishop Randall Davidson and his parents came through."

By January 1937, Lang had invited a thirteen-person committee to complete the task. The mission was "To investigate the subject of communications with discarnate spirits and the claims of Spiritualism in relation to the Christian faith." Three declined, and one, Evelyn— Francis Underhill's cousin—dropped out after the first meeting. Evelyn Underhill, a noted author on Christian mysticism, expressed her thoughts in her resignation letter: "The material so far circulated is, of course, the sort of thing we have been familiar with for many years. Reading it I am struck once more with the utterly sub-Christian, anthropocentric, hopelessly unsupernatural character of the Spiritualist outlook. It is all about man, his survival, prospects, etc., hardly at all about God ..."

The remaining committee members, who were sworn to secrecy, included Francis Underhill as chairman; a bishop; a master of the Temple; a secretary; a professor of Christian religion at Oxford University; a psychologist; and an attorney.

There were high expectations from Spiritualists and Christians alike. For the Spiritualists, the report would be a vindication of their claims that communication with those on the other side of the veil was a fact, while for some Christians, if it were true, Spiritualism provided evidence that their faith was not in vain.

For the next two years, the committee members conducted research that included conversing with mediums, consulting representatives of Spiritualist organizations, and attending séances, with each member required to attend at least one.

In January 1939, the report was delivered to Lang. Subsequently, it was circulated to Anglican bishops, marked "private and confidential."

Eighteen months went by, and Lambeth Palace—the official residence of the Archbishop of Canterbury—was silent on the matter. Then, in July 1940, Lang assembled a group of forty-one bishops to decide whether the report should be released to the public. After very little debate the bishops announced:

"In respect of practical guidance to Christian people on a subject fraught with grave dangers, the report does not seem to be so clear as to make its publication desirable."

In 1942, the publisher Psychic Press, no doubt sensing the frustration of its readers, published a booklet titled *The Silence of Dr Lang*, which criticized Lang's decision to withhold the report. It included a letter written in 1940 by the editor of *Psychic News* to Dr. Underhill which read: "It is now being freely stated that the reason for the report not being published is due to the fact that it presents Spiritualism in a favorable light. The suggestion is also being made that the report is deliberately suppressed for this reason."

Underhill defended the Church's position, saying: "The report of the Archbishop's Committee on Spiritualism, of which I was chairman, was presented to the archbishops and diocesan bishops of England some months ago. ... The report itself disclosed much difference of opinion, and it was consequently felt that there was need of further careful investigation into the subject. On that account it was decided that the report should not be made public."

Frank Hawken, secretary of the Marylebone Spiritualist Association, echoed the opinion of many Spiritualists, stating, "I am confident that the report would have appeared if it had been adverse."

A leading Churchman commented to Spiritualist author Arthur Findlay, "Spiritualism has won a great victory. The fact that the bishops had turned down the findings of their own committee meant that the committee decided in favor of Spiritualism, and the bishops were afraid to make the findings known."

"The Nazis suppress any news which is not favorable to their creed," replied Findlay, in a robust statement. "So do the Anglican bishops. That is why they will not publish the findings of their own committee on Spiritualism. It was stupid of them ever to set up a committee, but dictators always do stupid things. Doubtless they thought that the report would be adverse, and that they would kill, once and for all, this ever-recurring menace to their creeds and doctrines."

The media broke the story and the *Daily Sketch* quoting *Psychic News* reported: "Hundreds of clergymen, waiting for a lead, are disappointed by the decision. Spiritualists are jubilant. They believe that suppression of the report is clear evidence that the war against Spiritualism has crumbled in the face of facts. They will press for immediate publication of the report." Some thought the validation by the committee would strengthen Church congregations and criticized Lambeth Palace for its failure to make the report public. One contributor in the book wrote, "Now, a Church of England committee has come out *on the side of the angels*. It finds proof of Survival. Yet what happens? Shsh! says Lambeth Palace. Put it away! Don't publish it! Investigate, investigate, investigate! But we won't tell the public!

"Meanwhile all the churches are facing the problem of dwindling attendances, *a drifting away from religion*, as Dr. Lang called it. If Dr. Lang wanted the public to *drift back to religion*, then there was no surer means of persuading them than through the issue of the hitherto suppressed report.

"Fifteen thousand Anglican clergymen, bewildered by Dr. Lang's decision, know that mourners desert the Church because it cannot give them comfort in the hour of sorrow. The world to-day wants proof, not creeds nor theories."

"Religion attracts, but the churches repel."

"Who said that?"

"Dr. Cosmo Gordon Lang, believe it or not!"

"Who was in control of the Church?"

"Dr. Cosmo Gordon Lang."

The Silence of Dr Lang didn't result in the release of the report, but nine years later, part of it was leaked to A. W. Austen, the editor of *Psychic News*. It was revealed that the majority of the committee had a favorable opinion of Spiritualism, and he had been sent the "Majority Report."

Austen contacted a member of the committee known to be in favor of it being made public and declared, "I have a copy of the Majority Report, and I am going to print it."

The headline of the November 8, 1947, edition of *Psychic News* read:—ARCHBISHOPS REPORT:—"The Bishops Kept It Secret For Nine Years!"[3]

"The [Majority] report was printed in its entirety in *Psychic News* and, with the co-operation of the Press Association, extracts from it appeared in newspapers all over the world," said Austen. ... "Still the Church preserved a stony silence. Copies of the paper containing the report were sent to all the bishops and the two Archbishops. No comment came except for a protest from the Archbishop of Canterbury. ... My printing of the report gave to the rank and file of the Church of England the guidance that had been denied them by the House of Bishops.

"The leaked report stated: 'We cannot ignore the fact that at least one considerable Spiritualist organization is definitely anti-Christian in character' ... but conceded, 'when every possible explanation of these [spirit] communications has been given, and all doubtful evidence set aside, it is very generally agreed that there remains some element as yet unexplained. We think that it is probable that the hypothesis that they proceed in some cases from discarnate spirits is the true one.'"

The committee concluded: "There seems to be no reason at all why the Church should regard this vital and personal enrichment of one of her central doctrines with disfavor, so long as it does not distract Christians from their fundamental gladness that they may come, when they will, into the presence of their Lord and Master, Jesus Christ Himself, or weaken their sense that their fellowship is fellowship in Him."

Despite the publication by *Psychic News*, Lambeth Palace and successive archbishops kept the report pigeon-holed for forty years until 1979, when it was published in full by The Churches Fellowship for Psychical and Spiritual Studies. The report included the statements of nine witnesses who gave testimonies on their experiences with Spiritualism. They included members of the Society for Psychical Research and Spiritualist organizations.

One was Earnest W. Oaten, the editor of *Two Worlds*, a Spiritualist weekly newsletter. He stated that during a five-year period he attended almost 1,000 seances, in which he estimated 20 percent provided genuine phenomena. Oaten said that during his forty years as a Spiritualist "he had never known a single moment of doubt, concerning the love and purpose of God, or the actuality of the spirit world."

Another witness was the Honorable Mr Justice Atkinson, who was described as a typical Churchman. He said he hadn't paid any attention to Spiritualism until 1930 when his daughter died. He had been skeptical of psychic phenomena but his wife showed some interest in it, and after their daughter's death she attended sittings with various mediums. During one session, a communicator who identified as their daughter came through and asked her mother to bring her father along next time, which she did.

Atkinson said that during the séances he attended, their daughter communicated sometimes for an hour at a time and they discussed friends, relations, and other personal matters. He gave evidence to the committee of three particular incidents, which, according to the report, were beyond coincidence. When asked about the effect Spiritualism had on his religious life, he said he had been losing interest in religion because he didn't hear anything he hadn't heard before, and Spiritualism had "given him a new interest in spiritual things."

A third witness, Dr Oliver Gatty, a member of the Society for Psychical Research, stated from the outset that he didn't believe in spirit communication. He claimed he had spent hundreds of hours with the best mediums in the USA and Europe and was unaware of any evidence that would meet a scientific standard. His opinion was that there was no evidence for telepathy, precognition, or physical mediumship, and poltergeist activity was merely "lonely adolescents wishing to become the center of attention."

In 1939, after Great Britain entered the war in Europe, scientists were needed to address the challenges facing the armed forces and defense organizations. Gatty had a first-class honors degree in chemistry and was recruited by the Ministry of Supply to work on gasmask smoke filters.

He didn't get to see the final report. On June 5, 1940, while testing smokescreen apparatus in a field outside Cambridge, Gatty, aged thirty-two, and a co-worker were killed in an explosion while photographing a test.

Palmstierna was also chosen as a witness, and committee members were invited to meet those in his circle who had received the prediction outlined in his letter. His book detailing the event had already been published so it was deemed unnecessary to include it in the report. The report remained silent on whether any members accepted his invitation. It's evident he had issues with the Church and reportedly said, "We will never have peace or pure religiosity in the world until the military and priests are abolished."

∞

Spiritualist beliefs differ in some respects. For example, Spiritualism doesn't accept reincarnation, while Spiritism, which is popular in Brazil, does. It's understandable. Spiritual "truths" have been gleaned from afterlife communicators over time, and those communicators don't claim to be all knowing. But there is one thing which Spiritualists and Spiritists agree on: Jesus is not God and didn't die for our sins.

According to Spiritism: "Jesus constitutes the type of moral perfection that Humanity can aspire to on earth. God offers him to us as the most perfect model, and the doctrine he taught is the purest expression of the Lord's law because, being the most spiritually pure of all those who have appeared on earth, he was animated by the divine Spirit."

In an article in *Light* on August 2, 1919, titled "Jesus Christ and Spiritualism," Arthur Conan Doyle, the physician, author, and creator of Sherlock Holmes, wrote, "Every Spiritualist whom I know is convinced that Christ is the highest of Spirits. Upon that there is no contention. Why not leave it at that, and let each determine in his own soul and reason how far that highest spirit approached actual divinity?"

The seven principles of Spiritualism are:
1. That there is an Infinite Intelligence, who governs all.
2. That personal identity and all sentient forms of life survive physical death.
3. That continuous existence and eternal progress occur for all in the Hereafter.
4. That there is communion with the spiritual realms.
5. That all of humanity is spiritually linked.
6. That in the Hereafter, all must account for their actions on earth and will judge themselves accordingly.
7. That all are responsible for the way they conduct their earthly lives.

Spiritualism is primarily a set of principles rather than an organized religion. It's based on various forms of evidence, including personal experiences and historical accounts, relating to our existence after death. Its seven principles[4] state continuous existence and eternal progress for all. Jesus in the Padgett messages would concur. However, it says nothing about his mission—the kingdom—and being In Christ. Jesus would argue that it's incomplete and missing an eighth principle: the ultimate purpose of existence, which is not merely surviving death, but immortality. Maybe that's what the Lang report meant by saying it was being anti-Christian or maybe it was number six: the proposition that all have to account after death, Christians or otherwise. Whatever the reason, the prediction in Palmstierna's letter that the Church wouldn't have the courage to validate spirit communication had proved to be correct.

7

ESP

Real or Imagined?

One night, I woke up around four in the morning, eyes still closed on the edge of a dream. I picked up the pen and pad on the floor next to the bed and wrote, "I was in a place with all six grandparents and they were dressed in white," which for me meant they were dead. I grew up with my step-grandparents so six grandparents made sense. "We are waiting for someone to arrive who has dementia. The person arrives. I don't know who they are or whether they are male or female but everyone is cheering because the person has no sign of any disease." It was a happy dream. After I'd written it down, I went back to sleep.

A few hours later, around eight in the morning, my son called me to let me know that Auntie Valerie had died during the night. I didn't know Auntie Valerie. She hadn't seen me since I was a baby and we had never met or spoken, but I was aware that she had suffered from Alzheimer's for many years. You might be thinking I was expecting Auntie Valerie to die, but I wasn't. My son met Valarie's daughter at a funeral a few years before and they discovered they share a love of blues music and stayed in touch. She let him know, which is why he called me. The materialist calls it a coincidence—others call it a "shared death experience." If it's not a coincidence it suggests that in my dream state I was connected to my dead grandparents and Auntie Valerie during her transition after death.

The Wheels of Science

The dogmatism prevalent in some orthodox religions, driven by a perceived need for certainty, also exists within parts of the scientific community when it comes to the subject of life beyond death. Any attempt to explore our ultimate reality using the scientific method that deviates from materialist philosophy, is swiftly labeled fringe, woo-woo, or pseudoscience and treated with disdain.

In 2024, Richard Dawkins, one of the most outspoken atheists in the world today, was asked if he was scared of death. "I'm afraid of dying," he replied ... "I'm afraid of eternity ... it's a daunting thought that the universe goes on and on ... for billions, for trillions of years. ... I wouldn't mind living for two hundred years but I wouldn't like to live for eternity."[1]

Christopher Hitchens, another famous atheist—or anti-theist, as he referred to himself—now deceased, described the prospect of heaven as a place of "endless praise and adoration, limitless abnegation and abjection of self; a celestial North Korea."

Dawkins seemingly only contemplated the orthodox heaven, experiencing time as we do, an unimaginable hell for sure. One would think these intellectual titans might have explored other potential afterlife scenarios rather than just the Christian heaven or Islam's paradise, and maybe they did, but if one rejects the possibility of any kind of continuity of life after death, why look for another heaven?

According to NASA, the first recorded sighting of a meteor shower occurred in 687 BC in China. While meteoroids have bombarded planets since the solar system's formation, reports of meteorite sightings, until the mid-nineteenth century were often dismissed by intellectuals as superstition or delusion.

In September 1768, local inhabitants of Lucé, a small village in northern France, witnessed a hot rock whistling through the air and crashing to the ground. In 1772, a sample was sent to the Académie des Sciences, where it was examined by the prominent French chemist, Antoine Lavoisier. Reflecting the scientific worldview of the time, Lavoisier reportedly expressed skepticism about the idea of stones falling from the sky, attributing the burned rock to a lightning strike. He argued that solid objects could not fall from the sky.[2]

It would be the following century before the extraterrestrial origin of meteorites was widely accepted by the scientific community, by which time Lavoisier had been beheaded for being on the opposing side during the French Revolution.

Imagine you're an academic, and you've spent your whole career believing continents don't drift, and someone comes along and tells you they do. That is what happened during the first half of the twentieth century when tectonic plates were discovered. For one leading geophysicist, Sir Harold Jeffreys, "Continental drift was out of the question because no force even remotely strong enough to move the continents across the Earth's surface was evident." Reportedly, Jeffreys went to his death in 1989 still rejecting the evidence, long after it had been deemed a scientific fact.[3]

OBEs; NDEs; remote viewing; clairvoyance; electronic voice phenomena; mediumship; deathbed visions; precognition; telepathy; distant healing; and psychokinesis all come under the umbrella term *psi*. Either these phenomena occur or they don't, and there is plenty of evidence, both scientific and anecdotal, that they do. Studies have shown that two-thirds of Americans believe in ESP,[4] and like meteorites, people have been reporting occurrences of it throughout recorded history. Materialist philosophy denies the existence of these phenomena; therefore, contemplating psi necessitates a change in worldview, which materialist scientists and nonscientists are unwilling to consider.

Science has transformed the material world, and as a methodology, is second to none. But humans are emotional creatures who have beliefs, ideologies, and agendas, and even though belief shouldn't be part of the scientific process, invariably, the interested party believes something is possible and investigates it using the scientific method. Conversely, if they don't believe something is possible, they are unlikely to start that process or even look at the data, and when asked about it, they will often dismiss it.

The key difference between religion and science is that science isn't dogmatic: like nature, science is a self-correcting process. Science replaces old facts, which weren't really facts, with new facts, whereas religion is stuck with its doctrine and seems unwilling to self-correct even when presented with evidence, and therefore is unable to progress in any meaningful way.

A Meeting of Minds

One scientific objection to psi is that for it to occur, minds either need to be connected in some way or thoughts must travel faster than the speed of light. The scientific consensus is that faster-than-light travel is impossible in our physical universe, meaning mind-to-mind communication must also be impossible unless minds are somehow connected, a concept not currently accepted by mainstream science.

If someone in New Zealand has a dream, vision, or just a hunch that someone died in a car crash in New York, and then discovers that at that time the person died in a car crash in New York, if it's not a coincidence, it suggests connectivity between minds.

In his 1973 book, *Dream Telepathy*, co-author Alan Vaughan, reported an incident of his own in which he watched one of his favorite writers, Kurt Vonnegut, Jr., on a television talk show one evening, and had a dream about him two nights later. On March 13, 1970, he wrote to Vonnegut to tell him about his experience. "... You appeared in a dream I had this morning. We were in a house full of children. You were planning to leave soon on a trip. Then you mentioned that you were moving to an island named Jerome." (As far as I know there is no such place, so perhaps the name Jerome or initial 'J' has some related meaning.)

Vonnegut's answer came back in a letter dated March 28, 1970. "Not bad," he replied.

"On the night of your dream, I had dinner with Jerome B. [an author of children's books], and we talked about a trip I made three days later to an island named England."

Shared Dreams

In 2009, I had just finished producing a documentary[5] about a man who was having premonitions about terrorist attacks, and for the past year I'd been interviewing scientists, journalists, and hypnotherapists on the subject.

I had been keeping a journal since my accident and recording my dreams, and I noticed a few appeared to be precognitive. Because I had gotten used to waking up in the night and writing down a dream before going back to sleep, sometimes I would almost forget I had written them down.

One morning I woke up and opened up the notebook by my bed to see what I'd written. I had scribbled, "HARRY REID IS A UFO," and I had crossed out "REID," and written "REED." I didn't know what to make of it. I knew nothing about UFOs and I didn't know anyone called Harry Reed (pseudonym).

Later that day, out of curiosity I googled "Harry Reed." The first name that came up was a website with that name. It was a man in the USA who ran dream workshops. I had never heard of him but wondered if I had subconsciously come across his name while making the documentary. The dream made no sense: "Harry REED IS A UFO." What does that even mean? I noticed the website had an email address, and I emailed him and said something along the lines of "Dear Harry, last night I had a dream about someone with your name. It was to do with UFOs."

That evening I received a reply saying, "That's interesting because last night I had a dream that WE WERE A UFO." **Note:** I had not mentioned in my email that HE WAS A UFO. I just said it was about UFOs. What are we to make of that? I had never had a dream about UFOs before nor since.

On October 3, 1226, the Bishop of Assisi was on a devout pilgrimage to the church of St. Michael, on Mount Gargano in Italy. In *The Life of Francis of Assisi* by Saint Bonaventure it was reported, "The Bishop of Assisi at that time had gone on pilgrimage unto the Oratory of Saint Michael on Monte Gargano, and unto him the Blessed Francis, appearing on the night of his departure, said: 'Behold, I leave the world and go unto heaven.' The Bishop, then, rising at dawn, related unto his companions that which he had seen, and returned unto Assisi; there, when he had made diligent enquiry, he learned of a certainty that in that hour whereof the vision had notified him, the blessed Father had departed from this world."

If it can happen to Vaughan, the bishop, and to me, it can happen to anyone.

Multitudes of people from around the world and across different ages have reported similar experiences. I wouldn't call my example precognitive—which is knowledge of something happening in the future—but if it wasn't a coincidence, I seemed to have been sharing someone else's dream.

It made me wonder whether we knowingly or unknowingly do that all the time. After all, it was the only time I've ever written to a stranger about a dream. And if I hadn't (a) remembered the dream, (b) written it down, (c) looked up the name, (d) written to the person, and (e) received a reply, I would have never been aware of it.

Events foreseen

Anecdotally, premonitions are commonplace. In June 1947, the legendary boxer Sugar Ray Robinson arrived in Cleveland, Ohio, for a match with the twenty-two-year-old welterweight Jimmy Doyle. While staying at a friend's home before the fight, Robinson had a dream. In his autobiography, *Sugar Ray*, he wrote, "In the dream, Jimmy Doyle was in the ring with me. I hit him a few good punches and he was on his back, his blank eyes staring up at me, and I was staring down at him, not knowing what to do, and the referee was moving in to count to ten and Doyle still wasn't moving a muscle and in the crowd, I could hear people yelling, 'He's dead, he's dead,' and I didn't know what to do. Then I woke up."

The following morning, he told his trainer about the dream who brushed it off, telling him, "Forget it, Robinson. That's a dream, that's all. Don't have it on your mind. Nothing's gonna happen."

At the weigh-in he shared his fears with the promoter, who didn't want the financial repercussions of canceling the fight. "Don't be ridiculous," he told him. "Dreams don't come true. If they did, I'd be a millionaire."

Robinson had knocked out many opponents during his career without killing anyone, but he saw it as a warning. He threatened to tell the Boxing Commission he wasn't going to take part and a priest was sent to talk to him, and after some persuasion, he agreed to fight.

Robinson dominated the match but Doyle kept coming at him, and in the eighth round he recalled, "I saw the opening I had been waiting for, and I went for it. I threw a double right hand, first into his belly, then to his head. He sagged a little but he kept coming at me, and he started to throw a right hand when I beat him to the punch with a good left hook to the jaw. ..."

"I stood over him, transfixed, seeing my dream come true, horribly true ... You warned me, God, I was thinking; you told me. Why did I let everybody talk me out of it."

Doyle was taken to hospital where a priest administered the last rites, and he died shortly after. Feeling remorseful, Robinson sent the proceeds from his next two fights to Doyle's mother.

Robinson is known today as one of the all-time greats, and the Doyle fight may well have been his most memorable, for all the wrong reasons.

On April 8, 2024, a video was posted on YouTube about solar eclipses. In it, a pastor named Brandon Biggs was prophesying about climate, weather, and a new wave of patriotism: "A red wave coming to America."

"I saw Trump rising up," he told two other presenters. "I saw an attempt on his life. This bullet flew by his ear, and it came so close to his head that it busted his eardrum. He fell to his knees ... and he started worshiping the Lord; he got radically born again. He becomes really on fire for Jesus."

Three months later, on July 13, Donald Trump, the Republican presidential candidate in the 2024 election, was speaking at a rally in Butler, Pennsylvania, when a shot rang out. Trump dived to the ground, clutching his bleeding ear. He had been shot by a would-be assassin on a roof less than two hundred yards away.

Biggs was recalling an event that had yet to happen, and because the ear was important, he may well have embellished or misinterpreted the vision reasoning that Trump's eardrum had burst. Mediums warn against trying to interpret a psychic experience, as do remote viewers, who refer to it as "analytical overlay" (AOL). They see or sense something and then try to analyze it rather than simply reporting what they experience, which leads to errors and misreporting. There's no question that in the actual assassination attempt, the ear was a feature.

It could be argued that the most famous premonition in history is Jesus's prediction of his own execution, mentioned numerous times in the New Testament. His predictions reportedly included the manner of his death and the betrayal by one of his disciples. Jesus's premonitions are central to Christian belief and are cited as evidence that they fulfilled Old Testament prophecies—and, therefore, his execution must have been part of God's plan.

Due to Biggs's Christian beliefs, he may have assumed that God was giving him the information and concluded that Trump was God's pick for president. Later, Trump gave a speech saying, "I was saved by God to make America great again," which begs the question: Why didn't God protect the man sitting behind him, who died shielding his family from the assassin's bullet? And if God chose to intervene, why didn't He stop the shooter before the attack?

If the video is authentic, the pastor—like Robinson—may have gotten a glimpse of a potential future, as people report from time to time. And while that's anecdotally compelling evidence for a greater reality, it doesn't demonstrate that God had anything to do with it. In essence, a prophecy is a kind of premonition. The difference is that if the person believes it comes from God, they call it a prophecy, but without God, it's a premonition.

In the New Testament, Paul states: "Do not treat prophecies with contempt but test them all; hold on to what is good, reject every kind of evil" (1 Thess. 5:20–22).

"Test everything" sounds like good advice. One could argue that "reject every kind of evil," in this context, implies that some prophecies— such as the alleged attempt on Donald Trump's life as reported by Biggs, a disturbing dream recounted by Robinson, or even Jesus predicting his own execution—may point to troubling future events that are not necessarily part of God's plan.

There is currently no widely accepted scientific explanation for how premonitions might work, and mainstream science generally regards them as nonexistent. Nevertheless, the specificity of the experiences people report is not easily explained by coincidence alone.

It's often said that "the wheels of science move slowly"—and that certainly seems to be the case. Physicist Max Planck, a Nobel Prize winner often regarded as the father of quantum theory, said "science advances one funeral at a time." Quantum theory has been around for more than a hundred years, and debates about the nature of consciousness have been going on for centuries. In recent years, both have become hot topics.

A unified theory of everything remains elusive, while evidence for ESP continues to defy explanation. Perhaps a new paradigm is emerging. Maybe in another hundred years, science will have figured it out.

8

SPIRIT COMMUNICATION

A Tricky Business

In May 1959, during a session with Leslie Flint where Betty Greene and George Woods were sitters, a communicator came through who identified as Cosmo Lang.[1] Having died fifteen years earlier, it appears the former head of the Church of England now found himself on the other side of the veil trying to communicate ... the very thing he suppressed during his career.

"Cosmo Lang here."

Greene: "Excuse me, would you say that name again?"

Lang: "My name is Lang."

Woods: "Lang?"

"Cosmo Lang. Yes, Archbishop of ..."

Greene: "Oh is it ...?"

Lang: "Can you hear me?"

Greene: "Yes, just."

Lang: "I pray you forgive me if I do not manifest very well."

Woods: "You're doing very well."

Lang: "It's quite a complicated procedure to-to-to manage to s-s-speak in this fashion, through this apparatus."

Woods: "Yes."

Lang: "But I would very much like to talk to you for a few moments."

Woods: "Thank you very ..."

Lang: "There are many souls here ... like myself, who are most anxious to make contact with the earth and to be of some service."

Woods: "Yes."

Lang: "But we realize the manifold difficulties—difficulties on our side and, in a sense, also on yours."

Woods: "Yes."

Lang: "There are so few, unfortunately, in your Spiritualistic circles who seem to have any real aspiration in the true sense. And although I do not want to cause any alarm, I would give this warning; that in my opinion, it is very unwise for so many of these souls in your world, sitting in their circles, to sit in the fashion in which they oft-times do.

"If only they would realize the dangers all around and about. There are many earth-bound souls of a low order, who are only too anxious to take advantage and to distort and, in fact, I consider it highly dangerous to tamper with these things.

"By that I mean, that when you sit in a group or circle in your own home or wherever it may be, that you approach it in the right manner, in a truly spiritual way.

"... And you should aspire to the highest possible, that you might contact souls who can be of inspiration and help to you. I have been to many of these sessions—these séances, as you call them, and I realize only too well how dangerous they can be if they [are not] conducted in a true spiritual manner.

"... if you are to contact the highest forces, the good forces, those who can help the world, those who can uplift mankind, you must take instruments who are of like mind and of like thought. And as I have said it seems to me, that many of these instruments are of a very, unfortunately, low order.

"By that I don't want you to think I condemn. Far from it. I am anxious to help all, of course. But I do feel that only when that which you term Spiritualism, is placed in its right perspective—when it is used and applied in the right way, when it has the instruments who are of a higher mental and spiritual level, who will give up all in true service to God, looking upon themselves as mere instruments of his divine power to serve the children of the earth and who have that feeling of desire for self-sacrifice, to give up all in service, to tune in with the highest and the finest that can come through from our world ... then it seems to me that while you are, as it were, only scratching the surface of the astral worlds, of which 90 percent of your instruments seem to be doing—then, it is not only bad—but it can even be dangerous.

"Because like can attract like and also lower entities who are earth-bound, who cling to the earth, can come through and use instruments and also through instruments, speak to peoples and tell peoples of things which are not true and also be the cause of much unhappiness, much misery.

"If you could see, as I have seen, various low mentalities and entities haunting various places in your world ... I mean, for instance, you take some of those whom you call lunatics, some of those who are in places set apart from those whose mental condition is such, they are often controlled or used by low forces, low entities.

"You see, there are many who, in your world, are unconscious mediums and if those in charge, for instance, in certain institutions where the insane are placed, understood these things, these truths of communication, many of those patients could be rid of these entities.

"Even [as you know] in the time of Jesus, when he released those who were obsessed by the Devil. So it is, that obsession is very much in your world, in certain instances. And that is where it seems to me the dangers of these séances can be—that you can be obsessed by entities who will distort you and distort truth, who will give to you falsehoods and mislead you.

"I feel it's so important that when you sit, you should always conduct yourself in the right sense, in the right fashion.

"That you should first approach God, not only when you sit in prayer, but also in your lives, which is even more important. For it is useless to sit for an hour to pray, unless you yourselves, in your daily lives, endeavor to make it a living prayer, in thought and in action."

∞

A verse in the Old Testament reads:

When someone tells you to consult mediums and spiritists, who whisper and mutter, should not a people inquire of their God? Why consult the dead on behalf of the living?

Consult God's instruction and the testimony of warning. If anyone does not speak according to this word, they have no light of dawn.

Distressed and hungry, they will roam through the land; when they are famished, they will become enraged and, looking upward, will curse their king and their God.

Then they will look toward the earth and see only distress and darkness and fearful gloom, and they will be thrust into utter darkness" (Isa. 8:19–22).

Both Isaiah and Lang were advocating seeking God rather than the spiritually dead. "They look toward earth and see only distress and darkness" could be interpreted as those in the earth planes of the spirit world Lang warned about—who "will distort you and distort truth, who will give to you falsehoods and mislead you." Just as Jesus in John advises us to "test the spirits," so Isaiah and Lang are indicating spirit communication is a reality and warning us to be discerning.

If you spend time with a group or circle you will often find they claim to have deceased people in the levels beyond this one working as guides and controls. Their aim is to curate and authenticate who comes through and to protect the medium, the intermediary, much like a security detail would here. In today's world of podcasts, chatrooms, and online forums, perhaps we can think of them as moderators.

At the higher levels, communication might come from a group—a group soul some call it—and they will communicate via a spirit team.

The circles and groups I've met, sing, pray to God, and operate in a respectful, spiritual manner, and are aware of the dangers of being influenced by negative entities. But if someone doesn't realize they are psychic, we are told they can be susceptible to those entities and influenced to exhibit violent or psychotic behavior, or just exist in a negative, depressed, and sometimes suicidal state.

We often talk about being in *good* spirits, but rarely do we refer to someone as being in *bad* spirits. When someone acts selfishly, we might call them *mean-spirited*. But consider the word *acts*: it's as if we are saying it's not really them. For the most part these are just figures of speech. But maybe we aren't in good or bad spirits. What if, occasionally, the spirits are in *us*?

The natural inclination of most humans doesn't seem to be to kill, otherwise with the technology available we might well be extinct by now. When someone calmly talks about how they kill children and defenseless people, we find it abhorrent. We talk about them looking like they were *possessed* and wonder what *possessed* them to do it, or we ask what got *into* them.

Serial killers sometimes claim the Devil or some otherworldly entity made them do it. The cynic might think they are trying to get a lower sentence or better conditions by pleading insanity, and in some cases that may well be true.

David Berkowitz, the notorious serial killer known as Son of Sam, terrorized New York City in the 1970s, taking the lives of six innocent people. At one point, he claimed a six-thousand-year-old man named

Sam channeled messages to him via his neighbor's dog instructing him to kill. His horrific crimes, fueled by a twisted belief system, sent fear throughout the city.

Berkowitz was adopted by Jewish parents when he was a few days old after being given up for adoption shortly after birth. Although he grew up in a stable home he was described as a troubled child. From an early age he was aware that he was adopted, which reportedly left him feeling inadequate and isolated and may have contributed to his aggressive and disruptive behavior.

In a 2024 interview, Berkowitz[2] said that during his childhood years he had no knowledge of the Bible, yet later developed a morbid fascination with satanic themes and horror movies. He joined a group and recited a satanic bible. He believed that the Devil was reaching out to him and prayed to it to hasten the end times, the end of the world. Plagued by depression and anger, he inflicted self-harm, describing his experiences as "something taking over my mind." He believed he was a soldier for Satan, called up on a mission. His victims were randomly selected. It was nothing personal.

After a decade in prison he found God, accepted full responsibility for his actions, and since that time has dedicated his life in prison to teaching Bible studies, helping other prisoners, and corresponding with troubled, sometimes suicidal people who write to him. We will never know if Berkowitz was possessed by an unseen entity, and most westerners, including Christians, probably wouldn't entertain the idea.

Spirit attachment or possession is an ancient universal belief, and in countries such as Italy, Mexico, and the USA, certain church denominations continue to perform exorcisms.

In a 2024 interview, Fr. Vincent Lampert,[3] a Catholic priest and designated exorcist from Indianapolis, was asked what he had seen in an exorcism that led him to believe it was supernatural and anything other than a mental health condition.

"Only God is supernatural," Lampert replied. ... "Demons, we would say are preternatural, they're above our understanding of nature. That's why demons can do things that we would say are not humanly possible. How is a body levitating; ... a head spinning, a body climbing up a wall like a spider? These kinds of things."

The interviewer asked, "Have you seen anything remotely like these things?"

"I've seen 'em all," Lampert said, but clarified that the head didn't actually "spin" but turned beyond what is considered humanly possible.

Alan Sanderson, a pioneering consultant psychiatrist, helped develop spirit release therapy, which posits that certain mental health conditions are due to spirit attachment. Unlike exorcism, spirit release therapy doesn't involve a priest, holy water, or a crucifix. Instead, the patient is relaxed through hypnosis, and the therapist—sometimes aided by someone with psychic abilities—communicates with the offending spirit or spirits. They gently question the spirit about its harmful impact on the patient—something the spirit is sometimes unaware of. The goal is to persuade the spirit to seek help and move on.

Mainstream psychiatry and psychology reject the idea that individuals who hear voices in their minds might be receiving information from an external source. But spirit release therapy has shown results—whether or not an actual spirit is involved—and today, a significant minority within the psychiatric profession are open-minded on the subject.

In his 2003 paper: "A Case for Spirit,"[4] Sanderson gave an account of a woman named Pru who had been diagnosed with multiple personality disorder, now referred to as dissociative identity disorder (DID).

Pru was a married woman in her forties. She had no children and had spent long periods in hospital. She had undergone psychotherapy for many years as a result of being sexually abused by her father as a child.

She suffered from deep depression, suicidal thoughts, and missing time, and would often find clothes in her wardrobe with no memory of buying them. She had scars from self-harm, but despite the challenges she was motivated to try the treatment, and was a subject who was easily hypnotized.

"During the therapy sessions some very destructive spirits were identified. Most powerful among these was her [dead] father, Jason. Pru would sometimes see him in the consulting room and would recoil in terror. With Pru in hypnosis, Jason spoke through her, claiming her as his possession, to do with as he pleased. To me he was strongly antagonistic," Sanderson wrote. "During two of our sessions Pru rose from her chair and stood over me, threatening to kill me. Each time she responded to my steady gaze and the command, 'Sleep'. In deep trance, Jason agreed to look within himself, where he saw blackness. I called for angelic help. With the use of Baldwin's protocol for dealing with demonic spirits, the blackness left. Thereafter, Jason was amenable. He agreed to leave."

In time Pru made a full recovery. She stopped cutting herself, took up art, and Jason and the other entities disappeared.

∞

On one occasion, Padgett received a communication from a deceased woman who was suffering:

"I have been waiting so long to reach you and have you help me," she pleaded. "Oh, do help me if you can. I am in darkness and torment in a hell that I never believed in when on earth, but which I now see is more real than the fire and brimstone hell which my very earnest pastor used to tell us about."

She explained that she was suffering because during her time working at a hospital, she secretly poisoned many men, women, and children but was never suspected or arrested for her crimes. Usually it was thought that the patient had died of heart failure. "Why I did this, I don't know, except that I was possessed by a legion of evil spirits more wicked than myself."

She told Padgett she was considered a good nurse who had helped many patients recover from their illnesses, and still remembered the good work she had done, but this was marred by the memories that filled her mind of the harm she had done to others.

"I really gloated over the deaths caused by my awful deeds," she wrote, "and many a time I have sat beside the patient and watched his life go out, when it might have been prevented by an antidote of which I knew. ... Oh, it was pleasure to my evil cravings and to my evil spirits that I sometimes thought were around me. So you see, I was of all women the most wicked, and of all sufferers I have suffered the most."

Padgett asked if she had tried to resist the urges: "Yes, I have tried to fight against these desires when I felt them coming to me and I have even sought to avoid the awful deeds by leaving the hospital for a while, but all to no purpose. I would be drawn back as if a great chain was attached to me and was pulling me back to my awful work."

Padgett asked whether she had met her victims since her death: "I have met some of them since I have been here, but they did not know of my deeds, for when they took this poison, they, of course, thought it was the medicine given to help them. So you see whatever of accusation comes from seeing them, comes from my own conscience, and not from their lips or words."

He suggested she look for Helen and that if she accepted her help, she would be there for her. "Yes," she replied. "I will go with her and do as you say, only do not give me hope if there be none.

"Yes, I see some bright spirits.

"I have told her and she says that she will help me and love me too, and that I must go with her and believe in her, and I am going and will believe what she tells me; and oh, if she only does help me, how thankful I shall be to you."

Help from Above

In the world of fiction, we hear a lot about spirits of the dead influencing the living. It's a genre that has spawned an industry of horror movies, TV series, computer games, books, music, and plays—and it shows no sign of diminishing. It seems the more violent, creepy, and dark it is, the more popular it becomes. Terror sells. It's as if there's no good news coming from the spirit world. But is that really the case? Are we ever influenced for the better?

Squizzy Taylor[5] was a notorious Australian gangster from Melbourne in the 1920s. He was a career criminal whose crimes included pickpocketing, bank robbery, murder, and gang war. His luck ran out when in 1927, at the age of thirty-nine, he was killed in a shootout with John "Snowy" Cutmore, a member of the rival Razor Gang, who were part of the Sydney underworld.

Sometime after his death, a communicator came through via Stan Walsh (mentioned in Chapter 3) who identified as Squizzy. He said he was in great distress and looking for help. Walsh's group encouraged him as much as they could and as time went on he came back and reported on his progress. He said he had risen to a higher plane, was very happy, and helping others progress from the condition he once found himself in.

When asked about his work he said:

"I come down and mingle with the people I know on earth. I find them in criminal quarters, in jails and all sorts of strange places. I try to influence their minds and prevent them from committing crimes they are planning. Often, I am successful, although not always, of course. But if I am, I find that, knowing how they think, I can get into their minds and bring the understanding to them that they lack.

"Through progression and constant study over here I have acquired a 'new language,' and if I were to try and impress their minds as I think and understand now, they would ignore my thoughts. I must think in their language, not the language I have since learned.

"To explain a little more, if I were to try and impress their minds according to my present way of thinking, by saying: 'What you contemplate doing is evil in the sight of God' it would not register with them other than as a silly thought. But if I forcibly place a thought in their mind such as 'Listen, mate. If you break into that joint, you'll cop the lot. Dice it. It's a mug's game.' *That* thought registers. It might make him hesitate, through fear, or it might be taken as a premonition, and he gives up the idea.

"From then onward I keep working on his mind until I can induce him to turn to an honest living. It's hard work and I don't always succeed. But even though success is rare, I find when it does come, it gives me a wonderful feeling of exhilaration. I know that I am progressing spiritually as I help others to progress. That's why I need your constant prayers as they give me greater strength to succeed."

It's sometimes said, "To catch a thief you have to think like one" and Squizzy could be seen as an "influencer" helping people in the physical world make good decisions to atone for his bad ones.

∞

The Bible contains multiple references to possession, including the Greek term *Diamonizomai*, which translates as "to be possessed by a demon." In the Gospels, the term is used negatively, contrasting with the more positive concept associated with Socrates' "daimon," often interpreted by scholars as an inner voice or conscience rather than an external entity.

A verse in the New Testament reads:

"When an impure spirit comes out of a person, it goes through arid places seeking rest and does not find it. Then it says, 'I will return to the house I left.' When it arrives, it finds the house swept clean and put in order.

Then it goes and takes seven other spirits more wicked than itself, and they go in and live there. And the final condition of that person is worse than the first" (Luke 11:24–26).

If we get a flash of inspiration while writing a song or a poem, it's not unusual to think, *Where did that come from?* And creatives sometimes claim they are inspired from above and are happy to admit it.

If that's the case, could the same be said for extreme acts of violence or evil thoughts that appear out of nowhere? This is an old idea. In Roman times, the word *genius* meant an attendant spirit guiding the person through life, influencing their decisions—for better or worse. Many religions insist that demons, devils, and jinns are independent entities, yet Jesus insists there are no fallen angels, demons, or devils.

On March 26, 1915, he explained to Padgett:
"Well, the devil is with you all the time. He is not a person as many think, but merely the evil suggestions that result from the operations of the thoughts of the unregenerate man. Every man has his devils, who cling close to him, and can only be gotten rid of by the operations of the Holy Spirit. So do not think that the devil is something that has form or independent personality, for he is not. You are the creator and nourisher of your own devil, and until you get into a state which leaves no room for his presence, he will abide with you."

Padgett asked if those in the spirit world can influence us: "Well, the influences and suggestions that come from evil spirits would not have any effect if man were not in that condition of sympathy with such spirits as enables them to become, as it were, a part of him. I know that many men are possessed or obsessed by these evil spirits, but if they, the men, would only seek the higher spiritual conditions these spirits would not harm them."

Jesus was indicating that—similar to a gene which predisposes us to physical conditions and, when activated, can contribute to disease— our mind, when activated, has the potential to invite in entities, both negative and positive. It reminds me of the story in which a Cherokee elder explains to his grandson that there are two wolves fighting inside us all. One is bad, full of anger, envy, and bitterness. The other is good, full of joy, peace, and love. "Which wolf wins?" asks the grandson. "The one you feed," the elder replies.

In *A Course in Miracles*, Jesus tells us:

73 The 'Devil' is a frightening concept because he is thought of as extremely powerful and extremely active. He is perceived as a force in combat with God, battling Him for possession of the souls He created. He deceives by lies and builds kingdoms of his own in which everything is in direct opposition to God. Yet he *attracts* men rather than repels them, and they are seen as willing to 'sell' him their souls in return for gifts they *recognize* are of no real worth. 74 This makes absolutely no sense. The whole picture is one in which man acts in a way he *himself* realizes is self-destructive but which he does not choose to correct and therefore perceives the cause as beyond his control (3.IX:73–74).

Throughout history, popes, bishops, and priests have continued to insist that the Devil is an independent entity. "The Devil is a real being, a spiritual substance, endowed with intelligence and will, and separated from God by sin," said Pope Leo XIII in 1884.

On November 15, 1973, during an audience, Pope Paul VI warned his followers, "The Devil is our number one enemy, our preeminent tempter. We know that this dark, disturbing being exists, and that he is still at work with his treacherous cunning; he is the hidden enemy who sows errors and misfortunes in human history."

Spirits of deception

Satan, in the Old Testament, means "accuser" or "adversary." In the book of Job, Satan appears as a member of God's council, tasked with testing Job's faithfulness. He functions as a servant of God—not His opponent.

The passage reads:

> One day the angels came to present themselves before the Lord, and Satan also came with them.
> The Lord said to Satan, 'Where have you come from?'
> Satan answered the Lord, 'From roaming throughout the earth, going back and forth on it.'
> Then the Lord said to Satan, 'Have you considered my servant Job? There is no one on earth like him; he is blameless and upright, a man who fears God and shuns evil.'
> 'Does Job fear God for nothing?' Satan replied. 'Have you not put a hedge around him and his household and everything he has? You have blessed the work of his hands, so that his flocks and herds are spread throughout the land.
> But now stretch out your hand and strike everything he has, and he will surely curse you to your face.'
> The Lord said to Satan, 'Very well, then, everything he has is in your power, but on the man himself do not lay a finger.'
> Then Satan went out from the presence of the Lord (Job 1:6–12).

Over the centuries, Christian doctrine has portrayed Satan as God's enemy—an evil, fallen angel and the ruler of Hell. The ancient Jewish non-canonical text 1 Enoch describes "the Watchers"—angels who rebelled against God and mated with women "because they were fair." Some early Christians seem to have adopted this imagery, and over time Satan has been shaped into a cosmic adversary from whom the Catholic Church offers spiritual protection.

Another reason for this shift may lie in a verse in the Book of Revelation, which reads: The great dragon was hurled down—that ancient serpent called the devil, or Satan, who leads the whole world astray... For the accuser of our brothers and sisters, who accuses them before our God day and night, has been hurled down" (Rev. 12:9–10).

In modern political or militaristic terms, Satan could be likened to a war hawk—one of God's hardliners—yet Christianity has turned him into an enemy of the state.

∞

On January 3, 1916, Jesus commented on a book Padgett was reading:

"I am with you tonight to warn you against letting any doubt enter your mind or heart, as to our actually writing to you, for we and none other are actually in communication with you.

"The book that you read is a snare and a lie, for there are no angels who have become devils as the author of that book declares. Never were there any angels who through ambition or any other reason revolted against the power of government of God, and thereby lost their estate as angels. Never was there any Lucifer, and never were there any angels who were thrown from the battlements of heaven into hell, as it has been written and as I told you before, there are no devils and no Satan, considered as real persons and fallen angels.

"The only spirits in the spirit world are those who at one time were mortals and who lived lives on earth, shorter or longer, and whenever angels are mentioned in the Bible, or rather in the New Testament in places which contain my sayings or those of the apostles, and I mean those sayings which were actually said, the word angel always refers to the spirit of some mortal who had passed the line between life and death as commonly understood. ...

"It is true, that by the workings of the law of attraction, and the susceptibility of mortals to the influence of spirit powers, mortals may become obsessed by the spirits of evil—that is evil spirits of men who once lived on earth—and this obsession may become so complete and powerful that the living mortal may lose all power to resist this influence of the evil spirits, and may be compelled to do things that the mortal will not desire to do, and to show all the evidence of a distorted mind, and present appearances of a lost will power, as well as of the ability to exercise the ordinary powers given him by his natural creation."

On March 15, 1917, after Padgett had visited a séance, John also advised caution:

"I was with you tonight at the séance and heard what the medium said, and saw that as she delivered the various messages, she was being dictated to by spirits of a very low order of development, and that they enjoyed very much the deception that they were practicing upon the medium and upon the hearers.

"These spirits are not the kind that you should have the association of, and while your band was present and prevented any of these spirits from getting in rapport with you, or from affecting you by their influence, yet it does you no good to mingle with such spirits.

"The medium believes that the spirits who came to her are really the relatives of, or spirits interested in the people in the audience, but as a fact, these spirits are mostly impostors who have gotten possession of the medium and use her for their own enjoyment. When she attempted to describe the spirits present, she was not only imposed upon, but the spirits whom she saw, as she said, were not the spirits whom the sitters might suppose them to be.

"But there were some of these spirits whom she saw really were the ones that she described them to be, and were interested in the people to whom they came, but they were of the earth plane, having very little development. ...

"The spirits who she says came to you were not your grandparents, for you must know that none of your spirit band manifested themselves, and the ones that she saw and said were interested in you, were some of the spirits who are with her very often, trying to deceive the people. The medium has the powers of seeing and hearing the things of the spirit world to some extent, and is generally honest in her attempts to convey what she receives, but sometimes she exercises her own thoughts and fabricates the message that she delivers.

"It is a pity that such a condition of affairs should exist, but it is a truth and will continue so long as these spirits of deception are given the opportunity to manifest themselves."

During one of Julia's communications with Stead, she castigated him for his "Old Testament" fear of spirit communication and shrugged off the risks involved comparing it to traveling to a large city.

"You have had teaching as to the communion of saints," she wrote. "You say and sing all manner of things as to the saints above and below being one army of the Living God, but when any one of us on the other side tries to make any practical effort to enable you to realize the oneness, and to make you feel that you are encompassed about by so great a cloud of witnesses, then there is an outcry. It is against the will of God! It is tampering with demons! It is conjuring up evil spirits! ...

"Oh, my friend, my friend, be not deceived by these specious outcries! Am I a demon? Am I a familiar spirit? Am I doing what is contrary to the will of God when I constantly, constantly try to inspire you with more faith in Him, more love for Him and all His creatures, and, in short, try to bring you nearer and closer to God? You know I do all this. It is my joy and the law of my being. I should go on doing it even if you were to refuse to let me use your hand. I am more privileged than most because I can consciously interpret my action to you. But I am only doing consciously to you what is being done to others who are more or less unconscious of the influence they are subject to. ...

"I want to say one word now about the danger of the communications about which you hear so much. I have not much to say. That there is love on this side is true. The Devil and his angels are no mere metaphysical abstractions. There are evil ones, false ones, frivolous ones on this side, as there are on yours. You can never enlarge the scope and range of existence without at the same time enlarging the area of possible temptation and probable loss and peril. But the whole question is one of balance. And what I want to ask you is this: Do you or anyone else in your world ever cut off your communications with your children when they have gone into the larger life of a city, because they may bring you into the vortex of a city's temptations and the risk of evil and danger? You laugh at the suggestion. Why not laugh equally when those whom you love have passed on, not to New York, or Chicago, or London, but in the presence of God?

"I do not ask that you should open a door into your souls through which all who feel disposed on this side should enter in to possess it. You can, if you like, either on this side or that, enter into companionship with the good or the bad. And I dare say that it is as true, on this side as on yours, that there is a possibility of making acquaintances who may be difficult to shake off. But so it is in London. You do not shrink from coming up to London from the country because in London there are many thousands of thieves, drunkards, swindlers, and men of evil and vicious life. ...

"It is necessary to risk the danger of evil spirits for the sake of keeping in conscious touch with the loved who have gone before. And, believe me, the danger is monstrously exaggerated. It springs entirely from the false and foolish notions which have prevailed. *If only you grasp the idea of the continuity of existence;* if only you remember that, though the conditions of existence are altered, the life itself remains the same, you will no more have to face so many evils as those which come from believing that, when we speak to you, you are confronted by a kind of spiritual earthquake—a rushing into your life of something altogether supernatural. There is no such thing as supernatural. All is natural, and our Lord is the Lord of all."

Just because someone is psychic doesn't necessarily mean they are spiritual. From time to time, we hear of psychics and healers—both fake and genuine—who let their egos get the better of them, and it doesn't end well. Sometimes, people end up handing over their life savings, suffering abuse, or, in extreme cases, being driven to suicide.

Earnest W. Oaten, mentioned in Chapter 6, estimated that out of the nearly 1,000 séances he had attended, only 20 percent provided genuine phenomena. These days, there are highly profitable "psychic phone lines" populated by "psychics" who are happy to take people's money. Some may well be genuine, but since anyone can claim to be psychic, no doubt the opportunity to defraud vulnerable people is high. It's potentially a tricky business. But, as Julia elucidated, that doesn't mean we should ignore all communication and not take some messages seriously. As with everything in life, we discern, judge, reason, believe, have faith, and know—it's how we navigate the world around us.

Putting the Band Together

During May 1914, Padgett's father communicated and suggested he assemble a spirit team on behalf of his son. "I will try to tell you what you must do to form a band of spirit workers," he wrote. "Let me select them, and then you will not be troubled by bad spirits. You must not try to talk to everyone who may come to you, for that will work injury to you and you will not be able to get the best results." His father suggested the band should be Padgett's grandmother Ann Rollins, his mother, Ann, wife, Helen, Professor Salyards, and Albert Riddle. Padgett asked if he thought they would be willing to help and his father replied that he would ask.

"I will, and you will be a successful medium," wrote Ann Rollins, "and will not need to go to the séances where you went on Friday night, as they are not helpful to you in the way of progressing in your investigations."

"I certainly will," wrote his mother, "and you will not be troubled by bad spirits, for your father and grandmother will keep them away from you."

"I will be one of the band to help you," wrote Salyards. "You will be my mouthpiece in my writing to the world the thoughts that I desire to make known on subjects that are of interest to mankind. ..."

"I will be one of the band," wrote Riddle. "You will not be annoyed by any others than the ones your father has named. I will write you what my beliefs and thoughts are of the life here so that you may know that I am just a spirit in search of the truth. ..."

It had only been three months since Helen's passing, and Padgett was receiving messages daily. A spirit team had been assembled that he was told was fully capable of protecting him from potential interlopers intent on disrupting the quality of communication. In spite of all the talk of devils, demons, and evil spirits, it seemed he was in safe hands.

9

WHY PADGETT?

Imagine you have composed a piece of music for piano. It's your life's work: your magnum opus. You purchase the best piano money can buy and invite a number of pianists to perform the piece.

Time after time they bring your work to life but you're not satisfied. Some apologize saying they can't play it—it's too complex—too highbrow. Others say they are having a bad day. One man has an infection in a finger and it hurts when he pushes the keys, while another complains of sore feet and is unable to press the pedals. A few blame the piano. You are disappointed The music isn't coming out as you envisaged it.

Then a five-year-old walks in, sits down and plays the piece to perfection. It's a sublime moment. Why that child, why now? The child tells you she was walking past and heard music playing. She loves piano and felt compelled to come and see what was happening. She looked at the sheet music and understood it completely. She was feeling healthy, had no injuries and was in good spirits. The piano was perfect for her— the right height, the right stool—and tuned to her ear. The conditions were just right.

Psychic phenomena, similar to creative ability, are often subjective and difficult to predict. You can visit one medium and get evidence that's inexplicable by normal means, while another might give you nothing. And even the person who gave you good evidence might not get anything on another day, what's known as a blank sitting. In my limited experience, mediums who can give good evidence time and time again are few and far between, and even those who can, can't do it on demand. The conditions have to be right and we are told that could involve the medium, the sitter, the environment, and the conditions of those on the other side trying to get through.

Most people never visit a medium or experience anything otherworldly, and if they do, whether it's a positive or negative experience, it may well be a one-time event that's filed away in their memory bank and marked "interesting" or "disappointing," depending on the circumstance.

Padgett may well have asked himself: *Why me?* Communication wasn't without its challenges. It worked when, to use sports parlance, he was "in the zone," which meant a spiritual connection achieved through prayer and focus, undistracted by day-to-day concerns such as money and material well-being on this side, and interference from low-level spirits on the other. Helen mediated as a life coach and wife, continually showering him with love and asking him to do the same to her. It's as if love and prayer on both sides acted like an electric current, and whenever his thoughts were elsewhere the connection dimmed.

Communication Breakdown

By 1918, Padgett had been receiving messages for four years and was still trying to understand the process. In a message on January 4, 1918, John came through and explained why subjects of a mundane nature were easy to transmit, whereas higher truths were often not forthcoming:

"It may seem to you that if we control your brain and not use or transmit your thoughts but only the thoughts which come from our minds, it would be immaterial what the nature of our thoughts might be, and that as your brain is used by us as a mere instrument, we, having possession of your brain, would have the power to write anything we might desire. And upon a mere superficial glance at the assertion, it could be reasonably supposed to be true.

"But, as we have told you before, rapport and our ability to use your brain are governed by laws, and one of these laws is that a high thought cannot be transmitted through a human brain which is not in the condition that qualifies it to receive the thought, just as the brain, in matter pertaining to mere material knowledge cannot receive a conception or comprehension of some intellectual truth with which it has not had acquaintance, and transmit it. A brain cannot be used by the mind of the human to make known or present a problem in geometry, when that brain has never been used by the mind to acquire an acquaintance with or knowledge of the principles of geometry. This is an incomplete analogy but it may serve to illustrate what I mean. ...

"Swedenborg was the last and nearer perfect instrument for receiving these higher truths, and yet he, because of his want of soul development and his being bound, to a more or less extent, by his orthodox beliefs and scientific knowledge that caused him to coordinate and fit in these truths with his ideas of correspondence and such like conceptions, was a failure, and could not be successfully used to transmit these truth [*sic*] which we have been communicating through you.

"From all this you will comprehend why so very few messages containing high spiritual truths, or even moral truths, come through mediums. The mediums, mostly, are so developed that they can receive only messages dealing with the material affairs of life, and which kinds of messages I am compelled to and can truthfully say, are those that are largely desired by the mortals seeking information from the spirit world. ..."

Swedenborg's Error

John mentioned that Swedenborg had been the last and nearer-perfect instrument for receiving higher truths, but he failed to get their message across because of his entrenched orthodox beliefs. He was referring to the Swedish polymath Emanuel Swedenborg.[1] By many of today's standards, Swedenborg's achievements are impressive. Throughout his career, he wore many hats, excelling as a scientist, philosopher, engineer, mystic, and theologian.

Born in Stockholm in 1688 to a Lutheran bishop from a prosperous mining family, Swedenborg's early life was steeped in privilege and education. His mother, Sara, died during an epidemic when he was eight years old, and the following year his father, Jesper, married Sarah Bergia, a wealthy widow who had her own mining interests. Sarah appears to have taken a keen interest in her stepson, and after her passing in 1719, she left him part of her estate, which provided him with financial stability and allowed him to travel extensively.

In 1716, King Charles XII appointed him Assessor of the Board of Mines, a role to which he devoted three decades. His scientific endeavors included writings on anatomy, the design of a flying machine, and even a submarine. Moreover, he played a pivotal role in establishing Sweden's inaugural scientific journal which he titled *Daedalus Hyperboreus* (The Nordic Daedalus). For the greater part of his life he remained wholly engrossed in his professional activities, but that changed in his fifty-sixth year when he claimed Jesus came to him in a dream.

In his diary he wrote, "In the year 1744, on the night of the 19th to the 20th of March, I had a dream in which the Lord appeared to me and opened the world of spirits to me, so that I could see and converse with spirits and angels as if I were living in the natural world. This dream was the beginning of my intercourse with the spiritual world, which has continued to this day (Swedenborg, Spiritual Diary 1744:3)."

As with Paul, Schucman, and Padgett, from the moment Jesus communicated and was accepted as genuine, Swedenborg's priorities changed and his day-to-day activities were subordinated to second place, while understanding God, Jesus, Heaven, and Hell became the most important mission in his life.

His communion with the higher worlds didn't begin in 1744. There is evidence that he had mediumistic gifts during childhood. His father believed in the presence of angels and spirits, and it appears the young Emanuel was comfortable with that belief.

In a letter to Doctor Gabriel A. Beyer in 1769, he wrote, "From my fourth to my tenth year I was constantly engaged in thought upon God, salvation, and the spiritual affections of men; and several times I revealed things at which my father and mother wondered, saying that angels must be speaking through me. From my sixth to my twelfth year I used to delight in conversing with clergymen about faith, saying that the life of faith is love, and that the love which imparts life is love to the neighbor; also that God gives faith to everyone, but that those only receive it who practice that love."

Swedenborg is primarily known today for his book *Heaven and Hell* in which he described visiting the afterlife and communicating with what he believed were angels and God in dreams and clairvoyant visions.

In February 1772, the Methodist founder, John Wesley, was in a meeting with Rev. Samuel Smith and a group of ministers, when Wesley reportedly received a letter from Swedenborg which read: "Sir—I have been informed in the spiritual world that you have a strong desire to converse with me; I shall be happy to see you if you will favor me with a visit.

I am, Sir, your humble Servant, Emanuel Swedenborg."

According to Smith, Wesley was surprised to receive the letter and admitted that he had wanted to meet Swedenborg but had never mentioned it to anyone. Wesley wrote back saying he was about to embark on a six-month tour of his churches and that he would be happy to see him on his return. Smith reportedly learned later that Swedenborg wrote back saying that would be too late as he would go into the spirit world on the 29th of the following month.

On March 29, while visiting London, he suffered a stroke and passed away on that very day.

In 1915, Swedenborg communicated with Padgett to say that despite his achievements, when he arrived in the spirit world, life had been difficult due to his theological beliefs.

In his first message he admitted: "Well, I am sorry to say that my work was a failure, and that because of that fact, I have suffered very much since I became a spirit. I know now that what I attempted to do was injured by my preconceived ideas based on the orthodox teachings, and that I did not carry out the work of the great mission that I had been selected to perform."

Swedenborg saw Padgett as a kindred spirit taking on the work that he had attempted to do more than 150 years earlier.

"I will say now, though, and you must believe me," he continued, "that you have been selected to do the work which I failed to do, and I hope that you will permit me to give you one piece of advice and that is: take, record, and believe only the messages as they shall come to you from Jesus and the other high spirits, and let no opinion of your own mar or flavor these communications. The truths will be presented to you and you must accept them as they come.

"When I came to the spirit world and realized the failure that I had made, then everything was failure [*sic*] to my conscience.

"In your case, you have no such preconceived ideas to hamper you or prevent you from receiving the truths, for you are used merely as a conduit through which these truths are to be received, and they are to be declared in the very language of the writers.

"I am your friend and brother and co-worker in making known these truths, and write only, because I, as a failure, can speak from experience. So, my brother, turn your thought more to this work and, if necessary, sacrifice every worldly consideration to carry forward your work and make perfect your efforts to fulfill the great mission with which you have been blessed. I will not write more now.

"May the Father bless you with His Love.

"Your brother In Christ, Swedenborg."

As a result of his revelations and interpretation of Scripture, Swedenborg believed that Heaven and Hell were chosen spiritual states of being—a result of decisions made during life—and that faith, love, and good works lead to spiritual transformation. He rejected the Trinity, Original Sin, the concept of Hell as a permanent state, and Paul's faith-alone doctrine—all positions with which the high spirits would agree. However, his apparent error was in concluding that Jesus was God and should be worshiped as such.

Why Padgett?

On October 25, 1918, Jesus wrote and explained why Padgett was the subject of his attention:

"There are certain qualities in your constitution, both spiritual and material, that render you susceptible to the influence of our powers and to the use by us for the purpose of our design and work, which determines one to choose you for the work in the way in which I and the other high spirits have heretofore used you, and it may seem strange to you that in all the long ages preceding, I have not found one human with the qualification to fit him for the work.

"I have used others before, but they have failed to submit their minds and souls and beliefs and forethoughts to our influence and directions as you have so far done. Many humans have the qualified conditions of spiritual and material make up to perform our wishes and work, but as they all have free wills, which we cannot compel, and as circumstances and environments and education and beliefs are elements which affect and determine the possibility of our finding an instrument suitable for our purposes, we have not been able to find a medium who was qualified to be used for our work.

"You, of course, understand that you were not selected because of any special goodness or freedom from sin, or because you were more beloved by the Father, or naturally, and I mean according to your course of living, by reason of any spiritual condition that you were in, for there were many superior to you in goodness and more in at-onement with the will of the Father, and whose love and the results therefrom, were more perfect than yours. ...

"For know this, that for a long time I have been endeavoring to influence and mold your mind and beliefs, so that your soul might become developed in such a way that conditions might be formed that would enable us to make a rapport that would permit of our controlling your brain to convey these messages of truth. You were naturally a medium and, for ordinary purposes, it was not difficult for the spirits to control and communicate through you the truths of the spirit world, which are not of a nature such as I and others have communicated in reference to the soul spheres and the relationship of God to man in the higher spiritual sense. As you read John's message you will the better understand what I intend to explain at this point.

"There is another phase to all this, more personal to you, and this is, that while we have been developing you for the purpose of doing our work and helping make effective our mission, your soul, as you, has been developed in its spiritual nature and you have become in closer union with the Father and have partaken to a large extent of his love, and, to a degree, been transformed into his essence, so that you have become a very different entity from what you were when your development for our purpose commenced; and, as a consequence, you will derive all the benefits that flow from an experience such as you have had.

"You are now one of us in the progress towards the fountainhead of the Father's love, and have taken on a part of his immortality, and it depends only upon yourself how rapid your progress shall be towards a complete transformation such as spirits who are inhabitants of the celestial sphere possess. You need not wait until you come to the spirit world in order to make a rapid progression, although it will be more difficult for you to progress while in the flesh, as you understand, but wonderful progress may be made while in the flesh, and you have been told the secret of this progress.

"And I will further say that you have a closer association with spirits that are nearer the Father and more possessed of his essence and substance than have any humans of earth at this time. To you this may seem extravagant and improbable, but I declare to you that it is as true that I and many spirits, who come to you and write, are in the celestial sphere of God's immortality.

"Well, I have written a long time and you are somewhat tired.

"Remember my advice and pray often and earnestly, if but for a moment, and the condition will be yours and we will come and continue our revealments.

"With my love and blessing, I am, Your brother and friend, Jesus."

What Jesus and John appear to be saying is that a high spirit can only transmit higher truths to a mind that is spiritually developed enough to be able to accept those truths. If a medium is primarily focused on day-to-day activities and material well-being, and if the sitters are focused on the same, the medium may well pass on accurate information of a mundane nature, but high spirits might not be able to get through or have any interest in doing so.

There are also those people who are reluctant mediums, either knowingly or unknowingly. Some years ago, I was invited by a friend to his sister's home. His sister's husband was the son of a wealthy stockbroker. His external life was one of privilege. He had a beautiful home, a loving family, and more money and trappings than most people could ever dream of, yet his inner life was miserable. He was an unwilling medium and hated and feared the dead people who showed up in his life. In an effort to block them out he self-medicated on drugs and alcohol, which wreaked havoc on his mind and body.

His father, apparently, also had the same "gift" and slept with the lights on to try to avoid nightly encounters. Neither wanted anything to do with their communicators. For both, it was a huge hindrance in their lives.

Fortunately, Padgett was one of these unusual people for whom his ability wasn't a hindrance. He wasn't saintly or the most gifted psychically but he could do the job. On a good day he was highly receptive, which meant he could take long messages from high spirits, but on a day when he was distracted or engrossed in day-to-day living, those messages weren't forthcoming.

Like the five-year-old pianist, as well as ability, communication appears to depend on many things, not least, the conditions on the day.

10

RIDDLE

With the advent of family history websites that source information from government databases such as marriage, birth, and death registries, it's easier than it once was to trace connections between families going back centuries.

In the levels beyond the physical world, we don't exactly know how they connect with each other and us but they appear to be able to connect instantaneously if the motivation and conditions are right. From their vantage point—similar to our looking at an extended family tree—we can imagine them seeing connections between people in the physical and spirit world that we are unaware of.

In 2013, I was having a conversation with I.D., and she said, "I have someone here called Derek." By now I.D. and I had met several times and she knew I used to be in the record business and therefore, for me, anything evidential had to exclude information that could be found online. I said I didn't know anyone called Derek.

"He's connected to you through the record business."

"How do you know that?" I asked.

"I'm seeing a warehouse full of records."

I asked her what time period.

"Late seventies. ... He's a butcher."

I said I couldn't think of anyone named Derek and I didn't know any butchers.

"Well, he's connected to you."

None of it made sense, and the conversation moved on to something else.

On the drive home, a friend of mine popped into my mind. We shared a house for a while, and I had recommended him for a job at a record distributor where I worked. He worked there for a while as a salesman—it would have been around 1979-1980. The building we worked in was essentially a warehouse full of vinyl records and cassettes with offices on the side.

His father, whom I'd met a few times, was called Derek, and he had died the previous year. Derek had owned a butcher's shop in London's Mayfair, supplying meat to some of London's top hotels. I can't be sure if he tried to connect with me, but the information given fitted his description. However, in that case, there was no message because I didn't recognize him.

∞

Aside from the biblical and other historic communicators, many of those coming through to Padgett were lawyers, politicians, and presidents who had been working with or at the center of government in Padgett's hometown of Washington, D.C.

To understand why Padgett accepted communicators not known to him at face value, it's useful to know something about the people who communicated through him who *were* known to him—people who had played an important part in his life. One such figure who would prove to be a catalyst was Albert Gallatin Riddle.

On May 15, 1902, the *Baltimore Sun* reported:—DEATH OF ALBERT G. RIDDLE: End Of A Self-Made Career Which Was Full Of Interest. Special Dispatch to the *Baltimore Sun*: "The local bar lost another able advocate this morning in the death of Mr. Albert Gallatin Riddle, an ex-Representative in Congress, at his home on Thirteenth street. Death was due to a general breakdown from the infirmities of age. He was 86 years old. ... He took part in many famous cases, Including forty murder trials, during his practice at the local bar, and was attorney for the District of Columbia for twelve years, beginning in 1877."

Riddle[1] was an acquaintance of Abraham Lincoln, the sixteenth president of the United States, who was assassinated in 1865. In his 1895 book *Recollections of War Times: Reminiscences of Men and Events in Washington: 1860-1865*, Riddle recalled:

"In his famous progress as president-elect, Mr. Lincoln reached Cleveland on the 15th of February 1861, when I first met him at a great reception, and was by him invited to accompany him to Erie. This I was unable to do, but I attended him to Painesville, Ohio, where I was engaged in a trial. I was then and there afterwards treated by him with much kindness and consideration. I then formed and ever continued to have a cordial personal regard for Mrs. Lincoln."

Riddle was part of the prosecution team against John Surratt, Jr., the son of Mary Surratt, the alleged co-conspirator in the Lincoln assassination, who had been found guilty and executed by hanging in 1865. John Jr. was on the run for many years, and by the time his case was brought to trial, many of the original charges were beyond the statute of limitations and the case was dismissed.

In 1877, Riddle was appointed attorney for the government of the District of Columbia. Padgett, who already worked for him, was brought in as special assistant attorney. Riddle held that post until 1889 when he retired at the age of seventy-three. Padgett clearly respected and admired him, so much so that he named his first-born son, Edward Riddle Padgett.

Riddle first appeared in the communications in May 1914, when he sent a message to say he had agreed to join Padgett's spirit team. But it was seven months later on December 16, when he wrote a message sharing what his life had been like since he passed away:

"I am here, your old partner: I want to talk a little with you. You have not given me the opportunity before and I commenced to think that you did not wish to hear from me. Well I will try my best and will talk to you about the laws of control of spirits over human beings.

"You are not very different from us in your mental or spiritual conditions. We, of course, have no physical bodies but our spiritual bodies are very much like those we had on earth in former shape except that we are young and strong and not affected by those things which you are subject to.

"You must know, however, that we are all affected to a greater or less degree by the condition of our soul development. Your wife, for instance, is now a very beautiful spirit both as regards her spiritual body as well as her spiritual soul. She is one of the most beautiful that I come in contact with except your mother and grandmother who are beyond my ability to describe. I am also very different but not so very much changed as I have not yet made very great progress in the things pertaining to the involution of the soul.

"My ideas are not very much changed as I still think that I am a man who must depend upon himself for his advancement and that God is a way off somewhere in the heavens and not much interested in my welfare. But your father is now in another plane and I commence to wonder why he should progress and I be left to live in this earth plane, and as I think of this, I feel that there must be something more to my being lifted out of my present conditions through my own efforts.

"I hear what your mother tells me but somehow, I do not quite catch the import of her teachings, as I believe that her ideas are more or less the result of her training on earth and have no actual foundation for a belief in the help of the Holy Spirit to rest upon. But as I see the wonderful change in your wife and father, I cannot but think that there must be something more than my own efforts at elevating myself [that] is necessary to my rising out of my present condition. So I am thinking deeply on the subject.

"Your grandmother has also told me of the wonderful work of the Holy Spirit in her case, as well as in that of very many other spirits who were in my condition when they first came to the spirit world and it all makes me think that there is something in this wonderful transformation of these spirits beyond what I have ever thought of.

"I will try to learn what it is if I possibly can so if you can help me in any way, please do so for I do not want to remain in this state if there is any way for me to progress out of it. You seem to be in great favor with some spirits who have told me that they were benefited by you, and hence I say if you can help me do so.

"I have had a spirit come to me who said he was Jesus but I did not believe him even though he was of a most exceeding brightness and loveliness. I do not believe in his being Jesus even though your mother told me that he was. But until I can see that he is the true Jesus I do not care to listen to him, for I have never believed that Jesus is any more than man or that he can save anyone from sin or error. Yet as he seems so good and lovely, I sometimes think that maybe I am all wrong and that he is, in truth, what he claims to be. I will, in future, listen more to him and if he can show me the way to higher things as your mother claims he can, I will let his teachings linger in my thoughts for consideration. ..."

Having been in the spirit world for more than twelve years, Riddle could see that Helen, Padgett's mother, and grandmother were more advanced than he was, despite Helen having been there for less than a year. They were different from him, and progressing in ways he wasn't. But he still wasn't ready to accept that their beauty, radiance, and wisdom was a result of their thought processes, or that he could be helped by Jesus.

∞

Riddle served as a member of the Ohio House of Representatives between 1848-1850. He was succeeded by James A. Garfield. He authored a number of political papers including a biography on Garfield: *The Life, Character & Public Services of James A. Garfield.*

On March 4, 1881, Garfield[2] became the twentieth president of the United States, but his presidency was short lived. Four months later, on July 2, he was shot by Charles Julius Guiteau, who believed he played a part in Garfield's presidential victory and should have been rewarded with an overseas post. Garfield lived for another two months but died on September 19, from an infection likely caused by malpractice.

The following month, Guiteau was indicted for murder. His defense team argued that he was temporarily insane because he claimed God took away his free will, but nevertheless, he was found guilty and executed by hanging the following year.

On March 22, 1915, Garfield came through. He introduced himself to Padgett saying he was Riddle's old friend and that the two of them were in the third sphere and got together and philosophized about the nature of existence. Garfield referred to himself as an intellectual Christian. He said he had read the Bible but didn't understand the spirituality behind Jesus's teachings.

"My faith in prayer is not very strong," he wrote. "Nor in the possibility of becoming a spirit who may receive any great help from the operations of the Holy Spirit, which, as Riddle says, is the only influence that can surely redeem me from my sins or the result of them, and make me one with the Father. I cannot comprehend this teaching, and unless my reason can be convinced, I cannot be persuaded to accept the teaching as true. So you see, I am still in the position that I was on earth, that is, unless my reason tells me that such a thing is true, I cannot believe."

That same evening Helen came through: "Well, you had quite a letter from Garfield. He is certainly a wonderful spirit intellectually, as many spirits who come in contact with him say. But he is not very spiritual, I am sorry to say, and do hope that your conversation with him will help him and cause him to search for the truth. ..."

Padgett suggested Garfield connect with Ann Rollins, and asked Helen if she was party to the conversation. "Yes, I heard him," she replied. "And when he meets your grandmother, he will undoubtedly be impressed by her, for she is so beautiful and wise and powerful that he will realize that there is within her something that he knows not of."

Riddle, now being one of Padgett's band, was helping his friends and peers communicate for the benefit of all concerned. "You had a letter from Garfield," he wrote. "He was so anxious to write that I thought it would do no harm to let him try, and I am glad that I did, for what you said to him has impressed him very much, and, I believe, will lead to his seeking information on the subject of the New Birth. He is a wonderful spirit intellectually, and has progressed to a very great degree in the investigation of spiritual laws. So that on the whole his writing will do no harm to our band."

Padgett asked Riddle why Garfield didn't seek out Jesus after his death. "Well, I do not understand it, as he was a Christian on earth, and one would naturally suppose that he would have made inquiry for Jesus when he came over. But it seems he did not, why I don't know, but now that he realizes what you told him, he undoubtedly will seek the Master at the first opportunity."

It had only been a few months—as we measure time—since Riddle himself had rejected the suggestion that Jesus had come to him. He appeared to have changed. Padgett asked him about his own progress: "I am very happy and am progressing rapidly, and expect to soon be in the fifth sphere, where your father and Prof. Salyards are. Oh, my dear Padgett, I cannot tell you what happiness I am now enjoying."

When I write "as we measure time" it's a reminder that even though communicators report that they don't experience linear time as we do, they do describe past and future events as is evidenced by Riddle's comment above.

Having understood that spiritual laws differ from physical laws, Riddle was now sharing the good news with everyone, be they ex-presidents or ordinary people.

As well as breaking ties with the physical world, progress in the spirit world appears to come from service to others, and with no money changing hands, everyone's a volunteer.

11

BELIEF

Does it Matter?

My friend Jules was talking to me about writing a book and I mentioned I was writing one too.

"What's it about?" he asked.

"What happens after we die, except we don't die. No one's dead. You know, the trivial stuff, that's the premise."

"Very niche then," he joked. "For the fringes of society."

"Maybe," I replied. "Although most people think about it occasionally, after all, the death rate is still running at a hundred percent."

It is true that among the people I know, men in particular, the majority don't believe in an afterlife. They don't want to contemplate death and in that group I'm definitely on the fringe.

In my limited experience, many people who identify as Christian do so because they were born into it. It's tradition. But when you ask them what they actually believe, they don't elaborate. Then there are those who have rejected the dominant religion of their culture for one reason or another, and because they've rejected that particular story, they reject or at least ignore all the other stories.

Organized religions begin with a story. They become codified, then political, and often end up as control mechanisms. From the Church's perspective, any attempt to discover the nature of reality must be done within the confines of the institution. The Church might be fine for pastoral care and practical help, but when it comes to the question of existence beyond the physical world—the central theme of most religions—it has little to offer beyond its interpretation of the Bible. Some Christian groups, such as the Quakers and Pentecostals, encourage direct spiritual experience, but they are in the minority.

Throughout history, it's difficult to find a society that didn't—or doesn't—believe in dimensions, spirit worlds, or realms beyond our own. I say "didn't" because political systems such as Soviet communism once demanded absolute loyalty to the state, suppressing anything considered more important, such as organized religion. However, since the collapse of the Soviet Union, many Russians have turned their gaze to the heavens, leading to a resurgence of religious practice.

Thirty years after the communist era ended, a 2022 survey by the Levada Center, a leading independent polling organization in Russia, reported that 71 percent of the population identified as Orthodox Christian and 5 percent as Muslim, while 15 percent reported having no religious faith.[1]

Polls can be misleading because of how questions are framed. For example, someone might not identify as religious yet believe in life after death—or they might consider themselves religious but reject certain concepts, such as an eternal afterlife.

A 2022 Gallup survey of sixty-one countries found that two-thirds (62 percent) of respondents said they were religious, while one in four said they were not. Atheists made up 10 percent. Among the rest: 57 percent said they believed in life after death; 23 percent said they did not believe anything happens when we die; 15 percent were undecided. In the U.S., 60 percent said they were religious; in Japan, it was 15 percent.[2]

In the 2001 World Values Survey, 93.9 percent of Chinese respondents answered that they didn't belong to a religious denomination. In China, where the population is ruled by a communist government, aside from any cultural differences, being a member of a religious organization—at least publicly—can be potentially dangerous, so a low polling number is understandable. However, when a different question is asked, the percentage increases substantially.

According to a 2019 *Harvard Divinity Bulletin*, 75 percent of respondents in China reported participating in ancestor worship rituals, and other polls suggest that more than 70 percent of the population regularly engages in the practice. Ancestor worship (or reverence) often includes a belief in some form of continued existence or spiritual presence beyond death.[3]

BELIEF

Fear of Oblivion or What Comes Next?

During a conversation on the subject with my eighty-year-old father, I said, "You know, Dad, I think you're wrong about the whole death thing. The evidence is out there that ultimately there is no death other than the dissolution of the physical body." He didn't want to debate it, whereas we regularly debated everything else. He didn't even want to hear about it. It bothered him.

Similarly, I remember being at a dinner party and someone brought the topic up. A man sitting opposite me said he didn't believe any of it. His partner interjected saying he was fearful of death and refused to go to funerals, and that by avoiding the subject he thought he could deny death by putting it out of his mind.

During the conversation, I said, "If I told you Santa Claus is god and the elves are his angels, would you believe me?" He laughed. "No, of course not."

"You'd think I was crazy or having fun with you. Either way, the proposition wouldn't bother you because you know it's nonsense."

He agreed. But he wasn't laughing at the proposition that no one's dead, even though he said he didn't believe it. Just like the conversation with my father, it clearly bothered him. Both seemed certain of their positions and neither wanted to contemplate the possibility. The question is why? We weren't talking about death being the end—which many people understandably fear—we were talking about potentially carrying on, which one might think would be good news for lovers of life. Maybe it's because of what Shakespeare's Hamlet called, "The dread of something after death, the undiscover'd country, from whose bourn no traveler returns." In both cases it appeared that the fear of the unknown was as strong as the dread of annihilation, perhaps more so.

Imagine you are on your deathbed and someone offers you a pill. If you don't take the pill you die and that's it, but if you do take it, you'll continue in another body, in another world. Would you take the pill? Both of these men were what I would call adventurers. Both were the World War II generation, and I'm pretty sure they would have taken the pill, yet they didn't want to contemplate the undiscover'd country.

Shortly before his death in March 2022, Michael Cocks (mentioned in Chapter 3) and I had one of our regular video conversations. Michael had been an Anglican priest for more than sixty-five years. During the last nine years of his life, we had regular two-hour chats where we discussed religion, spiritual ideas, and whatever came to mind, but generally, we didn't bother with the mundane.

I feel very privileged to have had those conversations, and while we often challenged and questioned each other's ideas, I don't remember our ever exchanging a cross word. Michael said he felt he benefited from our conversations because we talked about anything, whereas in his church, subjects that weren't in the book of Common Prayer—reincarnation, for instance—weren't generally discussed. During one conversation, I asked him for his definition of a Christian. "It's the pursuit of Christ," he replied. I liked that. It seems like a goal anyone can reach, whether we call ourselves Christian or not.

Michael saw phenomena such as synchronicities, deathbed visions, spirit communication, and NDEs as a validation of his faith, but he said he was in the minority among his fellow clergy. Some of his peers had lost their faith while still in post but hadn't publicly "come out," while others had converted to Christian atheism, which sounds like an oxymoron. Having rejected Church dogma, they had thrown the baby out with the bathwater and were unwilling to contemplate a spirit world beyond this one, despite the abundance of evidence. It's understandable. Imagine spending your life convinced God is real and making a career of preaching Christianity to thousands of people, only to lose your faith. That sounds like an unnerving prospect. To then discover that there's good evidence that something might lie beyond death might be too much to contemplate.

During our conversation, Michael told me he'd been having nightmares.

"What are you fearful about?" I asked.

"Oblivion," he replied.

"Didn't you get the whole Jesus thing?" I joked. "The immortal soul and all that?" He laughed and that led to a more general discussion about the fear of death.

Having reached ninety-three years old and a lifelong man of faith, Michael's fear was of taking his last breath and ceasing to exist. My response was that if I had a fear of death, it was taking my last breath and finding myself in the basement of the many mansions Jesus talked about.

Before the accident, I was reasonably comfortable with the belief that one day I'll go to sleep and not wake up, or take a final breath and that will be it. After all, I go to sleep every night, and to date, I haven't worried about not waking up.

BELIEF

On the morning after I'd banged my head, I was lying in a hospital bed waiting for a general anesthetic. I'd read somewhere that a small number of people die from anesthesia (apparently around 1 in 100,000). I looked out a window at a small patch of grass and thought, *I've packed a lot in, and if this is the last thing I see, that's fine.* I'm not a particularly brave person, nor was I being stoic, but I felt very peaceful—as if everything was as it should be.

Since that accident, my worldview has changed. I feel there is a consequence for everything, and death doesn't change that. Death is the end of the chapter, but not the end of the story.

I remember watching a movie years ago. It was one of those old Hollywood gangster mafia movies. There's a scene in it where the don has been shot. He's lying on his deathbed and one of his lieutenants is sitting by his bedside trying to comfort him.

"How are you feeling?" the lieutenant asks.

"I'm scared," replies the don.

"You don't need to worry. No one can get you while I'm here."

"I don't mean that," snaps the don. "I ain't afraid of any man."

"What then?"

The don looks him in the eye. "What if the priests were right?"

My thoughts exactly. The one thing about being a materialist is when you get to the end of your life, you might think, *that's it. It's over.* I learned a lot from supporting people who were feeling suicidal and discovered early on that many were in so much mental and/or physical pain, that death presented itself as a welcome release. But what gave some pause for thought was the possibility that if death is not the end, killing oneself might just make things worse.

I empathize with the materialist's position. After all, we've had 2,000 years of what could rightly be called brainwashing—being told we are going to heaven or hell. When I was a materialist, I didn't accept the premise that there is a higher moral authority or that life has any inherent meaning beyond what we choose to give it. From my perspective, the Ten Commandments were just ten rules for life, created by humans, not given to humans. It's an easy position that requires no effort, other than the belief that the physical world is all there is.

Agnosticism also sounds like a cozy, secure, logical position. It seems reasonable to say I don't know and leave it at that. The question is, does it matter to us as individuals? A common answer to the question: "What happens after death?" is, "I'll worry about it when I get there." But is that a good idea?

Belief at the Point of Death

Imagine a five-year-old boy. He is playing a game and is fully immersed in his own world, not worrying about the past or future. He's living in the present, and all that matters at that moment is the game. Meanwhile, as a parent—someone who is a little further along the path—we might encourage him to eat healthily, learn to read and write, engage with others and be kind, because we know from experience that a friendly, engaging, literate, healthy child is more likely to have an easier journey through life. However, it takes work, and if the child was asked about the future, he might say, "I'll worry about it when I get there." If he takes no notice and does none of those things, he might still manage, he might even thrive, but for many, life will be more of a challenge. The communicators are telling us the same thing: "Sure, worry about it when you get here, but be prepared for a tough journey."

On April 13, 1915, Salyards[4] echoed other communicators observations, that at the point of death what we believe is important: "... Sometimes the mind of great learning (according to the standards of earthly learning) is more harmful," he wrote, "and retards more the progress of that man in the ways and acquirements of truth, than does the mind that is, as you might say, a blank; that is, without preconceived ideas of what the truth is on a particular subject.

"This unfortunate experience exists to a greater extent in matters pertaining to religion than to any other matters, because the ideas and convictions which are taught and possessed of these religious matters affect innumerably more mortals than do ideas and convictions in reference to any other matters.

"A spirit who is filled with these erroneous beliefs, that may have been taught him from his mortal childhood, and fostered and fed upon by him until he becomes a spirit, is, of all the inhabitants of this world, the most difficult to teach and convince of the truths pertaining to religious matters. It is much easier to teach the agnostic, or even the infidel, of these truths, than the hide-bound believer in the dogmas and creeds of the church."

In a communication with Padgett on January 4, 1917, Luke concurred: "The infidel who says he doesn't believe, the agnostic who says he doesn't know, the orthodox who believes, but whose belief is erroneous, and the free thinker who believes only what reason teaches him as he proclaims—if such beliefs are not in accord with the truth all come under the same penalty—that is, the impossibility of becoming the perfect man while such erroneous beliefs or want of true beliefs exist.

"So I say, belief is a vital thing in the progress of a man towards perfection, and men should cease to declare and rest on the assurance of such declaration that it makes no difference what a man believes if he does what he may consider to be right and just.

"Why, I, who know, tell you that the earth planes of the spirit world are crowded with the spirits of men who are in darkness and stagnation in their progress towards the perfect man solely from the causes that I have above written, and some men have been in that condition for many long years, and will not find progress except as such erroneous beliefs leave them and beliefs in accord with the truth take the place of the former.

"But for man and spirits there is this consolation, that at some time, how long in the future I or no other spirit know, these erroneous beliefs will all be eradicated and man will again come into his original perfection. But the waiting may be long and distressing, and wearisome to many. ..."

∞

In a 2011 interview with *The Guardian* newspaper, physicist Stephen Hawking said, "I regard the brain as a computer which will stop working when its components fail. There is no heaven or afterlife for broken-down computers; that is a fairy story for people afraid of the dark."[5]

Hawking might be correct about the brain being a computer, but if our minds are more than just brains—and centuries of anecdotal and scientific evidence suggest that's the case—then believing we simply cease to exist after death seems more like wishful thinking for those who are afraid of the light.

12

THREE BODIES

Physical, Spirit, Soul

At the age of twenty-nine, my great-granddad Harry was let go from his job and pensioned off due to a terminal illness.

Seventy-two years later, Harry, aged 101, organized a family gathering to make an announcement. Before the event, I remember discussing with my mother why he might have called the meeting. It was remarkable that he was still alive given his prognosis all those years ago. Had his time come, we wondered? Did he want to see the family one last time?

When we arrived, Harry was sitting up in bed wearing his trademark bobble hat. He grinned and called me over, and I introduced him to my one-year-old son, his great-great-grandchild. He seemed in good spirits and didn't look as if he was about to die.

Having dutifully filed into the room, his children, grandchildren, and great-grandchildren all stood around the bed, waiting with a sense of apprehension to hear what he had to say. No one seemed to know why we were there, not even his children who would have been in their seventies at the time.

A few minutes later, the door opened and a carer walked in pushing an elderly woman in a wheelchair. Harry gazed down at her, smiling. "I'm engaged to be married!" he said proudly.

"This is Emily."

Emily had long gray hair in pigtails. She beamed and said hello to everyone. She was ninety-four years old, blind, and unable to walk, but evidently still had much life in her. She had no other family present, and apparently it was the first time she had been engaged. It was a happy moment for both of them.

Unfortunately, the marriage never came to fruition because Emily passed away. Harry lived for a few more years and died a month before his 104th birthday. He was an incorrigible character who triumphed over adversity and lived a full life.

Conversely, my Uncle Derek (mentioned in Chapter 1) died when he was three weeks old—his life cut short—no doubt a tragedy for all concerned, and a common one in those days as it still is in parts of the world.

For many of us, physical life is everything. It's the only thing we can be certain of; it's all we know. Even among Christians I know, physical life is primary, and when it comes to the question of what happens after death, it's seen as something way off in the distance. It's a topic left unspoken—a taboo subject for many.

In 2003, during my first sitting with B.L., she said, "I have someone here presenting as a seven-year-old girl." One thing I was sure of: there was no seven-year-old girl on my list of people who had died. I didn't respond immediately because I didn't know what to make of it. But after the session, I asked who the girl might have been. "Oh, she's yours," she replied in a matter-of-fact way, as if it was obvious to me.

"Wouldn't I know if I had a child who had died?" I said, trying not to sound flippant.

"Not necessarily. She might be the result of a miscarriage or an abortion."

Then it hit me. Seven years earlier, I'd had a fling with a business acquaintance. We were both single and met up at a birthday party. The following year, I was at another party in London, and she came up to me in tears, telling me that after our brief encounter, she discovered she was pregnant and had a termination. I was shocked—although maybe I shouldn't have been. I felt bad for her because she went through that process alone, and I was partly responsible but could do nothing to help because I wasn't aware of her predicament. She later married and had children, which made me feel better, and I hoped she was happy. Life moved on, and I put it out of my mind. Now, seven years later, a medium I had just met was telling me I had a seven-year-old daughter in spirit, and she has been on my mind since that day.

It was interesting that B.L. said the communicator was presenting as a seven-year-old because, presumably, if physical bodies and time are manifestations of the physical world, and they don't experience time in the spirit world as we do, there are no seven-year-olds, seventy-year-olds, or seven-hundred-year-olds.

The Breath of a Moment

According to Jesus, physical life has only one primary objective. In a message to Padgett on March 21, 1920, he wrote:

"As I have told you before, man's existence in the flesh is only for the purpose of giving his soul an individualization, and all other apparent objects are only secondary, as you may say, accidental accompaniments of this process of individualization.

"Hence, you will observe, that this great object is accomplished equally in the case of the infant who dies young, and in the case of the man who lives to a ripe old age; in each case the object of the soul's incarnation in the flesh is effected. The old man, of course, has his experience, a longer and more diverse existence in meeting and overcoming or submitting to the exigencies of his living than does the infant, but the great object is not more perfectly accomplished in the one case than in the other.

"The soul becomes individualized the moment it finds its lodgment in the receptacle prepared by the laws of nature in using the human father and mother as its instruments. And time thereafter does not influence or have any determining effect upon that soul so far as its individualization is concerned; and neither does eternity, for that condition being once fixed never can be changed nor annihilated, so far as is known to the highest spirits of God's heavens. ... And at the same moment there is created for it or attracted to it, the form of the spirit body, which then and ever afterwards remains with it. Both of these bodies are of the material; one of the visible material of the universe, the other of the invisible but still of the material.

"As you know, that body which is made of the visible material lasts for a little while only and then disappears forever, while that which is of the invisible, and which is more real and substantial than the former and exists all the time of the existence of the visible, continues with the soul after the disappearance of the invisible body; and while changeable in response to the progress of that soul, yet the spirit body never in its composite form leaves that soul. This we in the spirit life know to be true, just as certainly as you mortals know the truth of the existence of the physical body. And as you mortals may in the short space of the life on earth identify the man—which is really the soul—by the appearance of his physical body, so we in the spirit world identify the same man by the appearance of the spirit body, and so this fact must be forever.

"Then such being the fact, it must be conceived that the soul has its existence in the physical body for an infinitesimal short time; that is, its life on earth is only the breath of a moment, and then it enters on its career through eternity, and after a few years, as you may say, it may cease to remember that it ever had a lodgment in the physical body."

At the time I found out about the abortion, if someone had told me that a fetus having been terminated was progressing in the spirit world, I would have dismissed it; it just didn't seem like something to be taken seriously, but these days I'm not dismissing it.

Physical Body or Spirit?

Jesus tells us the purpose of soul incarnation is individualization, the purpose of soul individualization is to obtain divine love, and the purpose of divine love is to achieve immortality. He didn't say at what point the soul attaches to or inhabits the embryo or fetus, but what he was saying is, once the soul has individualized, from the soul's perspective, whether the person survives for an hour, a day, or a hundred years, the job is done.

It's hard not to see ourselves and everything around us as separate and physical. Far better, Jesus tells us, to see ourselves for what we are: soul with a spirit body and physical body, experiencing the physical world.

In ACIM, he states:

62 You see the flesh or recognize the Spirit. There is no compromise between the two. If one is real the other must be false, for what is real denies its opposite. There is no choice in vision but this one. What you decide in this determines all you see and think is real and hold as true. On this one choice does all your world depend, for here have you established what you are, as flesh or spirit in your own belief. If you choose flesh, you never will escape the body as your own reality, for you have chosen that you want it so. But choose the Spirit, and all heaven bends to touch your eyes and bless your holy sight, that you may see the world of flesh no more except to heal and comfort and to bless.

63 Salvation is undoing. If you choose to see the body, you behold a world of separation, unrelated things, and happenings that make no sense at all. This one appears and disappears in death; that one is doomed to suffering and loss. And no one is exactly as he was an instant previous, nor will he be the same as he is now an instant hence. Who could have trust where so much change is seen, for who is worthy if he be but dust? Salvation is undoing of all this (31.VI: 62–63).

In a verse from the New Testament, Jesus instructs his followers to cross to the other side of a lake when, "Another disciple said to him, 'Lord, first let me go and bury my father.' But Jesus told him, 'Follow me, and let the dead bury their own dead'" (Matt. 8:21–22).

Over the years, biblical scholars have debated whether Jesus was referring to the "spiritually dead" or simply telling the man to reorder his priorities and put heaven above earth. But perhaps what he was really saying was, "Bury the dead if you believe in death, but if you don't, follow me. ... For who is worthy if he be but dust?"

Soul—The Image of God

Although little is said about the physical body, Jesus in the Padgett messages and in ACIM has much to say about the spirit body and soul. Where the Bible states, "So God created mankind in his own image, in the image of God he created them; male and female he created them" (Gen. 1:27), Jesus in the Padgett messages tells us what is meant by *man* is the *soul*, not the collection of cells we call a body.

To individualize, the soul splits into female and male counterparts, each inhabiting a host fetus in the physical world. The bipartite soul doesn't incarnate at the same time, but they don't say why that is. This all sounds like a mystical myth or science fiction, but much about our existence and origins is still largely a mystery.

Thanks to science, we can hypothesize, theorize, and calculate just about anything when it comes to this planet and the physical universe, but what we don't know very much about is us. In the same way a mechanic or engineer could eventually work out everything there is to know about a car, even if he didn't know its origins and had never seen one before, we can understand the brain's functions without fully understanding consciousness. While we know a lot about the physical body, and there is a correlation between brain function and physical activity, correlation doesn't scientifically demonstrate that the brain is the cause of our first-person subjective experience. Both the brain and the car can be reduced to their component parts, but consciousness appears to be more than the sum of the brain's parts.

We don't know how life began, the nature of time, how we experience subjective consciousness, or why we feel the way we feel. A fringe idea proposed by some physicists suggests that we might be part of a simulation. But even if we discovered that we are, we might not be any closer to understanding what that means, or what's behind the simulation, if anything.

Our brightest physicists, philosophers, and mathematicians continue to debate the nature of space and time, what consciousness is, how the universe came into being, and what the origins of life are.

It's hard to see how the scientific method could demonstrate the existence of the soul. Science relies on falsification, and the soul, if imperceptible in the physical world, presumably is unfalsifiable.

In a message to Padgett on February 15, 1920, Jesus explained:

"I know that many theories have been set forth as to how and when the soul became a part of the physical body and what was the means adopted by the laws of nature, as they are called, for the lodgment of the soul into that body, and the relationship that one bore to the other. Of course this applies only to those mortals who believe that there is a soul separate in its existence and functionings from the mere physical body. As to those who do not believe in the distinctive soul, I do not attempt to enlighten but leave them to a realization of the fact when they shall have come into the spirit world and find themselves existing without such body, but really existing, with the consciousness that they are souls."

Those In Christ tell us as fully functioning souls they can perceive God just as we can perceive a physical body, whereas those in the numbered levels can perceive a spirit body and remember their experience of inhabiting a physical body, yet in some cases still be unaware they are souls.

In a conversation with Padgett on May 25, 1917, Jesus wrote:

"We spirits of the highest soul progression are enabled by our soul perceptions to see God and His form. But here, I use the words 'see' and 'form,' as being the only words that I can use to give mortals a comparative conception of what I am endeavoring to describe.

"When it is remembered that mortals can scarcely conceive of the form of the spirit body of a man, which is composed or formed of the material of the universe, though not usually accepted to be of the material, it will be readily seen that it is hardly possible for me to convey to them a faint idea even of the soul form of God, which is composed of that which is purely spiritual, that is, not of the material, even though to the highest degree sublimated.

"And although I am not able because of the limitations mentioned to describe to men that form which they may glean a conception of the soul's form, as such form can be seen only with the soul's eye, which eyes men do not possess, it must not be believed that because men cannot understand or perceive the truth of the soul's form, therefore, it is not a truth."

Dead souls

We might equate the soul to a cellphone battery—the battery being the life force of whatever it's powering. A human, whether in a physical body or after transitioning to a spirit body, can charge its soul or leave it to die. Like the phone, when we say, "my battery died," we don't mean it's been annihilated; we mean it's without power and will remain dormant—or dead—until we charge it.

When it comes to the soul, the power needed to charge it is divine love. This isn't some mushy, vague statement. According to Jesus and the other communicators, love is a fundamental attribute and if we don't utilize it, when we leave this level we stagnate and our soul remains "dead" until its charged. Charging is achieved by living a life filled with love, both here and in the spirit world. Love is the juice, the power, and only when we have become free from negative human traits such as condemnation, hatred, fear, egotism, and ignorance, can the soul be fully charged. However, unlike a battery, once fully charged, the soul remains charged forever. It's immortal. This is because once Truth is *known* to the individualized soul it cannot become *unknown*, and nothing else can degrade it—it's become pure, its original, natural state.

On March 5, 1915, Ann Rollins wrote, "The soul does not learn all truths at once, but the truth that it does learn is one that never changes, and lets no revision alter or set it aside. No, truth of the soul's discernment is never shown to be error, and no error ever becomes a part of the soul's discernment of truth."

The following year, in a message to Padgett on March 23, 1916, Jesus reiterated: "The soul is the real human. Because it is the only thing, or part of human, that may become immortal. The only part of human that was made in the image of its Creator, and the only part of human that may become a part of the substance of its Maker, and partake of His Divine Nature."

In the *Course*, Jesus concurs with the idea that the soul can be spiritually dormant, but is never dead:

> 25 'What profiteth it a man if he gain the whole world and lose his own soul?' That means that if he listens to the wrong voice, he has *lost sight* of his soul. He *cannot* lose it, but he cannot *know* it. It is therefore *lost to him* until he chooses right. The Holy Spirit is your Guide in choosing. He is the part of your mind, which *always* speaks for the right choice because He speaks for God. He is your remaining communication with God, which you can interrupt but cannot destroy (5.IV:25).

The Divine Economy

On March 2, 1917, Jesus sent a message to Padgett on the soul and its relation to God:

"There is nothing in the material world that will afford a basis of comparison with the soul, and hence, it is difficult for men to comprehend the nature and qualities of the soul by the mere intellectual perceptions and reason, and in order to understand the nature of this great creation—the soul—men must have something of a spiritual development and the possession of what may be known as the soul perceptions. Only soul can understand soul, and the soul that seeks to comprehend the nature of itself, must be a live soul, with its faculties developed to a small degree, at least.

"First, I will say, that the human soul must be a creature of God and not emanation from Him, as a part of His soul: and when men speak and teach that the human soul is a part of the Over-soul, they teach what is not true. This soul is merely a creature of the Father, just as are the other parts of man, such as the intellect and the spirit body and the material body, and which before its creation had no existence. It has not existed from the beginning of eternity, if you can imagine that eternity ever had a beginning. I mean that there was a time when the human soul had no existence, and whether there will ever come a time when any human soul will cease to have an existence, I do not know, nor does any spirit, only God knows that fact. But this I do know, that whenever the human soul partakes of the essence of the Father, and thereby becomes divine itself, and the possessor of His substance of Love, that soul realizes to a certainty that it is immortal, and can never again become less than immortal. As God is immortal, the soul that has been transformed into the substance of the Father becomes immortal, and never again can the decree, 'Dying thou shalt die,' be pronounced upon it. ...

"While the soul of man is of the highest order of creation, and his attributes and qualities correspond, yet he is no more divine in essential constituents, than are the lower objects of creation—they each being a creation, and not an emanation, of their Creator.

"True it is that the soul of man is of a higher order of creation than any other created things, and is the only creature made in the image of God, and was made the perfect man, yet man—the soul—can never become anything different or greater than the perfect man, unless he receives and possesses the divine Essence and qualities of the Father, which he did not possess at his creation, although, most wonderful gift, with his creation, God bestowed upon him the privilege of receiving this great substance of the divine nature, and thereby become divine himself.

"The perfectly created man could become the divine Angel, if he, the man, so willed it and obeyed the commands of the Father, and pursued the way provided by the Father for obtaining and possessing that divinity.

"As I have said, the souls, the human souls, for the indwelling of which God provided material bodies, that they might live the mortal lives, were created just as, subsequently, these material bodies were created; and this creation of the soul took place long before the appearance of man on earth as a mortal, and the soul prior to such appearance, had its existence in the spirit world as a substantial conscious entity, although without visible form, and, I may say, individuality, but yet, having a distinct personality, so that it was different and distinct from every other soul.

"Its existence and presence could be sensed by every other soul that came in contact with it, and yet to the spirit vision of the other soul it was not visible. And such is the fact now.

"The spirit world is filled with these unincarnated souls, awaiting the time of their incarnation, and we spirits know of, and sense their presence, and yet with our spirit eyes we cannot see them, and not until they become dwellers in the human form and in the spirit body that inhabits that form, can we see the individual soul. ...

"The soul's home is in the spirit body, whether that body is encased in the mortal or not, and it is never without such spirit body, which in appearance and composition is determined by the condition and state of the soul. And finally, the soul or its condition decides the destiny of man, as he continues in his existence in the spirit world; not a final destiny, because the condition of the soul is never fixed, and as this condition changes, man's destiny changes, for destiny is the thing of the moment, and finality is not known to the progress of the soul, until it becomes the perfect man and is then satisfied and seek[s] no higher progress. ...

"*Then what is the spirit?* Simply this—the active energy of the soul. As I have said, the soul has its energy, which may be dormant or which may be active. If dormant, the spirit is not in existence; if active the spirit is present, and manifests that energy in action. So to confuse the spirit with the soul, as being identical, leads to error and away from the truth.

"It is said that God is spirit, which in a sense is true, for spirit is a part of His great soul qualities, and which He uses to manifest His presence in the universe; but to say that spirit is God is not stating the truth, unless you are willing to accept as true the proposition that a part is the whole. In the divine economy, God is all of spirit, but spirit is only the messenger of God, by which He manifests the energies of His Great soul. And so with man. Spirit is not man-soul, but man-soul is spirit, as it is the instrumentality by which the soul of man makes known its energies and powers and presence.

"Well, I have written enough for to-night, but some time I will come and simplify this subject. But remember this, that soul is God, soul is man, and all manifestations, such as spirit, and spirit body are merely evidences of the existence of the soul—the real man."

Jesus's explanation to Padgett—that the unincarnated, pre-individualized soul "had its existence in the spirit world as a substantial conscious entity, although without visible form, ... yet, having a distinct personality"—is not easy to picture. It suggests that having individualized, we become a new being—a new creation—with the potential to be an emanation of God: immortal.

When Jesus says that spirit is "the active energy of the soul," it suggests dynamic spirit worlds in which we manifest in different ways according to our stages of spiritual development. Throughout history, Hell has been associated with a gray, fiery world inhabited by demon-like monsters, whereas Heaven is portrayed as bright and beautiful, a realm where angelic beings reside. Perhaps we are all potential angels—and, like rebellious teenagers, some of us will go through a "demon phase" before we get there.

PART TWO

I AM NOT GOD
And Other Fallacies

13

THE BIBLE

Built on Shaky Foundations?

The Bible isn't just an ancient text; for billions of people it's a wellspring of solace, comfort, and joy. Its stories resonate across generations offering wisdom and guidance for navigating life's challenges, with an assurance of an afterlife in heaven for those who accept Jesus as their Savior. For its critics, it's a treasure trove of horrifying stories of genocide, incest, rape, and murder. Between these opposing worldviews are the scholars, whose task it is to analyze Christianity through a dispassionate lens.

Bart Ehrman[1] and Robert Funk are two scholars who, despite their initial Christian beliefs, after conducting extensive research, came to reject the doctrine of Jesus's immaculate conception, divinity, and sacrificial death—all cornerstones of Christianity.

Ehrman has authored numerous best-selling books, including *Misquoting Jesus, Jesus Interrupted,* and *How Jesus Became God,* all of which critically examine the Bible, and focus on how scribes' errors and alterations have shaped it into the text we know today.

Ehrman studied at the Moody Bible Institute in Chicago, where he embraced Christian fundamentalism, holding the view that "The Bible contains no mistakes of any kind, doctrinal, ethical, historical, or scientific." However, that profound sense of certainty appears to have been short-lived, as today he reportedly identifies as an agnostic atheist.

In his 2017 blog: "Leaving the Faith," he wrote that he had come to realize the Bible was deeply flawed and that Christianity had developed as a result of historical cultural forces rather than divine guidance. Yet despite that, he claimed his loss of faith wasn't due to historical inaccuracies, but that he couldn't reconcile the suffering in the world with the Christian claim that God loves people, answers their prayers, and intervenes when they are in need.

On September 10, 2005, *The New York Times* reported: "Robert W. Funk, founder of the Jesus Seminar, a consortium of Bible scholars who popularized a wave of studies that raised doubts about whether the deeds and sayings attributed to Jesus were historically authentic, died on Sept. 3 at his home in Santa Rosa, Calif. He was seventy-nine.[2]"

Before becoming a religious scholar, Funk was a teenage evangelist, preaching to crowded meetings. "I did that when I was starting out, sort of being a hotshot," he recalled in a 1998 interview. "I knew how to make people laugh, make them cry."

By 1985, Funk was questioning traditional Christian interpretations of the historical Jesus. He organized a forum and invited fellow scholars with the intention of improving religious literacy. At one early meeting, he shared his vision: "We are going to inquire simply, rigorously after the voice of Jesus—after what he really said."

The organization became known as the Jesus Seminar, operating under the umbrella of the Westar Institute, whose mission is "to foster collaborative, cumulative research in religious studies" and "communicate the results of the scholarship of religion to a broad, non-specialist public."

Like Ehrman, Funk questioned the divinity of Jesus based on his analysis of ancient texts. The Jesus Seminar scholars considered the Gospel of Thomas a potential "fifth gospel," as it contains sayings that may predate or independently parallel those in the canonical Gospels—Matthew, Mark, Luke, and John.

To compare sayings attributed to Jesus across different sources, they devised a color-coded voting system: red meant Jesus likely said it; pink, he probably said something like it; gray, he probably didn't; and black, he definitely didn't. Many sayings in Thomas received red or pink ratings, making it, in their view, a valuable source for identifying the historical Jesus.

Needless to say, Funk was not popular with many Christian peers, and was accused of leaving people "spiritually bankrupt and hopeless." Christian broadcaster Pat Robertson accused the Jesus Seminar of trying to "accommodate the Bible to their own unbelief."

"Jesus was one of the great sages of history," said Funk. "But he was not the man portrayed in a surface reading of the New Testament. ... I do not want my faith to be in Jesus, but faith in the really real—in some version of whatever it was that Jesus believed."

A year after Funk's death, the original Jesus Seminar was formally dissolved. Its website states:

Jesus was a mortal man born of two human parents, who did not perform nature miracles nor die as a substitute for sinners nor rise bodily from the dead. Sightings of a risen Jesus represented the visionary experiences of some of his disciples rather than physical encounters.[3]

There is a consensus among biblical scholars that Paul's epistles are the earliest writings in the New Testament, dating to around 50–60 CE, approximately twenty years after Jesus's death.

Before Paul's writings in the Bible, there is no strong evidence to suggest that apostles such as Peter and Jesus's brother James believed that Jesus was God or that those who failed to accept Jesus as their Savior would be confined to a permanent hell after death. Neither was the idea that Jesus's death was a sacrifice to forgive humanity for its sinful nature part of early Jewish-Christian thought.

James Tabor,[4] a prominent history scholar of early Christianity, asserts that as a result of Paul's personal revelations and his interpretation—or misinterpretation—of Old Testament Scripture, he radically changed the message of Jesus to the message of Paul. Tabor, author of *Paul and Jesus: How the Apostle Transformed Christianity* (2012), argues that Paul was the primary architect of the belief that Jesus was a divine figure who died for humanity's sins.

Tabor contends that Jesus's followers likely saw him as a messianic figure but not as a pre-existing divine being. In closing his book, he writes: "The task of a historian is to offer as clear a view of Paul's own testimony in this regard as is possible from his own letters, while recovering to whatever extent possible those now silent voices who represented an earlier and alternative 'Christianity before Paul.'" All three scholars agree that historic data suggests Christianity evolved into a belief system fundamentally different from what Jesus believed and taught.

∞

Martin Luther is one of the most influential Christian figures of the past five hundred years. By breaking away from the Catholic Church, he became instrumental in the Reformation, which led to the rise of Protestantism in Europe. He emphasized a personal relationship with God and rejected the Church's institutional authority.

Luther subscribed to Paul's doctrine of "faith alone" (*sola fide*) as the basis of salvation. He believed that the soul's eternal destination—heaven or hell—is determined at the moment of death. As such, he rejected the belief that the soul undergoes purification after death. Therefore, prayers for the dead had no efficacy, and the sale of so-called purgatorial indulgences—which, it was widely thought, were being used for monetary gain—was condemned and abolished.

He was a divisive figure and, like some of the early Church Fathers, was hostile to Jews, believing them to be Christ-killers.

Three years before his death in 1546, in his treatise *On the Jews and Their Lies*, he advised his Christian followers: "Set fire to their synagogues or schools and to bury and cover with dirt whatever will not burn, so that no man will ever again see a stone or cinder of them.[5]

Fast forward to the twentieth century, and the seeds of antisemitism continued to grow in Europe. Hitler praised Luther as a "great warrior," while William Ralph Inge, a retired Dean of St Paul's Cathedral, argued: "If we wish to find a scapegoat on whose shoulders we may lay the miseries which Germany has brought upon the world, I am more and more convinced that the worst evil genius of that country is not Hitler or Bismarck or Frederick the Great, but Martin Luther."

After Luther entered the spirit world, he discovered that the old adage, "The road to hell is paved with good intentions," was a truism.

On July 6, 1915, in his first message to Padgett, he wrote:

"I am here, a stranger, but a spirit interested in the work that you are doing for the Master, and also for many spirits, good and bad. I am writing by permission of your band. Hence, do not feel that I am intruding. So if you will kindly bear with me, I will say a few words.

"I am a spirit in divine love, with the efforts that you and your band, are making to help the unfortunates who come to you with such pitying tales of suffering and darkness and ask for help. I was once, when on earth, a human who suffered much because of my spiritual darkness. Not until late in life, did I find the way to my Father's divine love through prayer and faith. Even then, I had many erroneous beliefs, caused by the interpretations of the Bible, then obtaining in the church of which I was a member.

"Since coming to the spirit land, I have learned the truth. I have gotten rid of any old erroneous beliefs. Thank God, I am in the way that leads to life everlasting. I was a teacher when on earth, of what I thought were Bible truths. I know that some good resulted from my teachings, although they were mixed with errors. I have met many spirits of humans who listened to my teachings, and believed many things that I taught. So you see that even if the churches do teach many false doctrines in their creeds, yet mixed with these false doctrines are many truths. These truths often find lodgment in the hearts of the hearers, and result in their finding the light and divine love of the Father.

"I am still teaching mortals, whenever it is possible to do. I find that my task is a difficult one, because there are so few mediums who are capable of receiving the divine truths of the higher things of life."

∞

On March 12, 1917, after Padgett had attended a church, Luke sent a long message on the authenticity of the Bible, in which he wrote:

"I was with you at the lecture of the preacher on this subject, and was surprised that he could announce with such apparent confidence that the Bible is the authentic word of God, actually written by the men whose names appear therein as the writers of the same. The fact that he traced back the existence of certain manuscripts and versions to a hundred and fifty years subsequent to the time of the teachings of Jesus, did not establish the truth of his declaration that by such establishment the authenticity of the Bible, or the genuineness of the manuscripts as they now exist contain the real writings of the apostles, or of those persons who are supposed to be the writers of the same from the fact that their names are associated with these manuscripts. ...

"I was a writer upon these sacred subjects, and as I have before told you, I wrote a document which was called the 'Acts of the Apostles,' and left a number of copies of my writings when I died; but such compilation was merely a history of what I had heard from those who had lived with and heard the teachings of Jesus, and of their efforts to circulate and teach his doctrines after his death. I also had the benefit of some writings of the disciples about Jesus, but such writings were very few, for these disciples and followers of Jesus did not commence to place in the form of manuscript his teachings or the experience of his life until a long time after he had left the earth. They expected his speedy return when he would become their king and legislator, and hence, they saw no occasion or necessity for preserving in the form of writings the truths in which he had instructed them.

"I know that after my own death the writings that I had left were not preserved intact, and that many things that I had incorporated therein, were in the numerous copying and recopyings of my manuscripts left out and ignored, and many things that I did not write and that were not in accord with the truth were inserted by these various successive copyists in their work of reproduction. ...

"Even in epistles of Paul, which these theologians and Bible students claim have more authenticity and greater certainty than the Gospels or other epistles of the Bible, many changes were made between the times of their writings and the times of the execution of the manuscripts or of the sermons of the fathers of the early church.

"Within that one hundred and fifty years the truths of the spiritual teachings of the Master had become to a more or less extent lost to the consciousness and knowledge of those who attempted to reproduce the original writings, because these men had become less spiritual, and their thoughts and efforts had become more centered in building up the church as a church than in attempting to develop and teach and preserve the great spiritual truths.

"The moral precepts became the dominating objects of their writings and teachings and were more easily comprehended by them than were precepts that taught the way to the development of their souls and to a knowledge of the will of the Father, and the mission of Jesus to mankind as a way-shower and savior of souls, rather than as a Messiah to establish a kingdom on earth.

"No, I declare with authority that the authenticity of the Bible cannot be established as the word of God, for in very many particulars it is not His word, but on the contrary, contains many assertions of truth that are not truths and diametrically opposed to His truths, and to Jesus's teachings of the truth. ...

"Among these writings of the Bible there are many things declared to be truths, and embodied as the actual words of God, that are contradictory and unexplainable, and which, if they were the words of God, or even the teachings of Jesus, would contain no contradiction, or admit of any constructions that were not consistent one with the other. ...

"The Bible contains many truths, and enough to enable man to reach the Kingdom of Heaven, provided they are correctly understood and applied, but there are so many things taught therein as truths, which are just the opposite of truth, that they make it difficult for men to discern and apply the truth, and comprehend the will of God with respect to men, and the destinies that must be theirs according as they follow and obey that will or do not do so. ..."

A verse in Exodus, the second book of the Old Testament, reads: "God also said to Moses, 'I am the LORD. I appeared to Abraham, to Isaac and to Jacob as God Almighty, but by my name the LORD I did not make myself fully known to them'" (Exod. 6:2–3). In the Torah, "LORD" in all caps means YHVH (Yahweh or Jehovah), the personal name of the God of the Israelites.

Note: God told Moses that He appeared to Abraham, Isaac, and Jacob, but did not reveal Himself to them explicitly as LORD. Yet, in Genesis, the first book of the Old Testament, He seems to do exactly that. God tells Abraham, "He also said to him, 'I am the LORD, who brought you out of Ur of the Chaldeans to give you this land to take possession of it'" (Gen. 15:7).

And He tells Jacob, "There above it stood the LORD, and he said: 'I am the LORD, the God of your father Abraham and the God of Isaac. I will give you and your descendants the land on which you are lying'" (Gen. 28:13).

These verses are just one example of contradictions in the Bible, which, as Luke and others have noted, suggest inconsistency.

The Trinity

I don't know how many thoughts we have during any given day but some scientific studies suggest the number is around 6,000. If I have 6,000 thoughts a day, one thing I know for sure is that wondering whether the Trinity is real isn't one of them.

Jesus refers to God as "Father" more than a hundred times in the Bible, including: "I came from the Father and entered the world; now I am leaving the world and going back to the Father" (John 16:28), and: "You heard that I said to you, 'I go away, and I will come to you.' If you loved Me, you would have rejoiced because I go to the Father, for the Father is greater than I" (John 14:28). Then there's the verse about the rich man who asked Jesus:

"Good teacher, what must I do to inherit eternal life?"

"Why do you call me good?" Jesus answered. "No one is good except God alone" (Mark 10:17–18). That doesn't sound like Jesus is the Father or the Father is Jesus.

The word "Trinity" means a group of three, or three being one, and God, the Holy Spirit, and Jesus could be said to be acting as a group. Ultimately, if there is only "oneness" as some maintain, it could be said the Trinity is "one," but that doesn't mean Jesus, the Holy Spirit, and God are equal, or the same thing. Even if you believe every word in the Bible, "trinity" isn't mentioned anywhere, and the only reason it's one of my 6,000 thoughts today is because the Padgett communicators had something to say about it.

On September 24, 1914, in one of the earliest messages, Jesus explained:

"When I said, 'I am the Way, the Truth and the Life,' I meant that through my teachings and example men should be able to find God. I was not God and never claimed to be. The worship of me as a God is blasphemous and I did not teach it. I am a son of God as you are. Do not let the teachings of men lead you to worship me as a God. I am not. The Trinity is a mistake of the writers of the Bible.

"There is no Trinity, only one God, the Father. He is one and alone. I am His teacher of truth; the Holy Spirit is His messenger and dispenser of Love to mankind. We are only His instruments in bringing man to a union with Him. I am not the equal of my Father. He is the only true God. I came from the spirit world to earth and took the form of man, but I did not become a God, only the son of my Father. You also lived as a spirit in that kingdom, and took the form of man merely as a son of your Father. You are the same as I am, except as to spiritual development, and you may become as greatly developed as myself."

Contrary to the opening verse of the Gospel of John—"In the beginning was the Word, and the Word was with God, and the Word was God. He was with God in the beginning" (John 1:1–2)—Jesus is saying that he, like us, was created by God and was not with God from the beginning.

The Original Jews for Jesus: Heretics or Truth Tellers?

Long before the modern evangelical movement known as "Jews for Jesus," there were Jews who believed Jesus was the Messiah—but not God. Among the earliest of them were the Ebionites (the "poor ones"), some of the first known followers of Jesus in the first century. Today, little is known about them, and only fragments of their writings survive. Most of what we know comes from early Church fathers such as Epiphanius and Irenaeus, who regarded them as troublemakers and branded them heretics.

The limited evidence—though debated—suggests the Ebionites saw Jesus as the prophet Moses spoke of in Deuteronomy: "The Lord said to me: 'What they say is good. I will raise up for them a prophet like you from among their fellow Israelites, and I will put my words in his mouth. He will tell them everything I command him. I myself will call to account anyone who does not listen to my words that the prophet speaks in my name" (Deut. 18:17–19).

The Ebionites rejected Paul's teaching that faith alone was sufficient for salvation. They insisted on strict adherence to Jewish law, which they saw as essential to their Hebrew tradition. Judaism recognized 613 mitzvot (divine commandments) while Christianity focused on ten.

Much like Ehrman and other modern critical scholars, the Ebionites rejected Jesus's divinity, the virgin birth, and the idea that his death on the cross was a sacrifice. They believed he was divinely chosen and became In Christ at his baptism.

It was a hostile time for the Jews. Like other Church fathers, Ambrose of Milan—still regarded today as one of the most influential early Christian leaders—had harsh words for them, blaming the Jewish people for rejecting Christ.

In 379, he wrote: "The Jews are the most worthless of all men. They are lecherous, greedy, rapacious. They are perfidious murderers of Christ. They worship the Devil. Their religion is a sickness. The Jews are the odious assassins of Christ, and for killing God there is no expiation possible, no indulgence or pardon. Christians may never cease vengeance, and the Jew must live in servitude forever. God always hated the Jews. It is essential that all Christians hate them." [6]

In 379, the Bible had yet to be officially compiled, but in instructing Christians "to never cease vengeance," one wonders if Ambrose had read Jesus's teachings on forgiveness:

"And when you stand praying, if you hold anything against anyone, forgive them, so that your Father in heaven may forgive you your sins" (Mark 11:25).

Ambrose might not have been the first antisemite—the term didn't exist in the fourth century—but his demonization of the Jews was almost certainly a forerunner of its persistence today.

While adhering to the law, the Ebionites believed the Torah had been corrupted. It's thought they may have cited a passage from Jeremiah to support that view. Six hundred years earlier, the prophet Jeremiah had called out the scribes—the educated class responsible for copying and interpreting the law. A verse in the Old Testament reads:

"How can you say, 'We are wise, for we have the law of the Lord,' when actually the lying pen of the scribes has handled it falsely?" (Jer. 8:8).

There is a consensus among biblical scholars that Matthew was written later than Mark and incorporated a significant amount of Mark's material—possibly adapted to fit the writer's theology. For example, Matthew has its own version of the rich man story:

"Just then a man came up to Jesus and asked, 'Teacher, what good thing must I do to get eternal life?' Jesus replied, 'Why do you ask me about what is good? There is only One who is good'" (Matt. 19:16–17).

In Mark, Jesus is saying he is not good—only God is good—clearly differentiating himself from God. Whereas in Matthew, the man isn't calling Jesus good, he's asking about good things. The compilers of the Bible placed Matthew ahead of Mark, despite it being a later composition. So, was Mark's original account—indicating that Jesus isn't God—an inconvenient truth?

Some scholars claim that New Testament writers were trying to make Jesus fit the Isaiah prophecy in the Old Testament: "Therefore the Lord himself will give you a sign: The virgin will conceive and give birth to a son, and will call him Immanuel" (Isa. 7:14).

However, "virgin" is a translation of the Hebrew word *almah*, which means a young woman of childbearing age, unmarried or not. And while it can be translated as virgin, *almah* has a broader meaning that doesn't necessarily imply virginity.

Unlike Matthew and Luke, Mark and John say nothing about Jesus's virgin birth. If it was a widely accepted belief at the time, one might wonder why they didn't mention it.

It appears that, unlike mainstream Christianity, the Ebionite view of the historical Jesus—one of the earliest Jewish-Christian perspectives we have evidence for—is far more in line with the Padgett communicators and today's critical scholars. All unlikely bedfellows.

Messiah

In 587/586 BCE, the kingdom of Judah went to war with Babylonia in an attempt to escape its domination. During the siege that followed, Solomon's temple was destroyed and Jerusalem was razed to the ground.

Around that time, Daniel—according to the account in the Old Testament—was praying for the people of Judah and for the restoration of Jerusalem when he reportedly received a vision from Gabriel, the same figure he had encountered earlier. Gabriel said:

> Daniel, as soon as you began to pray, a word went out, which I have come to tell you, for you are highly esteemed. Therefore, consider the word and understand the vision:
>
> Seventy 'sevens' are decreed for your people and your holy city to finish transgression, to put an end to sin, to atone for wickedness, to bring in everlasting righteousness, to seal up vision and prophecy and to anoint the Most Holy Place.
>
> Know and understand this: From the time the word goes out to restore and rebuild Jerusalem until the Anointed One, the ruler, comes, there will be seven 'sevens,' and sixty-two 'sevens.' It will be rebuilt with streets and a trench, but in times of trouble.
>
> After the sixty-two 'sevens,' the Anointed One will be put to death and will have nothing. The people of the ruler who will come will destroy the city and the sanctuary. The end will come like a flood: War will continue until the end, and desolations have been decreed.
>
> He will confirm a covenant with many for one 'seven.' In the middle of the 'seven,' he will put an end to sacrifice and offering. And at the temple, he will set up an abomination that causes desolation, until the end that is decreed is poured out on him (Dan. 9:23–27).

In 538 BCE, Cyrus the Great, king of Persia, issued a decree allowing the Jews to return to Jerusalem and rebuild the city. Some interpreted this as the beginning of the fulfillment of Daniel's prophecy—and the coming of a Messiah: an "Anointed One," not God, but a leader or king sent to rescue Judah's beleaguered population from its enemies.

Scholars have suggested that the term "seven" refers to a symbolic unit of time—seven years. By this reckoning, "seventy sevens" would represent 490 years. Because the prophecy also mentions a final "half week," some interpret the timeline as "sixty-nine sevens," totaling 483 years. That 483–490-year span has been linked by some to the period between the rebuilding of Jerusalem and the life of Jesus. As with other Biblical scripture, the authorship and dating of the text have been debated, but the timeline is intriguing.

In the Padgett messages, "Messiah" is mentioned a number of times. Luke stated earlier that he viewed Jesus as "a savior of souls, rather than as a Messiah who came to establish his kingdom on earth."

In a communication on May 24, 1915, Jesus concurred:

"When I came to the world to teach the truths of my Father, the world was almost devoid of spiritual conception of the true relationship of God to man, and God was a being of power and wrath only. It was because of this conception of Him that the Jews were so devoid of the true knowledge of His nature and attributes. They only knew Him as a God who was interested in their material welfare, and did not realize that He was a God who wanted them to know Him as their Spiritual Father and Savior from the sins and evil natures that they possessed. And consequently when I came, they looked upon me—I mean those who accepted me as their Messiah—as one who would redeem them from the slavery which their Roman conquerors had placed them in and make them a great and independent nation, more powerful than all the nations of the earth, and fitted to rule the whole world.

"They had no conception of my true mission on earth, and even my disciples, until shortly before my death, looked upon me merely as a Savior of them from the burdens which the Roman yoke had placed upon them.

"The only one of my disciples who had any approximate realization of what my coming to earth meant, was John, and that was because of the great amount of love that seemed to be a part of his nature and being. To him I explained my real mission and taught him the spiritual truths, which I came to teach, and the only way in which mortals could receive that Love of the Father, which was necessary to make them one with the Father and enable them to partake of the divinity of the Father. Hence, only in John's Gospel is written the one necessary requirement to a full salvation and redemption of mankind. I mean the declaration that men must be born again in order to enter into the Kingdom of Heaven. This is the only true way by which a man can become a true child of the Father, and fitted to live in and enjoy the Father's kingdom to the fullest.

"The other disciples had more or less conception of this necessary truth, but not the full comprehension of what it involved. Peter was more possessed of this Love than were the other disciples, except John, and with it he also understood that I was the true son of my Father; but he never understood nor declared that I was God. He was a man filled with zeal and ambition, but his development of love was not sufficient to enable him to fully realize that my kingdom was not to be an earthly one, until after my death, and then the conviction came to him in all its truth and fullness, and he became the most powerful and influential of all my disciples.

"After the Pentecost, all of my disciples understood what my real mission was, and they went into the world and preached the true doctrines of my mission on earth, and the Love of the Father for His children, and the fact that that Love was waiting for all who should seek for it.

"So you see that many of my disciples when on earth were not possessed of the true conception of my mission, and were not true followers of me in that inner meaning of what the Love of the Father meant, and what I tried to preach to them."

Original Sin:
A mocking damnable lie

Jesus never mentioned it. Swedenborg didn't believe in it. Martin Luther did. Richard Dawkins called it a hideous idea. The term "Original sin" doesn't appear in the Bible, yet today it remains a cornerstone of Christianity. It's the idea that because the first humans transgressed, we are born flawed with evil inclinations, and are being punished by being separated from God. Jesus's death on the cross was a sacrifice to atone for our sins, and only by accepting him as our Savior, we are reconciled with God.

Ezekiel in the Old Testament reads: "The one who sins is the one who will die. The child will not share the guilt of the parent, nor will the parent share the guilt of the child. The righteousness of the righteous will be credited to them, and the wickedness of the wicked will be charged against them" (Ezek. 18:20).

In the New Testament, Paul states: "Therefore, just as sin entered the world through one man, and death through sin, and in this way death came to all people, because all sinned" (Rom. 5:12).

Islam teaches that Adam and Eve sinned but were forgiven by God, rejecting the notion of inherited sin. Judaism and other religious traditions also view humans as morally neutral, with free will determining our fate. Hinduism and Buddhism subscribe to the idea of karma—a moral law of cause and effect—but do not teach that humans are born inherently flawed. It's a doctrine that's unique to Christianity, particularly Catholic and Protestant Christianity.

If a child doesn't share the guilt of its parents, as Ezekiel states, why would it share the guilt of its ancestors? It's one of those seemingly theological contradictions that owes much to Saint Augustine, Bishop of Hippo, who influenced Christian doctrine during the fourth and fifth centuries. Augustine seized on Paul's letter to the Romans and concluded that we are born slaves to sin. In his *Confessions*, he wrote, "No one is free from sin in your sight, not even an infant whose span of earthly life is but a single day."

During Augustine's time, a British monk named Pelagius challenged his ideas and argued that humans are born morally neutral and capable of achieving perfection through their own efforts. "Surely, we are not nursed with sin, but are created free to choose good or evil," Pelagius wrote to his follower Rufinus. "How much greater to choose—and to freely choose good—than to be like the bees and the fishes. Every morning, we can awake and seize the day with our will, not wrapped in animal flesh, in the tyranny of our instincts, but awesomely free. Free to do great things, Rufinus."

Pelagius was smeared with accusations of heresy in what appears to have been an ecclesiastical witch-hunt, which led to the term "Pelagianism."[7]

In a letter to Pope Innocent I, Pelagius claimed he was being vilified and pleaded, "See how this epistle will clear me before your Blessedness, for in it we clearly and simply declare that we possess a free will which is unimpaired for sinning and for not sinning, and this free will is in all good works always assisted by divine help."

Before Innocent could resolve the matter, he died. Subsequently, Augustine doubled down on his assertions and sent word to other bishops encouraging them to do the same. He stated, "The Holy Spirit dwells only within the Catholic Church, and salvation is impossible outside it."

Pelagius was ultimately condemned as a heretic and excommunicated. He was reportedly expelled from Jerusalem in 418 CE, and details of his life after that are unknown.

Christian commentators sometimes point out that Christianity is evolving with the times, but even today, the theological doctrine that defines the beliefs of the Anglican Church, known as the Thirty-Nine Articles of Religion, states: "Original sin standeth not in the following of Adam (as the Pelagians do vainly talk) but is the fault and corruption of the nature of every man, that naturally is engendered of the offspring of Adam; whereby man is very far gone from original righteousness and is of his own nature inclined to evil, so that the flesh lusteth always contrary to the spirit ..."[8]

∞

On August 7, 1915, almost fifteen hundred years after his death in 430 CE, Augustine communicated with Padgett:

"I merely want to say that I am the Augustine who lived after the death of Jesus and was well acquainted with his teachings as they were preserved by the Church. At that time I never knew exactly what became of the manuscripts that were in existence when I lived, but the ones that are supposed to furnish the origin of many of the biblical writings were not the ones that I was acquainted with. Those that I used were all written in Greek and were written by the disciples of Jesus and by those of his followers to whom the disciples had communicated the teachings of the Master; and they were the genuine ones and were written from the actual communications of the disciples.

"Of course, the teachings of Jesus were never recorded at the time of his teachings but were merely the recollections possessed by the disciples of what they thought he really said, and consequently, as you may realize, they were imperfect and could not be relied on implicitly.

"I know that great controversies have arisen in the church as to what portions of these writings should be accepted as genuine, and many needless disputes have caused the officials of that church to differ as to what were really the writings of the disciples, and what were not. I, when on earth, joined in these disputes, and maintained that certain of these writings were genuine and certain were not, but I was as likely to be mistaken as any of the others.

"But even the ones that I thought genuine were more or less flavored by the spiritual knowledge and beliefs of those who wrote them. So I tell you that you cannot depend on these writings as a whole to learn what the Master actually did teach. He is now in condition to give you the genuine truths, and whenever what he may say conflicts with what is contained in the Bible, you must consider what he now writes as the truth and discard the Bible account as unreliable."

In a message to Padgett on April 17, 1916, Luke decried the doctrine, saying, "This doctrine of Original Sin is a mocking, damnable lie, and the sooner man realizes the fact that it is a fraud and deceit, the sooner he will be able to get rid of those things which have placed him in his present condition and held him there bound, as it were, hand and foot."

Two months later, Jesus concurred: "For the long years of misbelief in the idea of Original Sin, and that God created evil and error for the purpose of defiling man's nature and making a disobedient devil of him, without any inherent goodness or the possibility of becoming regenerated, unless by the operation of some miracle, will make it difficult for the acquiring of the true belief as to what he, and what his nature are, and enable him to become the master, and not remain the servant."

Pelagius's crime was to believe we are not born slaves to sin and free to make good and bad decisions. Today his name might be a footnote in history, but had his more optimistic view of humanity become Christian doctrine instead of Augustine's, the world might look very different today.

Vicarious Atonement

In 2016, during Pope Francis' Year of Mercy, he announced: "I henceforth grant to all priests, in virtue of their ministry, the faculty to absolve those who have committed the sin of procured abortion." [9]

According to Catholic teaching, a priest forgives sins by acting as Christ himself—that is, in the person of Christ (*in persona Christi*). It is as if, at that moment, he is Christ.

Personally, I can't imagine relying on anyone to forgive me on God's behalf. I'm a trusting person, but it feels like I'm being given a check I won't be able to cash.

My limited understanding of the Jewish tradition is that the fundamental goal is to know God, which is achieved through prayer and living according to His commandments. Good deeds, personal responsibility, and repentance are central. From a Jewish perspective, Jesus didn't die for our sins—those are on us.

During one of my conversations with Michael Cocks, we discussed this apparent conflict in the Bible between Jewish and Christian doctrine. Michael explained that the Bible is more like a library than a single book. I said, "That's fine, but surely some of it belongs in the fiction section, because both propositions can't be correct." And it's not a small thing—it's about whether the individual is on the right or wrong path, both in this life and after death.

In the New Testament, a verse attributed to Paul reads: "God made him who had no sin to be sin for us, so that in him we might become the righteousness of God" (2 Cor. 5:21). And: "God demonstrates his own love for us in this: While we were still sinners, Christ died for us. Since we have now been justified by his blood, how much more shall we be saved from God's wrath through him!" (Rom. 5:8–9).

In a message to Padgett on October 26, 1915, Paul commented on a book he was reading:

"The book on the 'Vicarious Atonement' that you have been reading, about the ransom price and the blood of Jesus and the sacrifice on the cross, as to these things is all wrong, and you must not believe what it says."

Padgett must have pointed out that the proposition that Jesus died for our sins was his.

"Well, I know the Bible ascribes to me the teaching of these things, but I never did. And I tell you now, as I have before told you, that the Bible cannot be depended on as containing things that I wrote, for there are many additions to what I wrote, and many omissions of what I wrote, and so with the others whose names are stated as the writers of the New Testament. Many things contained in that book were never written by any of the alleged authors of the book.

"The writings of any of us are not in existence, and have not been for many centuries, and when they were copied and recopied, great additions and omissions were made, and, at last, doctrines and dogmas were interpolated that we never at any time believed or wrote.

"I have to say this, and I wish to emphasize my statement with all the conviction and knowledge of the truth that I possess: Jesus never paid any debt of man by his death or his blood or vicarious Atonement. When Jesus came to earth his mission was given him as he progressed in his soul development, and not until his anointing was he wholly qualified to enter upon his mission or the work thereof. ...

"He emphatically never claimed that he came to earth to pay any ransom for mankind, or to save them by his death on the cross, or to save them in any other way than by teaching them that the Great Gift or privilege of obtaining immortality had been bestowed upon them, and that by prayer and faith they could obtain it."

The ransom Paul referred to was an early Church theory that Jesus's death was a ransom paid to Satan, who had imprisoned us because of our sinful nature. It was paid to free us and bring us back to God. According to one theory, Satan had a legitimate claim on us as a result of Adam and Eve turning away from God. If that were true, looking at the state of humanity today, both God and Jesus could be forgiven for wondering if it was all worth it.

In Christ

Many years ago, I was leaving a U.S. airport when a young man in a dark suit and tie approached me and asked, "Have you accepted Jesus as your Savior?" I told him I hadn't. He insisted that if I did, all my sins would be forgiven, no matter how bad, and I would be In Christ.

I said I couldn't bring myself to believe that being In Christ was that simple. The proposition that Jesus died for my sins seemed like wishful thinking. Want to bomb a country? Go right ahead. Feel like killing your neighbor? No problem—Jesus has already picked up the tab, as long as you repent before you die.

We shook hands and wished each other well.

∞

In a message to Padgett on March 3, 1918, Jesus clarified what it means to be In Christ:

"I desire tonight to write you in reference to the way in which, as the preacher advises, 'Christ may be in you,' I know that it is almost universal among preachers of the orthodox church to teach their hearers that the way to salvation is to get Christ in them and thereby they will be enabled to come into unity with the Father, and cease to remain subject to the effects of sin and evil.

"Well this teaching is the true foundation of salvation for the celestial heavens, provided it be understood by the preachers and the people what the true meaning of Christ in you is, and unless this meaning be comprehended, the fact that preacher or people may believe that they have Christ in them will not work the results that they may suppose or desire.

"Many, and I may say the most, of these professing Christians, have ideas of what this expression means in order to become effective, that are not in accord with the true meaning of this condition of the soul.

"They believe that all that is necessary is to believe on Jesus (*sic*) as their Savior by his sacrifice and death and that in so believing they have Christ in them, and that nothing else is required. They have no conception of the distinction between Jesus, the man, and Christ, the spirit of truth, or more correctly, the spirit that manifests the existence of the divine love in the soul. Christ is not a man in the sense that he is Jesus the son of the Father, but Christ is that part of Jesus, or rather quality that came to him after he fully received into his soul the divine love, and was transformed into the very Essence of the Father in His Love.

"Christ is thus, not a man but is the manifestation of this Love as bestowed upon Jesus, and made part of his very existence. And when men use the expression, having Christ in you, if they could correctly understand the true purport of the same, they would know that it, the expression, means only that the divine love of the Father is in their souls.

"The indiscriminate use of the words 'Jesus' and 'Christ' is the cause of much misunderstanding among these Christians as to a number of the sayings of the Bible.

"Jesus became the Christ only because he was the first to receive into his soul this divine love and to manifest its existence, and this Christ principle is one that all men may possess, with the result that they will become at one with the Father in His substance of love and immortality.

"It would be impossible for Jesus, the man, to get into or become a part of any mortal, and it would be equally as impossible for Christ, as the man Jesus, even though perfect and free from sin, to become a part of anyone.

"No, the meaning of having Christ in you is to have this Love of the Father in your soul, which can only be obtained through the working of the Holy Spirit as the instrument of the Father in bringing this Love into the soul.

"To many who hear the preachers' exhortations in this particular, the expression is only a mystery, which they accept merely intellectually, and feel that by such acceptance they have the possession of this Christ, which is the only evidence of the truth of the Father's love.

"Goodnight.

"Your friend and brother, Jesus."

Note: Jesus said that to be In Christ is the "true foundation of salvation for the celestial heavens." In this context, it has nothing to do with being in the physical world or even the spirit world. We can exist in the physical realm—and even in the upper echelons of the spirit world, such as the sixth sphere—and still not be In Christ.

My understanding is that to be In Christ is to be in a state of existence that transcends both worlds and enables entrance into the celestial.

It seems likely we can't know whether we are In Christ until we've left the physical world. And no matter how well-intentioned the man at the airport was—and I thank him for that—it appears to be a far more profound state of being. It's the ultimate goal—and merely accepting

Jesus as my Savior and sincerely repenting for past sins probably wouldn't have been enough.

The Sonship

In the New Testament, John said: "For God so loved the world that He gave His one and only Son, that whoever believes in Him shall not perish but have eternal life" (John 3:16). Some interpret this as God sacrificed Jesus for humanity. However, in ACIM, Jesus states the verse should read, "He gave *it* to His only begotten Son" meaning, God gave the offer of eternal life to the Sonship—every single human:

> 100 It should especially be noted that God has only *one* Son. If all the souls God created are His Sons, then every soul must be an integral part of the whole Sonship. You do not find the concept that the whole is greater than its parts difficult to understand. You should therefore not have too much trouble in understanding this.
>
> 101 The Sonship in its oneness *does* transcend the sum of its parts. However, this is obscured as long as any of its parts are missing. That is why the conflict cannot ultimately be resolved until *all* the parts of the Sonship have returned. Only then can the meaning of wholeness, in the true sense, be fully understood (2.V:100–101).

On September 24, 1914, in one of the early messages to Padgett, Jesus explained that what makes him unique is that, in the context of the Sonship, he was the first son:

"When on earth, I was the only son who had, until then, become vested with the divine love of God to the extent of being wholly free from sin and error. My life was not a life of earthly pleasure or sin, but was given wholly to my Father's work. I was His only son in that light. He was my Father as I knew Him to be. He is not a spirit of form like myself or yourself.

"I was born as you were born. I was the son of Mary and Joseph, and not born of the Holy Spirit as it is written in the Bible. I was only a human being as regards my birth and physical existence. The account in the New Testament is not true, and was written by those who knew not what they wrote. They have done the cause of God's truths much injury. Let not your belief in that error keep you from seeing that my teachings are the truth.

"Be only a believer of God and His truths and you will soon be in the Kingdom.

"You will soon be able to understand as I understand."

∞

Imagine that every soul who has individualized is a piece of a jigsaw puzzle. The pieces are scattered far and wide throughout history. Until the pieces are all back in place, the Sonship is not complete. Perhaps that is what "Thy kingdom come; thy will be done" in the Lord's Prayer means.

Baptism

In 2000, on the night I banged my head, my wife and I had guests staying who had traveled from the U.S. to the UK for the christening of our mutual friend's son. Later that day, my wife was with me at the hospital emergency room along with one of the other Godparents. The remaining Godparent went to the church, but when he told the vicar he was Jewish, the vicar decided he couldn't perform the ceremony, and they all went to the pub—including the vicar! The child in question is now around twenty-four years old and as far as I know has never been baptized.

I've never understood the assertion that Baptism is necessary for salvation. I can appreciate the symbolism of joining a person to a church and God, but the idea that a person can't achieve salvation because of the action or inaction of another seems illogical. If we are to enter into a relationship with God, how can it rely on our parents or anyone else?

In a communication to Padgett on September 9, 1915, Ann Rollins explained:

"Well, Baptism is not essential to a man's salvation. It is merely symbolical of the truth of a reuniting with the Love of the Father, and when you can receive that love in substance and reality, what is the need of resorting to a mere shadow. I tell you that no Baptism or drinking wine and eating bread in remembrance of Jesus is necessary to salvation, and are not even advisable so far as the actual salvation of man is concerned, because many persons when they are baptized believe that is all that is necessary to salvation, and neglect the real development of the soul, and the desire to have the inflowing of the divine love, without which there is no salvation. Have faith and trust in the master.

"So with all my love, I am your own loving, Grandmother."

On September 28, 1916, Jesus spoke to Padgett on the subject:

"I know that many men believe that the creeds of the churches are what is necessary for the salvation of mankind—I mean as to baptism and observance of the sacraments, and the belief that in my name men may be saved—are sufficient and all that are necessary to ensure them an entrance into the Kingdom of Heaven, and in such belief rest, with the feeling of assurance that nothing else is required or in any way to be sought for and acquired.

"The large majority of professing Christians are in this state of belief, and hence the greater number of mankind will not enter the Kingdom of Heaven, or become in their nature's divine."

Free Will

According to our current scientific understanding, Earth has existed for around four and a half billion years, and life has been evolving for over three billion years.

There is still much we don't understand about how our fellow creatures navigate the world. While some exhibit altruism and possess instincts that are superior to our own, they operate cognitively in different ways, and through observation, we can often predict their behavior. This is because we have will, a conscience, and self-awareness. In some sense, we appear to be more "conscious" than other creatures. We have the will to create, design, and destroy—we can be both altruistic and self-serving psychopaths. We possess a conscience that helps us distinguish right from wrong, along with the self-awareness to reflect on our actions and those of others.

A common question is: if God exists, why does it allow suffering? One answer might be: because we have free will. Without it—at best, we'd be operating on instincts—at worst, we'd be zombies.

Many scientists and philosophers argue that the world is deterministic, therefore, we have no free will. Every action is a reaction to a previous action. Like the moth to the flame, we are nothing more than sacks of animated meat wandering the planet, devoid of freedom of thought, responding to bodily needs, desires, and urges.

In 2018, Yuval Noah Harari, an author and historian, gave an interview to the *Guardian* newspaper in the UK. In it, he said, "Unfortunately, free will isn't a scientific reality. It is a myth inherited from Christian theology. Theologians developed the idea of free will to explain why God is right to punish sinners for their bad choices and reward saints for their good choices."[10] Harari believes that free will is a dangerous myth—dangerous because to believe we are free to choose makes us more easily manipulated. Think you have free will? Blame the Christians.

The scientific consensus is that our biology controls much of our actions—our sexuality, for instance, and other genetic predispositions. However, the idea that our subjective consciousness—the smell of a flower; the love of a child; the taste of food; the emotions we experience while reading a book, listening to a song, or watching a movie or play; and the decisions we make to do or not do something—is merely the result of brain processes is still the subject of ongoing debate.

Brain scans show correlations between brain processes and activity, but correlation does not always equal causation. If we are merely biological machines, it's reasonable to think we lack free will. After all, if you could look at a beating heart or a living brain in a petri dish, it would be hard to imagine it has free will. But in our day-to-day lives, it's hard to imagine we don't.

During a conversation with Padgett on December 25, 1915, Jesus said:

"Error does not exist in the world because God created it or permits it to exist, but solely because there belongs to man an unrestricted will, which controls and influences his thoughts and acts, and which in turn is influenced by the desires and appetites of the mortal.

"I know it is said that if God did not permit evil and carnal thoughts and desires to exist in the world there would be no reason or possibility for man to exercise his will in a way that would bring him to all these feelings of hatred, etc., that I speak of. But this is merely saying that if a man had not the power of free will he would commit no sin and indulge in no error, for you must know that in his creation he was given not only the privilege and the power, under certain conditions, to become a being entirely free from sin—which is merely the violation of God's established laws—but also the privilege and power to violate these laws. As he wills so shall he be. ..."

The materialist believes we are bodies, whereas Jesus insists we are souls inhabiting bodies. In this context, perhaps we can liken the body to a vehicle: it doesn't have free will, and we can only operate it within its limitations. We are controlling the body, but we are more than the body.

It does seem, at times, that thoughts occur which we do not create. We might say, "A thought just came to me," and then decide whether to believe, accept, or reject it—and act accordingly. Even if we are genetically predisposed to violence or suffer a brain injury that affects our decision-making centers, our lived experience still suggests we have the free will to say yes or no and to make simple choices.

The Rapture:
Vanities of vanities

In 2015, Michael Pompeo, a representative of the United States Congress, stood up in a church in Wichita, Kansas and gave a speech to a Christian congregation about God and country. In closing, he said, "We will continue to fight these battles. It is a never-ending struggle ... until the Rapture. Be part of it. Be in the fight."[11]

Two years later, Pompeo became director of the Central Intelligence Agency, and in 2018, the secretary of state for the U.S. government.

A 2022 survey reported that 39 percent of adults in the United States believe we are in the end times, and the popular novel and TV series *Left Behind*, based on the Rapture may have heightened that belief in recent decades.[12]

The premise of the Rapture is, at some point in the future during the end times after Jesus's return to earth, God will come and snatch him away to heaven, followed by his Christian followers. The Rapture idea dates back to the 1830s, when John Nelson Darby, a Bible teacher from Bournemouth, England, interpreted Paul's "First Epistle to the Thessalonians" as a forthcoming event. It reads: "For the Lord himself will come down from heaven, with a loud command, with the voice of the archangel and with the trumpet call of God, and the dead In Christ will rise first. After that, we who are still alive and are left will be caught up together with them in the clouds to meet the Lord in the air. And so we will be with the Lord forever. Therefore encourage one another with these words" (1 Thess. 4:16–18).

On October 1, 1916, John commented on a Church sermon Padgett had attended. As was often the case, the apostle was critical of the preacher's words. He said he had had misinterpreted the "end of the world," just as people have misinterpreted "end times" and "last days" prophecies since his time:

"If humanity would only understand that the world that was lost by the disobedience of the first parents was the world of man's immortality and happiness," he wrote, "and not the physical world. ... The material world is not involved in the plan of man's salvation, or in Jesus's mission, or in the declarations of Jesus as to the coming of the end.

"Men will continue to be born, live a short time, and die the physical death. ... All men at some time will have to die, then why should it be necessary to include the destruction of the material world in the plan of God?"

John was saying that the "end of the world" is the end of a thought process in which humans continually wage war against each other and nature. When souls are filled with love rather than fear, "this world" will end and be replaced by a heaven on earth—although heaven on earth is not the ultimate plan.

He continued: "Jesus is not seeking to establish a kingdom on earth ... but is working to lead men to the New Birth of the spirit ... to cast sin and error from their hearts ... so that love to God in the divine sense, and love to God in the created sense and brotherly love will cover the whole earth. ...

"Such a condition may be called the kingdom of God on earth—but it will not be the kingdom which Jesus came to establish. That is the Kingdom of Heaven. This kingdom has its seat and abiding place in the celestial spheres.

"Let mortals know that Jesus has already come to earth and is among men ... teaching them the way, the truth, and the life."

On the Rapture, John wrote, "Let men study the prophecies ... calculate the time of the end ... predict the near approach of the Master's coming in the clouds ... yet they will find that all these things are vanities of vanities. Only as each individual passes beyond the veil of flesh will he realize the end of his mortal world has come. ...

"So I say to men, prepare not for the passing away of the heavens and the earth, but for the passing of themselves ... for as they sow, so shall they reap—a certainty that is never changed."

During his term in office, Pompeo was seen by many as a war hawk. Evidently, he felt he was doing God's work and was possibly hoping that when his time comes, he won't be one of those *left behind.*

The Resurrection

The Resurrection is a cornerstone of Christianity. Without it, many Christians believe the whole doctrine would collapse. Scholars and theologians have long debated what Paul meant by the "Resurrection

Body." Did he mean that the physical body is raised or the spirit body? Or does the physical become spiritual?

His first letter to the Corinthians reads: "If Christ has not been raised, our preaching is useless and so is your faith" (1 Cor. 15:14).

And further on: "The body that is sown is perishable, it is raised imperishable; it is sown in dishonor, it is raised in glory; it is sown in weakness, it is raised in power; it is sown a natural body, it is raised a spiritual body. If there is a natural body, there is also a spiritual body" (1 Cor. 15:42–44).

And later: "Now this I say, brethren, that flesh and blood cannot inherit the Kingdom of God; neither doth corruption inherit incorruption" (1 Cor. 15:50).

Some scholars question the authenticity of portions of 1 Corinthians 15—commonly referred to as "The Resurrection of the Dead"—citing stylistic and thematic differences from the rest of the letter.

If flesh and blood cannot inherit the Kingdom of God, that would seem to rule out the physical body being raised. Although, like many concepts in the Bible, there's always room for ambiguity and endless debate.

In a message to James Padgett dated January 16, 1916, Paul explained:

"When the whole physical body dies, the spirit body, at the very time of death, becomes resurrected, and with all these faculties of which I have spoken, and thereafter continues to live free and unencumbered from the material body, which, these organs being destroyed, can no longer perform the objects of its creation. ...

"This resurrection is not the great resurrection upon which, in my teachings, I declared the great truth of Christianity to be founded. This is not the resurrection of Jesus that I declared 'Without which is our faith as Christians vain.' This is the common resurrection, applicable to all mankind of every nation and race, whether they have a knowledge of Jesus or not.

And many times in many nations has it been demonstrated before the coming of Jesus, that men had died and appeared again as living spirits in the form of angels and men, and were recognized by mortal men as spirits who had a previous earth existence.

"Many of the infidels, agnostics, and Spiritualists assert and claim— and truly—that the resurrection of Jesus as above referred to was not a new thing, and did not prove to humanity a future life any more convincingly than had been proved before his time by the experiences and observations of men and followers of other sects and faiths, and of no faiths at all.

"The great weakness of the church today is that they claim and teach as the foundation of their faith and existence this resurrection of Jesus as set forth above. The result is, as is plainly and painfully apparent to the churches themselves, that as men think for themselves—and they are doing so more than ever in the history of the world—they refuse to believe in this resurrection as sufficient to show the superiority of Jesus's coming and mission and teachings over those of other reformers and teachers who had preceded him in the world's history of faiths and religions.

"And as a further result, the churches are losing their adherents and believers. Christianity is waning—and rapidly—and agnosticism is increasing and manifesting itself in the forms of free thought societies and Secularism, etc."

Paul's message to Padgett is that the "great resurrection" is far more than merely surviving death—it's the key to the Kingdom: to immortality.

The whole premise of A *Course in Miracles* is that death—along with the physical world—is an illusion, so one might expect the resurrection to be an awakening to that.

Jesus tells us:

2 The resurrection is the denial of death, being the assertion of life. Thus is all the thinking of the world reversed entirely. Life is now recognized as salvation, and pain and misery of any kind perceived as hell. Love is no longer feared but gladly welcomed.

Idols have disappeared, and the remembrance of God shines unimpeded across the world. Christ's face is seen in every living thing, and nothing is held in darkness apart from the light of forgiveness. There is no sorrow still upon the earth. The joy of Heaven has come upon it (M.28:1–2).

In the New Testament, Jesus said, "I am the resurrection and the life." In the Gospel of Thomas, he said, "The kingdom is within you and it is outside you."

My understanding of those statements is that the resurrection is the recognition that we are not our physical bodies—that we are eternal and cannot be threatened. It is an awakening: a change of mind about the illusion of death—and that there is only life.

Until we accept this—whether in the physical world or while lingering, for what may feel like aeons in the timeless spirit world—the kingdom remains elusive.

Hell

A friend of mine went to a Catholic convent, and at the age of seven, after doing something trivial, was told by her teacher she would burn in hell. At such a tender age it traumatized her, and, like many others, as an adult she rejected Christianity and hasn't returned to it since.

If a figure of authority tells you at a young age you're going to burn in hell forever and there's no escape, once you grow up and think critically, looking for ways to debunk the whole thing is understandable.

A BBC news article in 2020, titled "hell—It's about to get hotter,"[13] cited *The Nature of hell*, a 140-page report drawn up by the Evangelical Alliance. The report defined hell as "a sphere of damnation, punishment, anguish and destruction." It stated, "Christian teaching on hell must be derived above all from Scripture, since Scripture is entirely trustworthy and supremely authoritative in all matters of faith and conduct."

Pope Gregory the Great seems to have set the benchmark for hell for centuries. During the sixth century, he described it as "A place of eternal punishment for those who have rejected God's love."

Fourteen hundred years later, Pope John Paul II said much the same thing, defining damnation as a "definitive separation from God, freely chosen by the human person and confirmed with death that seals his choice for ever."

Jesus and the communicators tell us "confirmed with death" and "seals his choice for ever" are fallacies.

Many of Padgett's communicators believed they were in hell, and two words sum up their experience: *darkness* and *suffering*. Padgett, for his part, spent a lot of time helping them to transcend that state, and succeeded if we are to believe the messages, by encouraging them to pray and change their thinking from hate, fear, and indifference to love.

In ACIM, Jesus places hell squarely in the domain of the ego:

> 8 The Holy Spirit teaches thus: There is no hell. Hell is only what the ego has made of the *present*. The belief in hell is what prevents you from *understanding* the present, because you are afraid of it. The Holy Spirit leads as steadily to heaven as the ego drives to hell.
>
> For the Holy Spirit, who knows only the present, uses it to undo the fear by which the ego would make the present useless. There is no escape from fear in the ego's use of time. For time, according to its teaching, is nothing but a teaching device for *compounding guilt* until it becomes all-encompassing and demands vengeance forever.

9 The Holy Spirit would undo all of this *now*. Fear is not of the present but only of the past and future, which do not exist (15.II:8–9).

It's an intriguing statement that time—compounds guilt. In a dream or nightmare, time seems to operate differently. We might wake from what felt like a long, in-depth dream only to discover we dozed off for just a few seconds.

Soldiers, after enduring the prolonged trauma of battle, are sometimes haunted by nightmares, frightening hallucinations, and flashbacks—known as post-traumatic stress disorder (PTSD)—a debilitating condition that can persist indefinitely without treatment.

In recent years, an approach called lucid dreaming therapy (LDT) has shown promise in treating PTSD. Lucid dreaming occurs when the dreamer becomes aware that they are dreaming. Imagine being in a nightmare, then realizing it isn't real. Simply put, lucid dreaming therapy encourages the patient to stay in the nightmare and recognize that it's unreal.

In one aspect, hell appears to resemble PTSD, in that sufferers relive past traumas in the present. But unlike the temporary nature of nightmares—where one can wake up to a beautiful environment—hell seems to be a self-imposed state in which thoughts and external surroundings merge.

One evening, when Padgett was helping the dark spirits, a communicator named Samuel Williams came through: "I am in darkness too, and need help so much," he wrote. "I was a man that lived a very wicked life in the way of causing many animals to suffer in order that I might get paid for my work in the way of helping the doctors to cut them up alive. I collected the animals and sold them to the doctors, and knew at the time what they were to be used for. So I was as much to blame as the doctors. ... I am now suffering for doing these things, and I want help, if you can give me any. I have been here a very short time as you might say, but to me it seems a century of years. Please help me if you can. I need it so much."

Padgett, as always, must have suggested he pray for divine love and look for the bright spirits. "Yes, I will do as you say," he replied. "I was a white man when on earth, but I am very dark now."

On December 17, 1915, Swedenborg wrote a message on Hell. He described it as a place and condition and a reality to those inhabiting it. That reality is created by a person's recollections—their conscience—and the degree of darkness they manifest as is determined by their memories.

"There are, of course, no fires and brimstone lakes, and devils with pitchforks, adding to the sufferings of the spirits," he wrote. "But yet, there are certain conditions and appearances which are outside of the spirits themselves, which causes their recollections to become more acute and to work in a manner to produce a greater degree of suffering."

Swedenborg explained that there were many earth planes close to the physical world that are populated by the like-minded. "These evil spirits live in communities, for the law of attraction operates in these dark and lower planes just as it does in the higher spheres, and causes spirits of like or similar conditions to congregate together and find consolation, or what they may at times think to be consolation, in one another's company. ...

"The inhabitants are not confined all the time to any particular hell; they have the privilege of moving at will along this plane, but wherever they go they find that they are in these hells, and they cannot escape from them, unless they accept the help from spirits who can instruct them [in] what they must do."

Padgett asked how many were there. "Well, there are thousands of millions of evil spirits," he replied, "and there is never a time when some of them, thousands of them, are not surrounding and trying to use their bad influences on mortals. We do not know why this is permitted, but only know that it is so."

Swedenborg described spirits travelling "along" the dark and lower planes, unable to escape without help. Barbanell described something similar in Chapter 4: "Wish I could go up! Little bit down, not much, more across," he told Beard.

During a conversation with William Stead, Julia explained that hell is a result of a lack of love, and a person without love in their heart is separated from reality. "He who dwells in perfect love is in heaven," she wrote. "Hatred is hell, and God is with all who love. God is love. Those who do not love are without God. ... hell is on this side as well as heaven, but it is the joy of heaven to be always emptying hell. We are learning always to save by love, [and] how to redeem by sacrifice. We must make sacrifices, otherwise there is no salvation. What else is the secret of Christ?"

∞

Jesus and the other communicators were certainly not advocating abandoning the Bible, one's faith in God, or Jesus. There is nothing in the Padgett messages or *A Course in Miracles* that should leave people—Christians or otherwise—feeling spiritually bankrupt or hopeless. To repeat Luke's message: "The Bible contains many truths, and enough to enable man to reach the Kingdom of Heaven, provided they are correctly understood and applied." However, the overall thrust of the messages is that the Bible, in its entirety, cannot be fully relied upon.

They are telling us that concepts such as the Trinity, the orthodox version of the resurrection, Original Sin, vicarious atonement, and eternal hell—all cornerstones of Christianity—are built on shaky foundations, and that has consequences in this world and the next.

14

PAST LIVES OR OTHER LIVES?

Imagine you're a widow with two sons living in the Middle East in a small town in Lebanon. Your husband was murdered in a civil war more than a decade ago and you are now doing agricultural work to provide for your family. One day a married couple and their six-year-old son arrive at your home and the boy tells you in a past life he was your husband. It's hard to take seriously, but that's what happened to Mrs. Khaddage in the late 1990s in a place called Qabr Chamoun, fifteen miles Southeast of Beirut.

In 2013, I was on a trip to India with Erlendur Haraldsson,[1] one of Iceland's leading researchers of anomalous phenomena, when he told me how he became involved in the case of Nazih al-Danaf, a boy born in Lebanon in 1992 who claimed to be Mrs. Khaddage's deceased husband reborn.

Haraldsson was a Professor Emeritus of Psychology at the University of Iceland and earned his PhD at the University of Freiburg, Germany, before relocating to the United States. His extensive research spanned more than a hundred papers and six books, which focused primarily on deathbed visions, cases of reincarnation-type experiences (CORT), and mediumship in Iceland.

Decades of research by a small group of dedicated scientists and researchers has produced evidence that some young children possess memories beyond their own life experiences. Occasionally, these memories align with those of deceased individuals unknown to the child or their family, which later have been verified, however, solid cases are rare.

While living in the USA, Haraldsson worked with Ian Stevenson,[2] a Canadian American psychiatrist at the University of Virginia. Stevenson is regarded as one of the first CORT researchers in the West. Having studied more than 2,500 cases of children recalling past life memories, his data forms the basis for much of today's research.

During the 1990s, Haraldsson worked in India and Sri Lanka. He decided he wanted a change, and traveled to Lebanon to study cases of past life memories among the Druze, a religious group that includes reincarnation as part of their doctrine.

By the time he arrived in Lebanon and met Nazih, the boy was eight years old and no longer talked about his "past life" unless asked. Nazih had many siblings and Haraldsson interviewed them independently as well as his parents who didn't pay too much attention to the boy initially. They had a large family and his siblings all had their needs. According to his mother, from the age of eighteen months he talked about his weapons, his pistols and hand grenades, and how he used to handle them. He said he had lived in Qabr Chamoun, a fifteen minute drive from his home in Baalchmay, and that he'd had a wife and two children and he would describe that life in great detail.

Eventually, his parents took him to Qabr Chamoun. When they reached the town, he was able to direct them to the street where he claimed he had lived in his previous life. His father parked the car and went to investigate. He met a young man washing his car who asked what he was looking for.

He explained that his son was convinced he had lived there in a previous life and they were looking for the house of a man who had been shot and killed in the past who might fit the boy's description. The man said it sounded like his father who had been murdered when he was a child. He ran and called his mother who was working in a nearby field and she came to meet them. Her husband, Fuad Assad Khaddage, worked for thirty years at the Druze headquarters in Beirut where he was employed as an office manager and one of three guards to the spiritual leader.

On July 22, 1982, during the Lebanese Civil War, assailants broke into the Druze headquarters and killed the two security guards on the gate. Fuad was shot in the head and neck at point-blank range, which, according to the autopsy, killed him instantly.

In his memoir, *Towards the Unknown*, Haraldsson reported Mrs. Khaddage's meeting with the boy:

"At first the widow was very skeptical and questioned Nazih closely. For example, who had built the gate to the house? Nazih answered correctly.

"She also asked whether she had had an accident while they lived in Ainab, which was not far away. He answered that she had dislocated her shoulder, which was correct. She asked him whether their daughter had become ill and he answered that she had become seriously ill from taking medicine that belonged to him.

"Then Nazih asked, 'Where is the barrel that I used when I taught you how to shoot?' She showed them a rusty barrel in the garden. ...

"She invited Nazih into the house. He said he wanted his weapons and walked to a cupboard in one of the rooms where they had been kept, but they were no longer there. The family had let go of the weapons after Fuad's death. His widow explained this to my interpreter, Majd Abu-Izzeddin, and me. Everything Nazih said proved true and Fuad's widow was convinced that he was her husband reborn.

"Fuad had a brother, who was still alive, and Nazih was taken to his home. The brother, Sheik Adeeb, also wanted to test the boy and asked how he could prove that he had been his brother. Nazih answered: 'I gave you a gun.' The brother asked what kind of a gun.

'It was 'Czech 16.' That was correct."

In summing up the case, Haraldsson said the boy made twenty-three statements about Fuad's life: seventeen were accurate and five were unknown. The only one that sounded incorrect was that Nazih had said that he (Fuad) was given an anesthetic in the ambulance after he was shot, whereas Fuad was shot in the head so that was thought unlikely. This may not be surprising—communicators who die violently or suddenly, such as in a crash—sometimes report that they have no idea how they died. One minute they were in their body, the next they weren't.

If the Nazih account is true, the statement about the Czech 16 is compelling evidence alone that Nazih had knowledge of Fuad's life that he couldn't have had access to by normal means, but does that mean he was Fuad in a previous life?

∞

The evidence that some young children have access to memories of other lives is compelling. In some cases they report memories of being in the womb and being guided by an entity on a choice of parents—so-called life between life—so-called because while there is evidence they are reporting a prebirth memory, that in itself isn't evidence for a life between life.

Even more intriguing are the cases where birthmarks matching the cause of death in the "past life" appear on the bodies of the children reporting the memories, but these are rare.

During a Silver Birch communication via Maurice Barbanell he explained: "There is reincarnation, but not in the sense in which it is generally expounded. There is in our world a spiritual diamond, which has many facets. These come into your world to gain experience and to add their quota to the diamond's luster and brilliance. Thus the personalities that are incarnated are facets of the one individuality. ... It is the facet which has its quota to contribute to the entirety of the diamond—in that sense there is reincarnation."

Barbanell was open to reincarnation, in part because of the information he received from Silver Birch. However, during the same communication Silver Birch conceded: "I speak of the laws of the Great Spirit as far as my own understanding reaches. I only speak the truth as I know it."

During the Marie Cherrie sessions with Beard (mentioned in Chapter 4), Barbanell admitted that having arrived in the spirit world, he was unsure about reincarnation. "I must confess in the early stages to a fear that reincarnation lay ahead of me," he said. "My feelings on this subject were very mixed, and as you know there was no way I could be assured. Whether this still lies ahead of me I do not know."

Prior to the Barbanell communication, Beard appeared to have accepted reincarnation. In his book *Living On*, published in 1980, he wrote, "It has become clear that an essential part of the overall picture presented from the discarnate world is that it treats reincarnation on to earth as a fact." ... In fact accounts of life after death, when put together, do not really make sense without it.

Beard asked Barbanell whether Silver Birch had enlightened him on the subject since his death. "He says I will understand later. It is too early to speak of this, but he did smile at my fear. I should so hate to lose this awareness and return again without the knowledge. At least this is how it appears to me. ...

"There seem to be no souls on this level that are reincarnating. I have checked back through my ancestors to see if any are missing. The line fades out."

Beard asked if there was a consensus among his peers on the other side.

"No," he replied. "There are many who discuss it over here much as you do there. This is why I went on my exploration and of course what adds to the confusion is the residue that is left over here, for the whole spirit does not return."

During one of their final sessions, Beard asked again, "May I ask if you accept reincarnation?"

"I am unsure on this point. I certainly have had no experience of it myself although I am trying to extend the boundaries of my knowledge. I cannot give you a yes or no answer on this."

In ACIM, reincarnation is mentioned briefly:

1 In the ultimate sense, reincarnation is impossible. There is no past nor future, and the idea of birth into a body has no meaning either once or many times. Reincarnation cannot, then, be true in any real sense. Our only question should be, 'Is the concept helpful?' And that depends of course on what it is used for. If it is used to strengthen the recognition of the eternal nature of life, it is helpful indeed. Is any other question about it really useful in lighting up the way? Like many other beliefs, it can be bitterly misused. At least, such misuse offers preoccupation and perhaps pride in the past. At worst, it induces inertia in the present. In between many kinds of folly are possible (M.24:1).

If reincarnation doesn't occur, how do we explain memories of other lives? Could the case of Nazih and Fuad have been the result of spirit attachment rather than a memory of a past life? Could Fuad have attached himself knowingly or unknowingly to Nazih, or could Nazih somehow have had access to Fuad's memories?

Swedenborg rejected reincarnation. In *Heaven and Hell* he wrote:

"Angels and spirits actually have memory just as we do. If a spirit were to talk with us from her or his own memory, then it would seem to us entirely as though the thoughts were our own, when they would really belong to the spirit. It is like remembering something that we have never seen or heard.

"This is why some of the ancients were of the opinion that after some thousands of years they would return to their former life and all its deeds, and that they had in fact returned. They gathered this from the fact that sometimes a kind of memory would come up of things that they had never seen or heard. This happened because spirits had flowed from their own memory into the images of these people's thoughts."

On January 13, 1916, Luke came through to Padgett and shared his thoughts on the subject:

"There is no such thing as reincarnation, and all the theories and speculations of men upon that question, which conclude that a soul once incarnated can again become incarnated, are wrong, for the incarnation of a soul is only one step in its destined progress from an invisible formless existence to a glorious angel or to a perfected spirit. A soul in this progress never retraces its steps—it is always progress, though sometimes stagnation takes place—but continues as an individualized spirit until it reaches its goal in fulfillment of the Father's plan for the perfecting of His universe."

In a message on June 13, 1916, Jesus commented to Padgett on a book he was reading on reincarnation:

"I know the substance of the book that you have been reading, and the falsity of these speculations that assert the doctrine of reincarnation. There is no such thing as the second embodiment of the soul into the human form, and no return to earth for the purpose of improvement of the soul's condition."

On August 1, 1916, Helen came through and shared her thoughts on *The Birth of Buddha*, a book Padgett was reading:

"There are in the spirit world a great number of spirits who believe in, and worship Buddha, who are satisfied in their beliefs, their manner of living, and the places in which they live," she wrote. "None of them are in the celestial heavens, but are in several spheres of the spirit world, according to the development of their moral natures, and their natural loves.

"I have never seen the founder of this sect. I am informed that he is in the sixth sphere, and is a very bright spirit, and pure. He is still engaged in teaching his doctrines. Of course, he has changed in some of his doctrines, notably, the doctrine of reincarnation. For all the spirits of his followers on earth, remain in the spirit world, and never become reincarnated."

Questions

Reincarnation is accepted among Hindus, Buddhists, some out-of-body travelers, near-death experiencers, hypnotherapists, and others, but there's no consensus on how it might operate. Beliefs include the idea that the soul is like an actor playing many parts—each incarnation a new body playing a new role to learn lessons.

Hinduism posits that we are souls (*Atman*), repeatedly incarnating until we eliminate karma (action, or to act) accumulated in this life and previous lives—the aim being to transcend the egoic state and achieve Brahman—the ultimate reality or divine consciousness. In Buddhism, the ultimate aim is Nirvana. In Islam, it's Paradise. In Christianity, it's the Kingdom of Heaven. All are described as ultimate states of existence beyond the physical world. While the paths to achieving these states differ, the overarching aim is largely the same: to transcend the physical world in order to attain salvation or spiritual liberation.

Some New Age teachings suggest that we choose roles in life— whether predator or prey. From a pre-birth, elevated, timeless perspective, knowing that death doesn't exist, it's easy to imagine someone choosing to incarnate to play a victim role. But if divine love is the very fabric of the pre-separation state—the God state—the idea that we would willingly choose to incarnate with the purpose of inflicting pain—or anything other than love—on others seems counterintuitive.

While life seems to be a continuous growth process, there is no indication from Jesus that we are here to learn lessons. Whether one has a wonderful life or one that is "solitary, poor, nasty, brutish, and short," as philosopher Thomas Hobbes described it, appears to be of no real consequence from a spirit perspective.

Reincarnation is a complex subject, and reportedly as controversial and hotly debated in the spirit world as it is here. But for those troubled by the idea of returning to earth, if you believe Jesus and the other communicators, it's not going to happen.

15

SENECA AND THE CRUCIFIXION

Lucius Annaeus Seneca the Younger, commonly known as Seneca, was an orator, Stoic philosopher, statesman, and dramatist at the forefront of Roman society during the reigns of Caligula, Claudius, and Nero.

Stoic philosophy teaches that life consists of *internals* and *externals*. Internals are our thoughts, judgments, and actions—our inner life—while externals include sickness and health, life and death, wealth and poverty, social status, estrangement, fame, and fortune. In essence, the Stoic path is to prioritize one's inner life, embrace our fate (*amor fati*), and accept life's inequities with calmness and fortitude.

In 41 CE, Seneca was exiled to the island of Corsica by Emperor Claudius, allegedly for having an affair with Caligula's younger sister, Julia Luvilla. After eight years, a reprieve came when Julia Agrippina, Caligula's older sister, now married to her uncle Claudius, persuaded her husband to bring Seneca back to Rome to tutor her twelve-year-old son, Nero, whom Claudius adopted a year later.

Nero's father died when he was three years old. Agrippina remarried, but after nine years decided the marriage wasn't working and poisoned her second husband.

Claudius died when Nero was sixteen. Allegedly, Agrippina hired a woman named Locusta, known as "The Crayfish," a convicted poisoner, to kill him. Later, Claudius's older son suffered the same fate, leaving the path open for Nero to become emperor at the tender age of seventeen.

Seneca tutored and advised the young emperor on ethics under Agrippina's watchful eye. He wrote Nero's speeches, penned the eulogy for him to read at Claudius's funeral, and appeared to have tried hard to convince him not to be a tyrant. Unsurprisingly, that didn't work out.

Agrippina died in 59 CE. The story goes that Nero killed her because he thought she was plotting to kill him. It's plausible. Given the success of The Crayfish, I imagine he was nervous about accepting her dinner invitations.

With Agrippina out of the way, Nero turned on Seneca. In 65 CE, he ordered Seneca to commit suicide, accusing him of taking part in a conspiracy against him. Seneca obliged by sitting in a hot bath, ingesting poison, and opening up his veins. (Note: Don't try this at home.)

Seneca's brother was Lucius Junius Gallio Annaeanus, a Roman senator also known as Gallio. Aside from being Seneca's brother, Gallio is more widely known today for an event that occurred when he was proconsul of Achaea in 51-52 CE. During this time, Paul of Tarsus (St. Paul) was brought before him on a charge of violating Mosaic law.

The evidence of Gallio's involvement comes from the New Testament:

> While Gallio was proconsul of Achaia, the Jews of Corinth made a united attack on Paul and brought him to the place of judgment. 'This man,' they charged, 'is persuading the people to worship God in ways contrary to the law.'
>
> Just as Paul was about to speak, Gallio said to them, 'If you Jews were making a complaint about some misdemeanor or serious crime, it would be reasonable for me to listen to you. But since it involves questions about words and names and your own law, settle the matter yourselves. I will not be a judge of such things.' So he drove them off (Acts 18:12–16).

The evidence of Gallio's status is further strengthened by an inscription to the Emperor Claudius in Delphi, an ancient sanctuary in Greece, which reads: "Lucius Junius Gallio, my friend, and the Proconsul of Achaia, to the god Claudius, a very great savior, the senate, and people of Delphi have dedicated this as a votive offering on account of their goodwill and his imperatorial power."

Today, Seneca is probably best known for his *Epistulae Morales ad Lucilium* (Moral Letters to Lucilius): a collection of 124 letters in which he shares his philosophical musings with Lucilius, who was thought to have been one of Nero's financial administrators.

The Crucifixion took place during Seneca's time in Rome, approximately thirty years before he wrote *Moral Letters to Lucilius*.

Yet he only mentions "crucifixion" in two letters:

In Letter 98: *On the Fickleness of Fortune*:

"Just say to yourself: Of all these experiences that seem so frightful, none is insuperable. Separate trials have been overcome by many: fire by Mucius, crucifixion by Regulus, poison by Socrates, exile by Rutilius, and a sword-inflicted death by Cato; therefore, let us also overcome something ..."

In Letter 101: *On the Futility of Planning Ahead*, Seneca explains to Lucilius that prayer and hope are not strategies for a good life: "There he is, praying for that which, if it had befallen him, would be the most pitiable thing in the world! And seeking a postponement of suffering, as if he were asking for life! I should deem him most despicable had he wished to live up to the very time of crucifixion."

We are familiar with the stories of Christians being thrown to the lions. In Letter 7: *On Crowds*, Seneca writes: "In the morning they throw men to the lions and the bears; at noon, they throw them to the spectators ..."

Nowhere in Seneca's letters does he mention "Jesus," "Christians," or "the Crucifixion," despite the Crucifixion being one of the most significant events in recorded history. At the time, it was still the early days of the new religion, and even in Paul's writings, the terms "Christian" and "Christianity" don't appear. Still, skeptics sometimes point to Seneca's silence as evidence that Jesus never existed.

∞

On January 22, 1917, a communicator wrote to Padgett:

"I am a Greek, or rather the spirit of a mortal who was a Greek, and I lived in the days when Jesus walked the hills and plains of Palestine, teaching his new doctrines of the divine love and the Kingdom of Heaven. I was not a follower of him or a believer in his teachings, for I was a disciple of Plato and Socrates, and was satisfied of the truth of their philosophy, and did not believe that there were other truths than what it contained. I was a traveler, and at times visited Palestine, and on several occasions heard Jesus teaching the multitudes of people who seemed to be so interested in his discourses. ... I saw and heard him teach only a few times, and then I heard of his crucifixion and death as a malefactor, and forgot about him.

"When next I saw him, it was in the spirit world, and this continued after I became a spirit; and then he was teaching the same doctrines that I had heard him teach on earth; but he was a wonderfully bright and glorious spirit.

"I don't think that I can write more tonight. I will come again.

"Your brother In Christ, Elameros."

In April 1921, after Padgett had attended an Easter church service, Samuel, a prophet in the Old Testament, communicated and said he watched the Crucifixion in spirit:

"When Jesus was crucified, there was no great concourse of people because he was considered as a common malefactor, paying the penalties that followed the violation of the law that he was charged with violating."

Samuel claimed that aside from the soldiers, a large group of Sanhedrin and a few of Jesus's followers were present at the execution. No words were heard from Jesus because onlookers were kept away from the immediate vicinity and his followers were only allowed to approach his body after it had been pronounced dead.

"The words that he is supposed to have uttered were not so uttered, and he did not call upon the Father for His help, or to cause the bitter cup to pass from him," he told Padgett. "And all reports of what he said or did at that time are not true, but merely the imaginings of those who wrote of him in later times. There was no sudden breaking up of nature or things material, and the accounts of the graves opening, and the bodies arising therefrom and being seen and talked with in the city are purely fiction, and have no foundation in fact."

The question is: Why would a loving God sacrifice his son leaving us to crucify ourselves and others without consequence? And why were Judas, Pilate, and the Jews who called for Jesus's death portrayed as villains? If it was all part of God's plan, shouldn't they be seen as heroes—since without their actions, it wouldn't have happened?

Jesus in ACIM points out the upside-down thinking that the Crucifixion was Jesus's atonement for humanity, and that God would sacrifice his loving son or anyone else:

11 The crucifixion did *not* establish the Atonement. The resurrection did. This is a point, which many very sincere Christians have misunderstood. No one who is free of the scarcity-error could *possibly* make this mistake. If the crucifixion is seen from an upside-down point of view, it does appear as if God permitted and even encouraged one of his Sons to suffer *because* he was good. Many ministers preach this every day.

12 This particularly unfortunate interpretation, which arose out of the combined misprojections of a large number of my would-be followers, has led many people to be bitterly afraid of God. This particularly anti-religious concept enters into many religions, and this is neither by chance nor by coincidence. Yet the real Christian would have to pause and ask, 'How could this be?' Is it likely that God Himself would be capable of the kind of thinking which His own words have clearly stated is unworthy of man? (3.III:11–12)

4 Do not make the pathetic human error of 'clinging to the old rugged cross.' The only message of the crucifixion was that we can *overcome* the cross. Unless you do so, you are free to crucify yourself as often as you choose. But this is not the Gospel I intended to offer you (4.I:4).

On May 20, 1960, The Beatles played their first concert at Alloa Town Hall in Scotland under the name "The Silver Beetles." It was a local affair and, by all accounts, a full house of around 200 people. Nearly six years later, in an interview, John Lennon famously said, "We're more popular than Jesus now."[1]

In 1966, the Beatles sold an estimated four million records—an impressive number. The first print run of the Bible in Germany in the 1450s is estimated to have been approximately 180 copies. In 2021, *The Guinness Book of Records* estimated that the Bible had sold five billion copies, and today it reportedly still sells millions of copies annually, particularly in the United States.

By some estimates, during Seneca's time, the population of the Roman Empire was 60 million, of which 7,000-10,000 were Christians. If we accept the communicators' version of events, the Crucifixion—like the first Beatles gig—was very much a local affair, which could be why Seneca never mentioned it.

Enter through the narrow gate. For wide is the gate and broad is the road that leads to destruction, and many enter through it. But small is the gate and narrow the road that leads to life, and only a few find it.

—MATT. 7:13–14

PART THREE

THE WIDE GATE
The Road to Nowhere

16

WAR

Not in God's Name

Killing in the Name of God

During the US-led wars in Iraq and Afghanistan, at an Israeli Palestinian summit in Egypt, President George W. Bush, a born-again Christian, reportedly said, "I am driven with a mission from God. God would tell me, 'George go and fight these terrorists in Afghanistan.' And I did. And then God would tell me 'George, go and end the tyranny in Iraq.' And I did. ... And now, again, I feel God's words coming to me, 'Go get the Palestinians their state and get the Israelis their security, and get peace in the Middle East.' And, by God, I'm gonna do it."[1]

During an interview with British Prime-Minister Tony Blair, also a Christian, he was asked about his decision to invade Iraq: "That decision," he replied, "has to be taken and has to be lived with—and in the end there is a judgment that—well, I think if you have faith about these things, then you realize that judgment is made by other people." When asked what he meant, he replied: "If you believe in God, it's made by God as well."[2]

By 2007, Iraq lay decimated. Hundreds of thousands of its population were dead or injured, and its president had been executed. Blair's term in office was coming to an end and he went on a farewell tour. One of his last official engagements was to meet Pope Benedict XVI at the Vatican. It was there that he expressed his desire to convert to

Catholicism. "Such an authoritative personality choosing to join the Catholic Church could only give rise to joy and respect," A Vatican spokesman reportedly said.

In 2016, an 85-year-old friar was stabbed to death in France by armed assailants while saying Mass. The murderers, who had pledged their allegiance to Islamic State, were shot dead by police.

In a speech on September 14, 2016, Pope Francis commented on the murder saying, "Killing in the name of God is satanic." Francis later blamed the rise of Islamic State terror and destabilization of Libya on western military interventions. He described the invasion of Iraq as a "true disgrace" and "not to say one of the worst cruelties."[3]

In 2020, Joe Biden became the president of the USA. In his victory speech, he said, "God bless you and God bless our troops." Biden's invocation of God wasn't surprising. The USA has the largest Christian population of any country, and no U.S. president has ever openly declared himself an atheist. To date, no president has self-identified as non-Christian, although some past presidents, such as those with Universalist or Unitarian beliefs, might not be considered Christian by some.[4]

In 2022, Vladimir Putin, the president of Russia, invaded Ukraine. The invasion resulted in the death and destruction of thousands of people, their homes and cities destroyed. After 300,000 Russian troops were mobilized, the Patriarch, Kirill, the head of the Orthodox Russian Church, reassured the public telling them, if someone dies doing his duty it would be considered a sacrifice and therefore, "We believe that this sacrifice washes away all the sins that a person has committed."[5]

In December 2024, after attending the Supreme Eurasian Economic Council meeting in St. Petersburg, Putin held a meeting with reporters. Answering a question from a Russian journalist about whether the war in Ukraine would end naturally in 2025, he said, "Yes. I believe in God, and God is with us."[6]

God Bless Those Bombs

In 2020, the *Moscow Times* reported, "The Russian Orthodox Church is considering to ban priests from blessing weapons of mass destruction, citing concerns that the practice goes against church tradition."[7] One might reasonably wonder what is going through a priest's mind when he blesses a weapon designed to destroy everything in its vicinity.

On May 3, 2019, hundreds of "Campaign for Nuclear Disarmament" (CND) protesters held up banners outside Westminster Abbey in London. Inside, the Dean of Westminster conducted a service to commemorate fifty years of the nuclear deterrent.[8]

Prior to the ceremony, the CND's General Secretary stated, "It is morally repugnant that a service of thanksgiving for Britain's nuclear weapons system is due to be held at Westminster Abbey. This sends out a terrible message to the world about our country. It says that, here in Britain, we celebrate weapons in a place of worship that can kill millions of people." A number of priests signed a letter of objection. The Bishop of Colchester said, "To celebrate a device that is designed to indiscriminately kill and destroy thousands of innocent civilians is totally incompatible with the gospel of Jesus Christ and with our commitment as a Church to peace and to the flourishing of all humanity."

Throughout history, leaders of countries have claimed to be doing God's work when going to war. They invariably claim the moral high ground—and if they believe God is on their side, then war is, presumably, always justified.

Former U.S. President George W. Bush famously called Iran part of the "Axis of Evil," while Iran's Supreme Leader Ayatollah Khomeini—and others since his death—have labeled the United States "the Great Satan" and cast themselves in the grand drama as the "Axis of Resistance."

In 2018, during a summit with US President Trump, Putin said that if Russia were ever attacked with nuclear weapons, "An aggressor should know that vengeance is inevitable, that he will be annihilated, and we would be the victims of the aggression. We will go to heaven as martyrs, and they will just drop dead because they won't even have time to repent."[9]

These leaders all appear to think God is on their side. But is that likely?

WWI: A Spirit Perspective

When Padgett received his first message in the spring of 1914, he might have been unaware that the world was on the edge of a global conflict, which would result in 9 million military deaths, 23 million injuries, and an estimated 8 million civilian deaths. Not surprisingly, the Padgett communicators had much to say about it. According to Jesus, going to war with anyone—however justifiable it might seem in the eyes of the instigators—doesn't seem like good post-physical life planning, and whoever or whatever *possesses* leaders to go to war, it isn't God.

In a message on December 24, 1916, Jesus explained to Padgett:

"Each nation claims that its war is right and that God is on its side, and prays to that God to assist it in overcoming its enemies. But I want to say here—and it may astonish those who believe that if they conceive that they are in the right and pray to God for success that their prayers will be answered—that God hears only the prayers of the righteous, or of the sinner who prays for mercy and salvation.

"Never in all the history of mankind has God responded to the prayers of men or nations to assist in the destruction of other men or nations, and this, notwithstanding the accounts in the Old Testament of the many times that he was supposed to have helped the Jews to destroy their enemies. ... Take that saying: 'I came not to bring peace to the world, but rather a sword.' Now, while it appears in Matthew's gospel as coming from me, I never said it nor used any expression that would convey the meaning that some of the commentators are endeavoring to place upon the words. I never taught war upon a man's neighbors, and never at any time was such a thought a part of my teachings to the disciples or to any others. No, militarism is all wrong and against all the precepts of truth, and it should not, for a moment, be believed by any Christian or by anyone else that such action was ever advocated by me. ..."

In ACIM, Jesus concurs: "20 There are two glaring examples of upside-down thinking in the New Testament, whose whole gospel is only the message of love. These are not like the several slips into impatience which I made. I had learned the Atonement prayer, which I also came to teach, too well to engage in upside-down thinking myself. If the Apostles had not felt guilty, they never could have quoted me as saying: 'I come not to bring peace but a sword.' This is clearly the exact opposite of everything I taught" (6.II:20).

On November 2, 1917, John gave a warning to leaders engaging in war:

"The men who are directing the war must understand that this law is operating in the conduct of the war, and that evil thoughts put into execution will inviolably bring evil consequences. You may look for an earlier determination of the struggle than some men now believe possible, yet ere that end comes many mortals will become spirits and find their homes, some in the darker spheres, and some in those of light and love, but all are the children of God and will not be forsaken by Him in the great eternity."

During WWI, deceased presidents, emperors, royalty, and other interested parties were reportedly observing what was going on from their respective levels in the spirit world. It's as if the physical world is their theater or TV set, for those who choose to engage in it.

It's reasonable to assume that those in the lower levels, having made less progress, might be rooting for a particular side whereas one might expect the high spirits, particularly those In Christ, not to judge or condemn any person.

On August 1, 1915, George Washington, the first president of the United States who died in 1799, communicated with Padgett:

"I came to tell you that I am a spirit who is now a follower of the Master and that I have found the love of God and am an inhabitant of the first celestial sphere, where my home is one of happiness and love.

"I am not so much interested in the affairs of earth as I once was, and I do not attempt to influence the men who are at the head of public affairs as I did a few years ago. Now I see that the things of the earth are only temporary and need not the oversight of spirits who have advanced to the higher spheres, and consequently I don't at this time take an interest in such matters. But I am interested in the individual souls of men and in their spiritual welfare and I am doing what I can to help them develop their soul qualities. ...

"As to the present terrible war, I do not see that it had any excuse much less justification, and the results that will follow are beyond the conception of the wisest statesmen. I do not know how or when it will end, but to me it seems that the allies must prevail, and the Germans and Austrians be compelled to submit to the dictates of their antagonists.

"But ere that time comes, many a man will become a spirit, and many an orphan and widow will be made to hunger and suffer the pangs of distress.

"So my friend, I must stop.

"Thanking you for your kindness, I will say goodnight.

"Your brother In Christ, George Washington."

∞

In August 1915, Gilbert du Motier, Marquis de Lafayette, a French aristocrat and officer who fought in the American Revolution and the Revolutionary War, in which he served under Washington, wrote a message predicting the outcome of the war:

"I am the Frenchman who was a lover of liberty and a soldier of both your country and mine, and who was an aide to your great general and father of his country—I mean Washington.

"I came because I want to tell you that in the great war that is now going on I am interested, and want to express my opinion as to its causes and its ending. ...

"In the end Germany will be defeated and her Kaiser will be killed and his family disappear from the face of the earth as a ruling family. Germany will become in a few years after the war a republic, but its territory will be much reduced. ... But the sad thing is that before these results come, many a human will become a spirit, and many a happy family will be broken up and poverty and distress cause much suffering. But such is war and such a war never was.

"So my friend, I thought that I would write to you tonight and express my views. I will not take up more of your time. I live in the sixth sphere and have a home of much beauty and many friends in whom I find much happiness and entertainment."

Those in spirit sometimes prophesize forthcoming events. From their vantage point, they appear to see potential outcomes unknown to us.

Imagine you are standing on the corner of the roof of a high-rise building. Down below you can see two cars hurtling toward each other at high speed on a single-track road from either side of the building, each one unaware of the other. The closer they get the more certainty there is they will collide, but they have free will to change direction and avoid a collision. Similarly, from a spirit world perspective, in which time as we experience it is absent, the future in the physical world appears to exist as probabilities rather than something fixed.

When Lafayette said, "Her Kaiser will be killed," clearly, he was wrong because Kaiser Wilhelm wasn't killed. He abdicated the throne in 1918 and lived in exile in the Netherlands until his death in 1941.

Padgett asked Lafayette if he'd seen Washington. "I sometimes see him but not so often as formerly," he replied. "He is living in a sphere higher than where I live and I don't often see him. Our attractions have not continued as you might suppose, and where this attraction does not exist, spirits do not often come in contact with one another."

Presumably, Padgett suggested that with Washington's help he could move to the higher spheres. "I never thought of that view of the matter," he replied, "and the next time I meet him I will make the inquiry. I know that he is a more beautiful spirit than I am and more beautiful than when he lived close to me in a lower sphere. I have never thought to ask the reason for his improvement but will do so as you suggest."

Civilization

In the spring of 1916, the United States hadn't yet entered the war in Europe. On May 27, President Woodrow Wilson, who was seeking reelection, made a speech at the "First Annual Assemblage of the League to Enforce Peace,"[10] in which he said:

"If it should ever be our privilege to suggest or initiate a movement for peace among the nations now at war, I am sure that the people of the United States would wish their Government to move along these lines: First, such a settlement with regard to their own immediate interests as the belligerents may agree upon. We have nothing material of any kind to ask for ourselves, and are quite aware that we are in no sense or degree parties to the present quarrel. Our interest is only in peace and its future guarantees."

The previous month, Thomas Ince's silent movie, *Civilization*,[11] had opened in Los Angeles. *Civilization* was a Christian pacifist drama about a peaceful mythical country in Europe, whose monarch, King Wredpryd, takes his country to war to increase his power and influence over the population. It was billed as: "Thomas H. Ince's Million Dollar Spectacle!" The dramatic scenes were enhanced by a soundtrack composed by Hugo Riesenfeld and Victor Schertzinge. Both would go on to become pioneers of the film score industry. It was reportedly one of the first films to feature Jesus on the battlefield.

The movie depicts young men being forcefully conscripted into the military. Mothers are left helpless, and children weep as their fathers march off to the battlefield. Intertitles such as "Blood spurting from their wounds, they pray for death!" and "The cries of the outraged women reach all parts of the earth," flash across the screen underscoring the horrors of war.

King Wredpryd commandeers Count Ferdinand, the protagonist in the story, who has invented a submarine with technology that can overpower the king's enemies. The king promises him a wife and riches if he will join the war effort. Accordingly, Ferdinand meets a lovely young woman, and they quickly fall in love. However, she's a pacifist and not impressed with his pro-war worldview. When he explains that going on a mission will curry favor with the king, she replies, "Yours is but an earthly king, while mine is king of peace and brotherly love. How can you prove a traitor to a cause—so unjust—so unholy?" Ferdinand is now torn between his new love's pacifism, her love of God, and his duty to the king.

While at sea, he is ordered to fire on a ship carrying enemy ammunition and innocent passengers, he refuses, and during a fight with the crew, he opens a torpedo tube and scuttles the sub. Miraculously, he is later pulled from the sea and taken to a hospital.

While in an unconscious, deathly state, he has what today we might call an out-of-body experience, in which he meets Jesus who tells him, "Peace to thee, child, for in thy love for humanity is thy redemption." Ferdinand is shown humans suffering in a cave-like environment that resembles one of Dante's Nine Circles of Hell. Jesus points to one of the "miserable wretches" and tells him, "Here is he who scattered the seeds of hate and mocked at love."

Ferdinand sees the error of his ways and promises, "In thy earthly body, I will return and with thy voice plead for peace."

"Much evil is being wrought in my name," Jesus replies.

In the next scene, Ferdinand wakes up in the hospital, and the doctors announce, "A miracle has happened! The Count lives!"

Meanwhile, on the battlefield, the king's forces are losing the war, and the bodies are piling up.

Ferdinand leaves the hospital and walks among the general population, preaching a gospel of love, charity, and peace, which stirs up pro- and anti-war sentiment, leading to riots. He tries to quell the rioters, telling them, "Blessed are the peacemakers, and cursed is he who raises a hand against his fellow man." *But he suffers the taunts of those who would again crucify him.*

He is brought before the king, who's portrayed as a modern-day Pontius Pilate. The king tells him, "Traitor! Stand before me and hear your sentence: IT IS DEATH! And may God have mercy upon your soul." Ferdinand looks the king in the eye and replies, "Repent for thy sins, O king, or thalt lose thy soul!"

The king looks decidedly uncomfortable. It's a scene reminiscent of Daniel in the Old Testament telling King Belshazzar he's been weighed in the balances and found wanting.

Ferdinand is put in a cell to await his execution. A bright light floods the room bathing him and the women protesters outside in what's described as heavenly glory.

The King visits Ferdinand in his cell, only to discover he has died. Looking shocked, he too goes into a trance and meets Jesus, who tells him, "O king, let me reveal the harvest thou hast sown. See thy handiwork. Under thy reign, thy domain hath become a raging hell!"

Jesus opens the "Book of Judgment" and tells the king, "Those whose deeds have been weighed in the balance are recorded here." The king asks, "And is my name among them?"

"Yea, verily," Jesus replies. "Upon a page stained with the blood of thy people. And as ye have denied them peace, so must ye be caused to suffer."

The king looks fearful and kneels before Jesus, who fades away. Coming out of his trance state, the king finds himself back in the cell, staring at Ferdinand's lifeless body.

In the final act, Jesus moves through the battlefields amongst the *victims of greed.* The king repents and calls for unconditional peace talks, and they all live happily ever after.

The End.

Civilization was a blockbuster. The budget was $100,000 and reportedly it took $800,000 at the box office. It is said to have contributed to Wilson's reelection later that year. His campaign slogan was "He kept us out of war." However, the movie's antiwar propaganda was short-lived. Having won the election, Wilson decided to join the war the following year and the film was pulled from distribution for a time.

Jesus at the Movies

Six months after the movie's debut, during a conversation with Jesus, Padgett asked whether he really did move through the battlefields weeping for the dead:

"Of course, the scenes in which I was represented are creatures of the imagination, and intended to impress upon the observers of these scenes the belief or thought, that because of my teachings of peace and good will to men, I would necessarily be interested in those things that violate my teachings, and consequently would be present at the fields of battle and the destruction of human life.

"But I may surprise you when I tell you that I do not visit these scenes, because my mission as a spirit is not to help those who fall in battle and come to the spirit world as the result of was destruction [*sic*] and murder of human beings. There are many spirits whose duty it is to look after the spirits of those who are so suddenly ushered into the spirit world, and to help them to a realization of their changed conditions, and to lead them to the knowledge that they are no longer mortals. ...

"But my work is different. I deal only with the souls of men irrespective of their spirit condition, that is, of the condition of spirit as mere spirit. On the field of battle the souls of men are not generally open to the influence of my teachings, and my work is not among the physically dead, but among the living, who are in that state of mental and soul equipoise to receive the influences of my suggestion and love. ...

"I am interested in the peace of mankind and the love of one brother for another, and my teachings on earth and in the spirit world are given for the purpose of bringing about this peace. But the wars of nations or the hatred of battles will never result in bringing peace, merely because of the horrors and desolation that flow from such wars and battles.

"Men may think that when mankind looks upon these things of destruction, it will also look upon them with such horror and dread, that never again will war take place, and that only peace will follow and forever remain the heritage of men. But I tell you that in this they are mistaken, for in the passing of a few years all these things will be forgotten, and then, men's hearts being the same, with all the hatred and envy and ambition that existed in the hearts and minds of those who were responsible for the forgotten wars, these things will be repeated, and the fact that men are of the same carnal minds and desires will be demonstrated. ...

"And hence, you may understand that I am not so much interested in having peace come to man as a result of the horrors of war as I am in having it come as the necessary result of the transforming of men's hearts and souls from sin to purity, from the merely natural love to that of the divine love, for when this latter love is in men's souls, they will not cease from war and hatred, and carnal appetites will not be satisfied, because of the horrors that may attend these things, but because of the love that exists in their souls, which will not permit wars. Love will rule and men will forget hatred and all things, which now form a part of their very existence. ...

"I see that many centuries may pass before a man will attain to this state of purification of his natural love, that will enable him to say that because of his love, wars cannot come again and peace must reign, and hence, the great necessity for him to know that only with the coming of the divine love will come the impossibility of war and strife, individually and nationally.

"... A dead body is of small consequence as compared to a dead soul, and there are so many that pass into the spirit world [and] bring with them their dead souls. As the dead bodies lie on the fields of carnage, I know that there is nothing there that needs my help or sympathy: and the souls that leave these bodies are not in condition, at that time, to listen to my ministrations or consider their future existence. ...

"Physical death in view of eternity is not of much moment, and while I know that to the ordinary mortal it is one of the most momentous of their existence, yet as I say, it is of comparatively little importance. But, oh, the importance of the death of the soul, and the great necessity of striving to awaken that soul to life! ..."

While *Civilization* may have had peaceful intentions, if Jesus is correct in suggesting that it could take centuries for us to evolve to a point where war and conflict are inconceivable in our minds—on the current trajectory—characterized by increasingly advanced weaponry and heightened fears among populations, without a shift in our thought process, the idea that we will survive in significant numbers in the coming decades might be considered optimistic.

Some think this pacifist way of thinking is naïve, but most of us have never attacked another during our lives, so it's not unreasonable to think we can evolve into a more peaceful species. Equally, one could argue that it's naïve to think that we can continue in a state of endless wars without the day coming when the weapons at hand are used by accident or design and life as we know it comes to an end.

A quote widely attributed to Einstein is: "I know not with what weapons World War III will be fought, but World War IV will be fought with sticks and stones." Apparently, there's no written evidence to back up his authorship but it's a reasonable statement.

In certain situations, it's understandable why someone might kill or order the deaths of others. Injustice is everywhere, and for many, revenge may feel like justice. If one believes justice is only available in the physical world because there is nothing else, injustice can seem intolerable.

If morality is a human construct, then anything could be considered acceptable, and values are whatever we as individuals and societies decide they are. Over the centuries, those values will likely change as society evolves. However, if one believes morality is a divine law, why would a true follower of Jesus's teachings attack anyone, particularly a leader ordering the deaths of many? Nevertheless, some zealous Christian leaders and commentators advocate for war. Perhaps they believe that since Jesus died for their sins, they are on safe ground.

Warlike Christians

Mahatma Gandhi famously said, "I like your Christ but not your Christianity." In an interview with Dr. J. H. Holmes in 1927,[12] he said, "I believe in the teachings of Christ, but you on the other side of the world do not. I read the Bible faithfully and see little In Christendom that those who profess faith pretend to see. The Christians above all others are seeking after wealth. Their aim is to be rich at the expense of their neighbors. They come among aliens to exploit them for their own good and cheat them to do so. Their prosperity is far more essential to them than the life, liberty, and happiness of others.

"The Christians are the most warlike people."

I wouldn't go as far as to say Christians are the most warlike, although I'm probably biased.

According to recent trends, the countries with the highest homicide rates—excluding war zones—are Jamaica, Honduras, Belize, Venezuela, Saint Vincent and the Grenadines, Trinidad and Tobago, South Africa, Lesotho, and Saint Kitts and Nevis. All are predominantly Christian-majority nations. Sunny Jamaica also has one of the highest numbers of churches per capita in the world. In contrast, countries with low homicide rates include Indonesia, the world's most populous Muslim nation, and China.

While factors such as poverty, inequality, organized crime, and competition for resources play key roles in homicide rates, it's noteworthy that Niger, a Muslim-majority African country with a GDP per capita of just $590—one of the lowest in the world—has a lower homicide rate than the United States.[13]

Gun ownership and access to firearms also play a role, although it's unfair to blame guns alone. Finland and Switzerland, which have some of the highest gun ownership rates in the world, have low homicide rates and are ranked among the safest countries in the world in terms of overall crime rates and personal security.

Why do many countries with predominately Christian populations have higher homicide rates than non-Christian countries? Could one reason among many be because Christianity promises immediate forgiveness for all as long as you are part of the club, a bit like the "get out of jail free" card in the board game, Monopoly?

In ACIM, Jesus highlights the error in assuming that his death and belief in him absolves us from our actions:

13 The best defense, as always, is not to attack another's position but rather to protect the truth. It is unwise to accept any concept if you have to turn a whole frame of reference around in order to justify it. This procedure is painful in its minor applications and genuinely tragic on a mass basis. Persecution is a frequent result, undertaken to justify the terrible misperception that God Himself persecuted His own Son on behalf of salvation. The very words are meaningless.

14 It has been particularly difficult to overcome this because, although the error itself is no harder to overcome than any other error, men were unwilling to give this one up because of its prominent 'escape' value. In milder forms a parent says, 'This hurts me more than it hurts you,' and feels exonerated in beating a child. Can you believe that the Father really thinks this way? It is so essential that all such thinking be dispelled that we must be very sure that nothing of this kind remains in your mind. I was not punished because you were bad. The wholly benign lesson the Atonement teaches is lost if it is tainted with this kind of distortion in any form.

15 'Vengeance is Mine sayeth the Lord,' is a strictly karmic viewpoint. It is a real misperception of truth by which man assigns his own 'evil' past to God. The 'evil conscience' from the past has nothing to do with God. He did not create it, and He does not maintain it. God does not believe in karmic retribution. His divine Mind does not create that way. *He* does not hold the evil deeds of a man even against himself. Is it likely, then, 'that He would hold against anyone the evil that *another* did? (3.III:13–15)

Jesus asks:

19 A simple question yet remains and needs an answer. Do you *like* what you have made? A world of murder and attack through which you thread your timid way through constant dangers, alone and frightened, hoping at most that death will wait a little longer before it overtakes you and you disappear? *You made this up.* It is a picture of what you think you are, of how you see yourself. A murderer is frightened, and those who kill fear death. All these are but the fearful thoughts of those who would adjust themselves to a world made fearful by their adjustments. And they look out in sorrow from what is sad within and see the sadness there (20.IV:19).

In Chapter 4, Silver Birch said: "There is war in your world of matter, war that need not be, for if your world knew these truths and lived them, men would not kill." He didn't say why they wouldn't kill, but one reason could be—fear.

At the beginning of this chapter, John told Padgett, "The men who are directing the war must understand that this law is operating in the conduct of the war, and that evil thoughts put into execution will inviolably bring evil consequences."

If leaders who profess to be Christian had truly known they would face severe consequences after death—even if they didn't face them here—would they have invaded Iraq, Afghanistan, and Ukraine, putting their own troops and countless lives in jeopardy, knowing that these countries presented no existential threat to their own? Would that personal fear of what comes after death have outweighed a political decision? Only they know.

Killing and death is an activity *of* the world. Jesus is reminding us we are *in* the world, but not *of* the world. He's pointing out that the "get out of jail free" card is not valid in the spirit world, and provides no "escape value"—regardless of religious affiliation or lack thereof. The sooner we accept that and stop killing each other, the better it will be for all of us.

17

THE DIVINE RIGHT

A Reckoning?

In 2009, a Ugandan politician—a born-again Christian—introduced the Anti-Homosexuality Bill to Uganda's parliament, proposing that homosexuality, in certain cases, be punishable by life imprisonment or death. After years of debate and revisions, the bill passed in 2013, and the following year, Uganda's president—also reportedly a Christian—signed it into law.

In response, the Archbishop of Canterbury, the head of the Anglican Church, said, "Jesus taught us to love our enemies and to forgive those who wrong us. He also taught us that the greatest commandment is to love one another. These are the values that should guide our actions, not hatred and discrimination."

After widespread condemnation from Christians and others within Uganda and beyond, the law was struck down by Uganda's Constitutional Court in 2014 due to a lack of parliamentary quorum. In 2023, a new Anti-Homosexuality Bill was introduced in parliament and subsequently passed into law.[1]

Homosexuality is still a crime in some African countries, having been introduced by the British during the days of empire under the auspices of Christian lawmakers.

How is it that some Christian leaders and law enforcers who are told to love one another, turn the other cheek, and forgive others, think they are doing God's work by putting people to death? Do they think as Christians they have a God-given right to order the deaths of others? And if so, one wonders if they are representing Yahweh in the Old Testament, who said: "If a man has sexual relations with a man as one does with a woman, both of them have done what is detestable. They are to be put to death; their blood will be on their own heads" (Lev. 20:13), or Jesus, who said: "But I tell you, love your enemies and pray for those who persecute you" (Matt. 5:44)?

Jesus doesn't specifically mention homosexuality in the Bible, the Padgett messages, or ACIM, and there's no suggestion it's a punishable sin because according to Jesus in the Course, ultimately, there are no punishable sins. Similarly, contrary to Christian teachings, Jesus in the Padgett messages insists there are no unpardonable sins. However, that doesn't mean there aren't consequences after death for our thoughts and actions.

Like many people, given the situation, I can envisage killing a person—perhaps a predator, or during a war, or while trying to defend someone. I remember watching a TV series called "Inside Man." It's about a convicted serial killer on death row who helps solve crimes from his prison cell in a bid to atone for his own. During one episode, the governor of the prison asks the protagonist, Jefferson Grieff—who's a likable character—why he kills people. "Everyone's a murderer," he replies. "You just have to meet the right person."

In the New Testament, 1 John 4:16 reads: "And we have come to know and to believe the love that God has for us. God is love, and he that abides in love abides in God, and God abides in him." If God is love, then logically, God is incompatible with violence.

If we are to evolve spiritually, and Jesus is the benchmark, it looks as though we have a long way to go, although when we look at life a few hundred years ago, it seemed more violent than today. That said, leaders of some countries continue to order the deaths of others en masse, albeit in slightly more humane ways. However, that could be due to advancements in technology rather than any change in the mindset of the person ordering the killing.

That's not to say a bomb is more humane. But if we read about a terrorist, or just someone with an axe to grind (no pun intended) beheading a single person, there's an outcry—a visceral response—particularly in the West. It's seen as barbaric and cruel, and the perpetrator is viewed as a monster—an evildoer—and many of us, with no personal connection to the victim, will remember the event decades later. Contrast that with an anonymous drone operator sitting in an office who drops a bomb on a village and kills hundreds of people, it's seen as a legal killing—collateral damage—a statistic, and quickly forgotten by those not caught up in the drama. This is nothing new.

Beilby Porteus, an abolitionist and Church of England reformer who became Bishop of London, was one of the first senior clergy to criticize the Church's role in the slave trade. In his 1759 poem, "Death: A Poetical Essay"[2] he called out the ruling elites:

To sate the lust of power; more horrid still,
The foulest stain and scandal of our nature
Became its boast—One Murder made a Villain,
Millions a Hero.—Princes were privileg'd
To kill, and numbers sanctified the crime.
Ah! why will Kings forget that they are Men?
And Men that they are brethren?

By some estimates, during the past sixty years, the United States—often alongside my own country, Great Britain—has participated in wars and interventions, including conflicts in Vietnam, Afghanistan, Iraq, and Libya, resulting in approximately 2.4 million deaths.[3]

The question is, will the leaders, participants, and those of us who called for war pay a price after death?

Back in 1981, when Argentina tried to take the Falkland Islands from Great Britain, we went to war. At the time, it seemed like a necessary intervention, and I certainly wasn't antiwar in those days. But by 2003, I was protesting for the first time against our government, which seemed determined to invade Iraq. The protesting didn't make any difference to the outcome, but at least it felt as if I'd done something.

Will I suffer after I die because I voted for the government that voted for the war in the Falklands? Will my conscience extend to those affected directly and indirectly? Will the politicians who voted to have homosexuals executed in Uganda feel the pain and fear they inflicted on others when their time comes?

And what about the keyboard warriors who make anonymous death threats to politicians, celebrities, or anyone they don't like the look of— which seems to be a growing trend? If the subject of their hatred suffers, or worse, takes their own life, will they feel that pain when their time comes?

And then there are the professional skeptics—or rather, debunkers— who spend their careers trying to convince others that there is no afterlife, and often succeed. In the secular West, where the skeptic is often regarded as high in the intellectual hierarchy, it's easy to portray people with spiritual beliefs as gullible and inferior—it can even provide a dopamine hit. But so does junk food.

If it turns out that there is an afterlife, and those the debunkers persuaded now drift, stagnant, in the spirit world—appearing as clouds of witnesses—will the skeptic, faced with the consequences of their influence, be held accountable? If that's the case, debunking might be described as junk food for the spirit body. It feels good momentarily—but after death, there's a consequence.

Similarly, if the words of Jesus and the other communicators in this book turn out to be incorrect, and someone reads it and acts accordingly, will my conscience cause me to suffer? There's a verse in the New Testament: "For by your words you will be acquitted, and by your words you will be condemned" (Matt. 12:37).

∞

On September 5, 1916, Luther came through to Padgett and explained that those who think they have a divine right will have a reckoning after death: "I have met both the popes who were in the papal chair at the time that I went to Rome and when I was afterward persecuted and brought to trial before them."

The popes Luther was referring to were Pope Leo X and Pope Adrian VI, who died in 1521 and 1523, respectively. "They are not in the celestial heavens," he told Padgett, "but before they left the earth sphere, they were in very great darkness and suffering intensely, and thus repentance was very thorough and sincere." He explained that since that time, the popes had been devoting their lives in the spirit world to undoing the "great errors" they had taught and trying to influence priests, both dead and alive, to change their thinking.

"The state of the ignorant Catholic laymen is a very deplorable one when he comes to the spirit world," he added. "But that of the pope and the priest is beyond all description. They are forever branded by the results upon their followers of their evil teaching and consequently suffer very much."

On December 26, 1917, Jesus came through and shared his thoughts with Padgett on institutions and individuals wrongly assuming they represent God:

"Well, I have no vicar on earth. In the first place, I am not God but a mere spirit—a child of God—and one that worships Him with all the devotion of my soul, praying for an increased bestowal of His Love and for a complete unity with Him, and with the longings to progress eternally in the development of my soul.

"In the second place, the pope is a mere man, and he can only represent God to the extent that he has in his own soul the divine love and the consequent soul development. The mere fact that he is the head of the Catholic Church gives him no greater privilege or no greater commission to represent God on earth than is possessed by any other man with the same amount of soul development. His claimed infallibility is a delusion and a snare, and he is just as much subject to sin and sinning, even as pope of the Church, as is any other mortal; and this claim, which is an attribute belonging only to God, will be one of the sins for which he will suffer very much when he comes to the spirit world and has his soul opened up to the truth."

Imagine that at this very moment, you could press a button and have access to all your memories from birth to this point, seeing how your thoughts and actions have rippled through the lives of others. Even for a peace-loving person, who has lived an uneventful life, that might be an unnerving prospect. Near-death experiencers while out-of-body and in dream states, sometimes report experiencing a life review in which they feel the suffering they inflicted on others, either knowingly or unknowingly. Is this what Jesus meant by having our souls opened up to the truth after death?

The Queen is Dead:
Long Live Elizabeth

In 1603, Queen Elizabeth I died at Richmond Palace, Southwest London. She was sixty-nine years old.

After her father, King Henry VIII, broke away from the Catholic Church to annul his marriage to Catherine of Aragon, he founded the Church of England. Elizabeth, for her part, revised the Book of Common Prayer and the Thirty-Nine Articles of Religion, firmly establishing the Anglican Church we know today. This was the era of the divine right of kings: the widely accepted belief that monarchs were appointed by God and therefore had God-given power of life and death over their subjects, with no earthly accountability.

In those days, the death penalty didn't seem to be an issue. During Elizabeth's reign, it's reported she had more than two hundred people executed. Common methods included hanging, boiling in oil or water, starvation, being hung, drawn and quartered or burned at the stake. If you were from the aristocracy, family, or friends, and you were lucky, you were beheaded. That was the humane option. Given that her mother, Anne Boleyn, was beheaded by her father we can see where she might have gotten her violent inclinations from.

On May 12, 1915, Elizabeth communicated with Padgett. During the long message she lamented:

"I am not a spirit who thinks that because I was a ruler that therefore I could do no wrong. I knew at the time that many things I did were wrong and consequently my sufferings have become so much the greater. Many a poor soul has been sent to damnation by my commands, a damnation on earth as well as here.

"Even murder I was guilty of, although it may have had a legalized form, but it was murder nevertheless, and I am suffering the penalties. Why, some of my truest and best friends in moments of jealousy and envy I sent to the block, to afterwards bitterly regret my deed. Oh, I tell you that a queenly crown makes no difference in the penalty that must be paid for evil deeds. Many a humble subject of mine is now where I cannot go, and where they find happiness and love, as I am told.

"I loved once truly and deeply, but I sacrificed the object of my love through pique, and what I wanted in my blind rage to have him do, and he would not, and how bitterly I regretted the deed and suffered even while on earth. Yet I was to all outward appearances callous and without feeling. But God knows how my heart bled, and how my very soul was wracked with remorse and torture. But I was a queen and had no right to have the feelings of a human being. I loved and love had to be hid. He knew it and died in the knowledge that love wept while I killed him. Sometimes I hope that this love will meet again with the love of the victim, and be one throughout all eternity."

Padgett must have asked Elizabeth what she had done on earth that resulted in her suffering:

"Well, I will not relate the vast number of evil deeds that I did," she replied, "but only say that as my opportunity for committing evil without fear of punishment was great, so the number of my deeds was great. But I have suffered in darkness and torment and love has been absent from me all these years of the travail of my soul. I have lived alone, as I saw no pleasures in what other spirits who lived near me were engaged in.

"When I first entered the spirit world, I was still a queen as I believed and many of my subjects who had become spirits and knew me still believed I was their queen and worshipped me as such; but as time passed they saw that while on earth I may have been of divine creation, yet as a spirit I was without any evidence of divine right and no better than themselves, and they soon ceased to look upon me as superior to themselves and as is usual, as you on earth say, they went to the other extreme and treated me with neglect and even taunted me for having been on earth a fraud and deception. I soon hated them all, and so sought my consolation in silence and isolation.

"What a mockery is nobility on earth and what a leveler is the spirit world! I many times have wished that they had let me remain the simple country girl and not made me the queen of a great nation. I can now see that if my life had been that of a subject living in God's pure and uncontaminated country air, I would now be a much happier spirit. But it is now too late. As I made my bed I must lie in it, and there is no remedy."

It appears that, having died and discovered she was very much alive, Elizabeth assumed she was in hell; and because, according to her Christian theology, there was no remedy, she accepted that was her lot.

Padgett must have explained that her condition wasn't permanent and suggested she look for his band and help would be there. "Yes, I will do as you say," she responded. "Yes, I see the beautiful spirits. I see your mother and she says that she will take me with her and show me the way to light and happiness and will love me, as God loves me as He does all His children. So I am going with her and now I want to say that as you are my true friend and well-wisher, I believe what you told me and want you to think kindly of me as not many do."

After the message, Padgett asked Helen if it really was Queen Elizabeth communicating: "Yes," she replied. "It was a spirit who was once a queen, but she is so poor now that there are none to do her reverence. Your mother will help her, though, and she will get out of her darkness. She has long years of remorse and suffering and is in condition to grasp the truth."

He was surprised by the attention he was getting from so many famous people: "This may seem surprising to you," Helen replied, "but it should not. For in spirit life all these persons are mere spirits, and are not considered to be presidents and kings and queens. ... And some are not so high in the spheres as mortals might naturally suppose. ... You must not be surprised that so many spirits of presidents and rulers of Europe are here tonight writing to you," she continued, "for in the spirit life, space is as nothing, and the attraction of kindred thoughts brings together spirits who you might suppose are far apart in their habitations."

Elizabeth said that during her life she believed because she was a ruler, the "opportunity for committing evil without fear of punishment was great." Some things never change. Leaders today seem to operate under the same belief. When Christian commentators who advocate war are challenged about the commandment, "Thou shalt not kill," they often point out the Old Testament command is "Thou shalt not murder" and doesn't apply to war, "defense," or legalized killing, as if it's a technicality. If Elizabeth's experience is genuine, that might be an incorrect assumption.

Jesus puts it succinctly in ACIM:

41 Attack in *any* form is equally destructive. Its purpose does not change. Its sole intent is murder, and what form of murder serves to cover the massive guilt and frantic fear of punishment the murderer must feel? He may deny he is a murderer and justify his savagery with smiles as he attacks. Yet he will suffer, and will look on his intent in nightmares where the smiles are gone, and where the purpose rises to meet his horrified awareness and pursue him still. For no one thinks of murder and escapes the guilt the *thought* entails. If the intent is death, what matter the form it takes? (23.IV:41)

For Elizabeth, even though the smiles that justified the savagery were long gone, the nightmarish memories were still pursuing her. From our linear time perspective, it is hard to understand how she had not progressed for three hundred years; yet we hear these examples from communicators time and time again, so perhaps there's something to it. It seems that the spirit world, as has long been thought, is the great leveler where justice, often unavailable in this world, finally occurs.

Elizabeth's remains lie in a vault at Westminster Abbey, in the same tomb as her half-sister, Mary I. The Latin inscription on the vault reads: "Partners in throne and grave, here we sleep Elizabeth and Mary, sisters in hope of the Resurrection." Hopefully, by now they have made it home.

18

EVERY DAY IS JUDGMENT DAY

When I trained as a volunteer for the suicide prevention charity mentioned elsewhere, one of the prerequisites for the job was being nonjudgmental at all times when interacting with a caller.

On one occasion during a roll-play training session, the trainer said, "Imagine you take a call from a man who tells you he's having sex with his eight year-old daughter." I could feel the tension in the room, and at that moment we were all processing our thoughts trying to imagine that call. The idea was abhorrent to me and I'm guessing to everyone else in the group, and we were being asked whether in such a case we could treat the caller with respect, empathy, and without condemnation, despite how we felt about the subject being discussed. Understandably, some said in that situation they couldn't do it and left the organization.

A few months later, by then fully trained, I was doing a shift one night and took a call from a young man, a teenager, in a suicidal state. He told me in the past he'd had feelings for his niece, who was a child, and on one occasion touched her inappropriately and was caught. As a result, he was ostracized by the family and his mother had thrown him out of the house. He was charged by the police, convicted as a juvenile and put on the Sex Offenders Register.

Since that time, he had been having therapy and the thoughts had gone away. His mother had forgiven him. He had moved back home, and his life was moving forward.

As part of his therapy, he was asked to participate in group sessions which he found difficult because people talked about their experiences, and the thoughts, albeit momentarily, returned. He was fearful because he hated those thoughts and didn't want to continue with group therapy. He was certain he had them under control and was no longer a danger to anyone, but leaving the group meant having to explain his reasons to his therapist and his mother, and the repercussions of that terrified him, which is why he was contemplating killing himself.

I'm a father and grandfather and I can't imagine having those feelings, and like many, I think harming a child is one of the worst sins. But it was a good lesson because as much as I found what he was experiencing despicable, it made me more appreciative that it's unwise to condemn a person because we never know their whole story. His reality was not my reality. Some might say they were only thoughts, but in his case, they had led to actions, which had caused others to suffer, and potentially wrecked lives, and now those thoughts were causing him pain and distress to the extent where he was contemplating ending his life to get them to stop.

It's hard not to judge others when every day we are making judgments.

I used to shoot game, pheasants mainly, and I had no hesitation in running over to a wounded pheasant I'd shot and wringing its neck to put it out of its misery. I thought I was being humane even though I'd caused that misery. I never had a desire to kill a large animal and I've never considered myself a violent person, although it could be argued that killing an animal for recreation is a violent act.

Compare that with an article I read recently about a man working at an abattoir who had been caught on camera hammering pigs to death. His justification was, "The hammer is as quick as a bullet," and he appeared to have no problem carrying out the task. It made me feel sad as I read it. The man has probably done so much of it that he's numb to the pain he's inflicting on the animal, and from his perspective he's probably just getting the job done. In reality, I was no different from the man with the hammer. In fact, it could be argued that my sin was worse than his because he was being paid to kill pigs, which were presumably required for food, whereas I was killing pheasants, and while many might be eaten, I was killing them primarily for recreation. Until I wrote this, that hadn't occurred to me. I didn't see myself as the man with the hammer. I thought I was better than that. Although it's been more than twenty years since I deliberately killed an animal, it's taken me this long to figure that out. I have some atoning to do.

In order to be nonjudgmental, it seems we have to play the role of observer, observing our body interacting with the world, like watching a movie in which we engage with the experience without getting entangled in the plot. Of course, in "real life" that's not so easy, but according to the communicators, none of what we experience here is reality in the ultimate sense and therefore we shouldn't judge it as such.

If we can get through life without condemning others, albeit while condemning actions, we are told that we will have an easier journey through the higher levels. We don't have to start now, but the common message is, "I wish I knew then what I know now and started before I died."

In ACIM, Jesus tells us: "4 Remember how many times you thought you knew all the 'facts' you needed for judgment, and how wrong you were! Is there anyone who has not had this experience? Would you know how many times you merely thought you were right, without ever realizing you were wrong? Why would you choose such an arbitrary basis for decision-making? Wisdom is not judgment; it is the relinquishment of judgment" (M.10:4).

Certainly, after spending eleven years listening to all kinds of traumatized people—from child rape victims to murderers in prison—I feel less judgmental than when I started. I realize that's easy for me to say. My children haven't been murdered or molested, and I don't know how I'd react to that. But I do know that when I hear people describe atrocities they've endured, for instance through war, and yet they've forgiven the perpetrators, I'm hugely impressed and hope I would do the same. For the most part, we hold judges in high esteem while accusing others of "being judgmental," which is often seen as a negative trait.

Memory is Man's Storehouse of Good and Evil

The old idiom: "The writing's on the wall," is the idea that we've made a decision—usually a bad one, and that's it—our fate is sealed. The origin of the expression is the book of Daniel in the Old Testament. Chapter 5 tells the story of King Belshazzar of Babylon, who having not learned the lessons from his father's reign, held a great feast and invited his lords, wives, and concubines. They drank wine and praised the gods of gold, silver, and brass, but the king did not see the God that gave him breath and life, and his heart was not humble.

At the end of the feast a hand materialized in the room and wrote on the wall: "*MENE, MENE, TEKEL, UPHARSIN.*"

Daniel, a man who had the spirit of God in him, was brought before the king to translate the words. The king said that if he fulfilled the task, he would be given riches and land and made the third ruler of the kingdom. Daniel replied that he had no need of the king's riches or gifts but agreed to translate the writing.

MENE, he explained, meant "God hath numbered thy kingdom and finished it."

TEKEL: "Thou art weighed in the balances and art found wanting."

UPHARSIN: "Thy kingdom is divided and given to the Medes and Persians."

Later that night the king was killed.

Judaism emphasizes living a good and meaningful life according to God's commandments, but little is said about judgement in the afterlife: the world to come (*Olam Ha-Ba*).

In the Old Testament, there's a verse which reads: "At that time Michael, the great prince who protects your people, will arise. There will be a time of distress such as has not happened from the beginning of nations until then. But at that time your people—everyone whose name is found written in the book—will be delivered. Multitudes who sleep in the dust of the earth will awake: some to everlasting life, others to shame and everlasting contempt" (Dan. 12:1–2).

Similar to Judaism, according to the Islamic tradition, everyone is judged after death. The Quran reads: "And the record of deeds will be laid open, and you will see the wicked in fear of what is written in it. They will cry, 'Woe to us! What kind of record is this that does not leave any sin, small or large, unlisted?' They will find whatever they did present before them. And your Lord will never wrong anyone" (Surah Al-Kahf–49).

The idea of judgment by God has been passed down to us for centuries. If you believe in God, it's reasonable to assume that if there is judgment after death, God is doing the judging—and judgment equals punishment. But according to Jesus in the Padgett messages and ACIM, that's not the case. God isn't punishing anyone.

We are told there are spiritual laws in the spirit world just as there are laws of nature in the physical world. We don't fully understand the nature of gravity but it could be described as a physical law of attraction. It doesn't push or pull, yet we talk about "gravitating" to someone or something. If we fall off a roof we don't complain about gravity—it's nothing personal—it's a consequence of a law not a punishment. Similarly, judgment in the spirit world appears to be a natural law rather than a punishment by God.

∞

In a message to Padgett on February 25, 1918, Jesus wrote:

"Well, the judgment of the human soul is an important accompaniment of the human life, both in the flesh and in the spirit world, and as regards the questions and punishments, hardly anything demands more of the thought and consideration of men, for it is a certainty that beliefs, true or false, he cannot avoid them. Judgment as certainly follows what men call death as does night the day, and no philosophy or theological dogmas or scientific determinations can alter the fact, or in any way change the character or exact workings of this judgment.

"Man is his own bookkeeper, and in his memory are recorded all the thoughts and deeds of his earth life that are not in accord with the harmony of God's will, which is expressed or manifested by His laws. The judgment is not the thing of a day or a time, but is never ceasing so long as there exists that upon which it can operate, and it diminishes in proportion as the causes of inharmony disappear.

"Then, as I say, the judgment day is not a special time when all men must meet in the presence of God, and have their thoughts and deeds weighed in the balance, and then, according as they are good or evil, have the sentence of an angry, or even just God pronounced upon them. The judgment day is every day, both in the earth life of man and in life in the spirit, where the law of compensation is working. In the spirit world time is not known and every breathing is a part of eternity, and with every breathing so long as the law requires, comes the judgment, continued and unsatisfied, until man, as a spirit, reaches that condition of harmony, so that for him, no longer the law demands a judgment.

"But from what I have written, men must not suppose, or beguile themselves into that state of belief that will cause them to think that because there is no special day of judgment when God will pronounce His sentence, the judgment, therefore, is not so much to be dreaded or shunned. No, this state of thinking will palliate only for the moment, for the judgment is certain, and is and will be no less to be dreaded, because the immutable law demands exact restoration instead of an angry God.

"No man who has lived and died has escaped, and no man who shall hereafter die can escape this judgment unless he has, in a way provided by the Father in His love, become in harmony with the laws requiring harmony. 'As a man soweth so shall he reap' is as true as is the fact that the sun shines upon the just and the unjust alike.

"Memory is man's storehouse of good and evil, and memory does not die with the death of the man's physical body, but on the contrary, becomes more alive—all alive—and nothing is left behind or forgotten when the spirit man casts off the encumbrance and the benumbing and deceiving influences of the only body of man that was created to die.

"Judgment is real, and men must come to it face-to-face, and want of belief or unbelief or indifference or the application to men's lives of the saying 'sufficient unto the day is the evil thereof' will not enable men to avoid the judgment or the exactions of its demands.

"There is a way, though, in which men may turn the judgment of death into the judgment of life—inharmony into harmony—suffering into happiness—and judgment itself into a thing to be desired.

"Elsewhere we have written of this way open to all men, and I will not attempt to describe it here.

I have written enough for tonight. You are tired and must not be drawn on further.

So with my love I will say good-night."

A Kind of Trinity

Forgiveness is central to all moral teachings and is generally seen as a virtue. In this context, those who feel they have been wronged sometimes refuse—or simply cannot bring themselves—to forgive, either because they don't feel virtuous or because they wish to withhold forgiveness in order to exact some perceived justice. Jesus tells us that forgiveness is more than a virtue; it's essential—it's a state of being which, in order to be present, can never be conditional. After death, that refusal—that unwillingness to forgive—holds us back and leads to stagnation. This is reportedly one reason some people appear to languish in the lower levels for long periods—as we experience time—while others move up the ladder in no time at all.

In ACIM, Jesus asks: "38 How willing are you to forgive your brother? How much do you desire peace instead of endless strife and misery and pain? These questions are the same in different form. Forgiveness *is* your peace, for herein lies the end of separation and the dream of danger and destruction, sin, and death, of madness and of murder, grief and loss. This is the 'sacrifice' salvation asks and gladly offers peace instead of this" (29:VII:38).

"Condemn and you are made a prisoner. Forgive and you are freed" (W–198:2).

The word *atone* means to reconcile or bring into harmony. It is a continual process of undoing—replacing ego-based errors with thoughts of love. A sin is simply an error or mistake—nothing more. Forgiveness is the means by which these errors are undone, both in this life and the spirit world. As the Lord's Prayer teaches, "Forgive us our trespasses [that which is owed], as we forgive those who trespass against us." Jesus explains:

25 28 Miracles are part of an interlocking chain of forgiveness which, when completed, is the Atonement. This process works all the time and in all the dimensions of time.
29 I am in charge of the process of Atonement, which I undertook to begin. When you offer a miracle unto any of my brothers, you do it unto *yourself* and me. The reason you come before me is that I do not need miracles for my own Atonement, but I stand at the end in case you fail temporarily. The purpose of my part in the Atonement is the canceling out of all lacks of love, which men could not otherwise correct. The word "sin" should be changed to "lack of love" because "sin" is a man-made word with threat connotations, which he made up himself. No real threat is involved anywhere. Nothing is gained by frightening yourselves, and it is very destructive to do so.
26 30 Miracles represent *freedom* from fear. 'Atoning' really means 'undoing.' The undoing of fear is an essential part of the Atonement value of miracles.
31 The purpose of the Atonement is to restore everything to you, or rather to restore it to your awareness. You were given everything when you were created, just as everyone was. When you have been restored to the recognition of your original state, you naturally become part of the Atonement yourself. As you share my inability to tolerate lack of love in yourself and others, you must join the Great Crusade to correct it. The slogan for the Crusade is 'Listen, learn and do.' Listen to my voice, learn to undo error, and do something to correct it (1.I:25–26).

In ACIM, the question is asked, "Is each one to be judged in the end?"

1 Indeed yes! No one can escape God's Final Judgment. Who could flee forever from the truth? But the Final Judgment will not come until it is no longer associated with fear. One day each one will welcome it, and on that very day it will be given him. He will hear his sinlessness proclaimed around and around the world, setting it free as God's Final

Judgment on him is received. This is the judgment in which salvation lies. This is the judgment that will set him free. This is the judgment in which all things are freed with him. Time pauses as eternity comes near, and silence lies across the world that everyone may hear this judgment of the Son of God (M.15:1).

4 You who are sometimes sad and sometimes angry, who sometimes feel your just due is not given you and your best efforts meet with lack of appreciation and even contempt, give up these foolish thoughts. They are too small and meaningless to occupy your holy minds an instant longer. God's judgment waits for you to set you free. What can the world hold out to you, regardless of your judgments on its gifts, that you would rather have? You will be judged, and judged in fairness and in honesty. There is no deceit in God. His promises are sure. Only remember that. His promises have guaranteed that His judgment, and His alone, will be accepted in the end. It is your function to make that end be soon. It is your function to hold it to your heart and offer it to all the world to keep it safe (M.15:4).

Non-judgment, forgiveness, and atonement could be seen as a kind of trinity. All three serve as means to an end. Each offers individual benefits during life—fostering empathy, healing through the release of resentment, and taking responsibility for one's actions. Without all three, the end may not be fully achieved.

If we take these ideas seriously, we are all being weighed in the balances. On one side of the scale is divine love; on the other, our memories. Our conscience does the weighing. Most of us understand the expression, "My conscience is clear." After death, it appears that conscience clearing is part of the atonement process. Physical life, then, seems to involve something like a spiritual credit score, which sets our existential baseline. When we no longer have a physical body, we discover what our score is—and the next stage of the journey begins.

19

SUICIDE

Poor Perry Sees the Light

On July 18, 1915, *The New York Times* reported: R. R. PERRY KILLS HIMSELF.—Washington Lawyer Follows Example of His Two Brothers. Special to *The New York Times*.[1]

WASHINGTON, July 17.—Richard Ross Perry, one of the leaders of the Washington legal profession, committed suicide in his office here today by shooting himself in the head with a revolver. His son, R. Ross Perry, Jr., left the office to get his motor car to take his father home for luncheon. When he returned, he found his father dying with a revolver beside him. Mr. Perry had told friends recently that he believed that when a man was incurably ill he should kill himself. He had been on the verge of a nervous breakdown from overwork.

Mr. Perry was born in Washington in 1846. He was admitted to the local bar in 1868 and had been one of the most successful and prominent lawyers in the national capital. The latest important cases in which he was engaged were the suit to break the will of Stilson Hutchins, the millionaire newspaper owner, and the suit of the Riggs National Bank against Secretary McAdoo and Controller Williams. Mr. Perry was a Director of the Riggs Bank and for a number of years was its counsel: During the Hutchins trial he suffered from several severe heart attacks. Seaton Perry, an older brother and successful dry goods merchant here, committed suicide seventeen years ago. Charles Perry, a younger brother, killed himself about thirty years ago.

Perry had been an acquaintance of Padgett. On September 24, 1915, two months after his death, during a communication with Riddle, Padgett must have asked how he was doing. "Poor Perry is still in darkness," Riddle replied. "It is a hard matter to convince him of the truths of salvation, but we are all trying to help him."

The following week on October 1, Perry communicated directly:

"I am here, your late friend, Perry. I want to tell you that I am in a condition of great darkness and suffering and I am not able to find a way out of the darkness or to relieve myself from my tortures.

"I know that you may think it strange that I did not listen to Mr. Riddle when you brought him in contact with me a short time ago, but I could not believe what he told me—or understand in what way the darkness would leave me by merely praying to God—and trying to believe that there is such a thing as divine love, which I might obtain by letting my belief in what he said become sufficiently strong to cause me to forget the recollections of my awful deed. I saw that he was a wonderfully bright spirit, and seemed to be so very happy in his condition of belief, but nevertheless I was not able to believe that it was the result of what he told me, and so I am in the same condition that I was when I wrote you last. My friend, for such I believe you to be, or you would not be able to interest yourself in me as you have. I want to tell you that if I only again could shoot myself and by that means end my existence, I mean annihilate my spirit and soul, so that they would go into nothingness, I would gladly and quickly pull the trigger and send the bullet into that spot which would bring about the desired effect.

"But I realize now that I must continue to exist and to suffer for how long I don't know, but it seems to me for ever and ever.

"Oh, why did I do such a thing? I had no occasion to take my life so far as earthly things were concerned, for I needed nothing of the material to make life satisfactory."

Padgett asked why he took his own life.

"Well, I will tell you. As you may know I was as I thought, something of a philosopher on earth, and to me life was a thing to retain or put off just as I might think it had served or not its purpose, and when I felt that I could no longer do any special good to the world or to those who were near to me, I thought that there was no reason why I should longer continue the life which was one of monotony in a certain sense.

"And besides, I felt that I had arrived at the height of my mental powers, and that they were on the decline, and the thought that I should decrease in what I had so striven to cultivate and display to my acquaintances, caused me to believe that the object of my creation had been fulfilled, and that I would gradually become not only an encumbrance, but a person to be looked upon with a kind of pity which would cause me much unhappiness. To have others point their finger at me and say: 'there goes poor Perry who used to be such a brilliant and capable man, and who is now a mere wreck of his former self intellectually. Isn't it a pity that such a man should come to a condition that he has come to.' These are some of the thoughts that entered my mind; and in addition as I have told you. I thought that death was the end of all, and that in the grave I would know nothing, and sleep in utter oblivion.

"These thoughts I fed on some little while before I decided to die, and the more I thought the greater became my condition that what I had said would prove to be true.

"Just before I fired the fatal shot, I thought intensely of all these things, and saw that what I supposed would be an end to everything was the true solution of life's decay and to mental as well as to physical decrepitude. And when I prepared to do the deed, I was never more calm in all my life. It did not require any courage on my part, for conviction of the correctness of my conclusions was so strong that the question of courage was not a part of the equation. ..."

Presumably, Padgett suggested again that he connect with Riddle:

"I have not seen Mr. Riddle since my first interview," he replied, "and I do not think that I would be benefitted by seeing him, because, for one thing, the great contrasts in our conditions only intensifies my sufferings, and, hence, I prefer to remain to myself or among spirits like myself. You know, that on earth the poor are much happier with the poor, than when thrown into the company of the rich, and this because of the apparent greater happiness of the latter. And so with me, when I see Riddle in his happiness, I feel that my misery is the greater."

Perry's stark realization was that annihilating himself was not an option. But at least now he could see that Riddle, one of his peers, was evolving into a happy, bright spirit, even though he hadn't yet accepted that he could do the same.

Padgett asked if he had connected with Ann Rollins: "No, I did not see your grandmother at that time and I do not know her now. But why do you ask that question?" We can assume Padgett told him what he told everyone else—that his grandmother could and would help him out of his predicament if he were open to it.

"Well, if what you say is true, I should like very much to meet her and listen to her, and if you will tell me how I can meet her, I will make the effort. I will certainly take advantage of your invitation and be with you tonight, and hope that I may meet your grandmother."

On March 4, 1917, Perry sent a message: "I am very weak, but I must tell you that I am feeling better, for now I do not believe that I am doomed for all eternity to the damnation of darkness and suffering and when I think back that but for you and the loving spirits that you brought to me, I would be without hope, my heart is so filled with gratitude that it seems as if it must break asunder."

A year later, almost three years after his death, he communicated again:

"I was at the séance tonight ... and besides me there were Carrington and another spirit whom I did not know, named Silsby, who had committed an act similar to my own. ... Hutchins was also present, and he also is in a very bad condition and needs help very much, but I believe it will be more difficult to help him, because the sins of his earth life had a long continuous and accumulating acquirement.

"He is very dark and repulsive looking, and has not yet had any spiritual awakening. His thoughts and interests are still connected with the money that he left and the fight that is going on between his children and wife. He has attempted to discuss the matter with me just as he did on earth, but I tell him that he must forget these things and think of things that are more vital to his happiness and progress. But he says, he cannot, for as he loved the accumulation and possession of money while on earth, he still loves them and as on earth they took the place of God, so now, he has no other God.

"It is very pitiable and it seems as if it were not possible for him to get rid of his thoughts and desires with reference to these things, and it is hard to induce him to make the effort. When tonight, he said he was happy, he only meant that he had that supposed happiness, which he imagined he had on earth by reason of his love for these material things.

"I have observed frequently that spirits who are in a condition of darkness, with all their old loves and imagined happiness which they had on earth, say that they are happy, but it is not so, and they are merely without an awakening as to their true condition which will surely come to them, sooner or later, and then they will see themselves, as spirits in the more advanced condition see themselves to be. ..."

Hutchins was almost certainly Stilson Hutchins,[2] the publisher who founded the *Washington Post*, and died on April 23, 1912. As stated in Perry's obituary, he was Hutchins' attorney and presumably knew him well. In his case, it appeared that clinging to earthly affairs was keeping him in his lowly condition.

During his life, Hutchins was at the top of the tree. He was one of the richest and most powerful people in the richest and most powerful country in the world. But now Perry described him as "very dark and repulsive looking." Maybe this is what is meant by the third saying in The Gospel of Thomas, which reads: "But if you do not know yourselves, then you live in poverty, and you are the poverty." Perhaps Hutchins *was the poverty.*

Fortunately all was not lost. Apparently, it never is. Perry, having been helped to rise out of the darkness, was now able to help Hutchins do the same, should he choose to accept that help.

On April 27, 1918, Perry said to Padgett, "Well, since last I wrote you, I have been praying to the Father with all the longing of my soul for an increase of His Love and realize that it has come into my soul in greater abundance and I am correspondingly happy. I shall soon be in the third sphere, so the spirit friends who have been so kind and loving to me tell me, and it gives me much happiness to know that such a prospect is opened up to me, for I can, because of the progress that I have already made and realize to some extent what a home in that sphere will mean to me. ..."

∞

In the Padgett messages Jesus mentions suicide once. He says it's a grievous sin, and time and time again we hear that all destructive actions have to be accounted for, and presumably, suicide is no exception. I don't like the idea of someone who takes their own life suffering after death, particularly if it's a child who succumbed to bullying or someone with a mental illness, it seems unfair. However, if the person in question in their new elevated state sees and feels the consequences of their actions, and how it's affected the people in their lives who are still living, it's hard to see why they wouldn't suffer to some degree, even if they are guided and helped, which, we are told, they are.

In ACIM, Jesus doesn't mention suicide specifically, but he does mention death wishes: "90 There is a real dilemma here which only the truly right-minded can escape. Death wishes do not kill in the physical sense, but they do kill spiritual awareness. *All* destructive thinking is dangerous. Given a death wish, a man has no choice except to act upon the thought or behave *contrary* to it. He thus chooses *only* between homicide and fear" (2.V:90).

During the Barbanell sittings, Silver Birch was asked if suicide is ever beneficial: "No," he responded. "You must live your lives according to the law, for the law is always perfect in its operation. It is controlled by perfect love and by the Great Spirit who is in all things and who works through all things. You have no right to interfere with the operation of the law, and if you do you must pay the price for cutting yourself off.

"If you force the apple to drop from the tree before it is ripe, then the apple has no sweetness. If you force yourself to go into the next stage of life before your spirit is ready, then you will have to pay the price in the long adjustment that you will have to make. It will also have the effect of causing you to be separate from the ones you love, for you will have made a gulf." When asked if all suicides are treated the same, he replied: "You cannot answer that right away. It depends on the earthly life that has been lived; it depends upon the qualities that have been developed; it depends upon the soul's progress, and above all these things it depends on the motive. The churches are wrong when they say that all suicide comes in the same category; it does not.

"While you have no right to terminate your earthly existence, there are undoubtedly in many cases, ameliorating factors, mitigating circumstances, to be considered. *No soul is better off because it has terminated its earthly existence.* But it does not automatically follow that every suicide is consigned for aeons of time into the darkest of the dark spheres."

When asked if the person is set back as a result, he said, "Of course. Although there are always exceptions, but they form the minority. As you know, in all cases I always say the motive is the dominating interest. But your soul is judged on its own conduct. You write with your own hand your own book of life. The entries are indelible; you cannot cheat. You judge yourselves. The law is fixed and unalterable. We say face up to your responsibility. No situation is as dark as you think it is."

A Momentary Lapse of Reason

In 2002, I had an experience that nearly resulted in my ending my life. It was two years after the accident, during a period I now look back on as one of confusion and chaos. Amid that chaos, my new, serene self was observing the self-inflicted turmoil I was creating in my daily life. It was as if I were two people. At first, the observer made me feel uneasy, even though I was the observer. I didn't understand or like it since it devalued aspects of my life that I valued, such as my business, material possessions, pleasure seeking, and other external pursuits. Now, to the observer, these were trivial, unimportant and not to be placed on pedestals. It was as if my whole worldview had collapsed, and I didn't understand why.

In a vain effort to cling to my old, ego-driven existence, I partied harder, which no doubt contributed to my marriage breakdown and elevated my stress levels, although at the time, I felt I was taking it all in my stride.

One day, during a business meeting, for no apparent reason, I became tearful. Feeling embarrassed, I made my excuses and headed for the restroom. During the next week or so, it kept happening, even though I wasn't feeling particularly unhappy. It reminded me of a movie that came out in the 1990s called *Analyze This*, in which a stressed-out mafia mobster breaks down in tears in front of his henchmen and seeks the help of a psychiatrist, who diagnoses him with depression. I have been fortunate to have experienced good mental health, and I wondered if this was depression. I made an appointment to see the doctor, but that day, my doctor was away, so I saw a locum.

I described my symptoms and (stupidly) suggested it might be depression. Within a minute or two, I was prescribed antidepressants (SSRIs), a medication I knew nothing about.

After a month or so of taking the pills, I found myself having daily suicidal thoughts, which seemed completely rational. One day, I even stuck a shotgun barrel in my mouth to see if I could reach the trigger. It tasted oily and strangely comforting. Maybe it was the certainty that I could "escape" whenever I felt like it. Like Perry, when contemplating the deed, I felt calm. Courage wasn't an issue, and the fear of pulling the trigger was absent. I had no thoughts of the impact it would have on my children, family, and friends—with the exception of my mother, who I felt wouldn't be able to cope. To my mind that's what stopped me from going through with it.

By that time, my wife had moved out, and my son, who had sold his apartment, had moved in. A friend of mine, who had also recently split up with his wife, came to stay while he got back on his feet.

The house had three floors, including a basement, which housed utilities, an office setup, and a shotgun cabinet. I rarely used the basement, but my son used the computer down there every day. One morning he came into my bedroom and said, "Dad, did you know your shotgun is lying on the floor in the basement?" I said I didn't. He suggested that maybe my friend, who liked guns, had left it there.

"Yeah, maybe," I replied, because, at that moment, I didn't have an answer. But I knew that wasn't possible. I was the only person who had access to the keys to the gun cabinet, which were hidden in my bedroom. The only person who could have taken that gun out was me, and leaving it lying on the floor for days was something I would never have consciously done. That scared me. I had no memory of taking the gun out of the cabinet, and to this day, I still don't. It's what one might call "missing time."

Later that day, feeling shaken up and wondering what was going on with me, I researched the side effects of the antidepressant and discovered that one of them was suicidal thoughts. I immediately halved my dosage for the next few days before weaning myself off it.

Within a week or so I felt fine. The suicidal thoughts ceased and so did the tears. I felt as if I'd literally dodged a bullet. (**Note:** Discontinuing medication should at all times be done under medical supervision.)

During the next few years, I pushed the incident from my mind. I put it down to "a momentary lapse of reason," a phrase I borrowed from a Pink Floyd album of the same name. Had I committed the deed, I can envision the ripple effects on those left behind, causing me pain and suffering proportional to their pain and suffering, although that's pure speculation on my part.

If there can be a silver lining to entertaining suicidal thoughts, it's that I feel I have more empathy and understanding for those who are going through it, and strangely, I look back on it as a valuable life experience—though not one I'd recommend.

While writing this book, a colleague took his own life. It felt like a tragedy then and still does. I don't like the idea of his suffering after death, but if he's aware of the impact his actions are having on the people who love him, it's not hard to imagine that he would be feeling their pain. Assuming he survived death, I hope he and others like him are getting all the help they need.

PART FOUR

THE NARROW GATE
The Road Ahead

20

CROSSING OVER

First Steps

Reading the accounts of despair and hopelessness of many of the Padgett communicators, it doesn't paint a rosy picture of what's waiting for us on the other side. However, this bleak portrayal might not be the whole story.

Many of the communicators known to Padgett were business acquaintances, and in the early twentieth century, law and politics in Washington, D.C., were dominated by men.

I remember having dinner with a couple one evening whom I didn't know well. The woman was friendly and had a sunny disposition. Her husband was warm and engaging but I got a sense that he liked to control his environment. In my circle of friends and acquaintances, the subject of life after death is not one that usually comes up during a get-together, but on this occasion it did. His wife shared an experience she had a short time after her father died in which he "appeared" one night in her bedroom. As soon as she began to tell the story her husband became agitated and attempted to silence her. I tried to intervene saying I was happy to hear about her experience but he demanded that she stop talking about it. He didn't say why it bothered him, he just didn't want to go there.

On another occasion, I was introduced to a couple whose son had passed away in his twenties. No doubt it was a tragic event for the family, but the boy's mother came to feel that when she quieted her mind her son could communicate, and that helped her deal with her grief. However, her husband wasn't interested and didn't take her seriously. It seems to be a male trait to use mockery, ridicule and aggression to assert a position we don't believe, don't want to believe or are uncertain of. In my experience it's common and I'm sure I've been guilty of it.

We are told that ego, denial, and incorrect dogmatic beliefs all impede progress after crossing over. Studies have shown that women are more likely to believe in God and be affiliated with a religion or spiritual philosophy. They pray more often—are more empathetic—more altruistic, and more likely to volunteer than men. Conversely, men exhibit higher levels of violence—engage in more criminal activity and murder—and are more likely to take their own lives. Of course, these could be said to be generalizations, but given the statistics, it seems reasonable to postulate that women and children might adjust more easily after death, therefore, those who are suffering, at least in the early stages, are more likely to be men—although, again, that's speculation on my part.

Padgett was always eager to help those in trouble, despite occasional protestations from his band that he had more important work to do. The dark spirits needed help and he allocated time every week for them. Given that his band's job was to protect him from unwanted influences and prioritize who was coming through, it might explain the dearth of happy spirits.

Unlike many of the Padgett messages, if you read enough after-death communications (ADCs) from around the world, you find people reporting that they are having a wonderful life and experiencing joy they never imagined possible during their physical lives.

∞

On November 15, 1967, at a sitting with Lesley Flint, George Woods, and Betty Greene, an acquaintance of Woods who identified as George Olsen[1] came through.

"How are you getting on?" asked Woods.

"Very well," Olsen replied. "No regrets. I'm very happy. I wouldn't come back if you offered me all the gold in China! I'm perfectly well and perfectly happy and I can't tell you how marvelous it is to be dead!"

Flint laughed.

"Oh, well I never!" said Woods.

"Well, you know I was very interested in all this and I used to go to the meetings and the séances."

"Yes," said Greene.

"What are you doing Mr. Olsen on that side?"

"Oh, I'm not doing anything in particular. Just—I suppose everything's a matter of adjustment and time but I'm perfectly well, perfectly happy in my own way of life over here. Met all my people and lots of my old friends and companions, you know."

Olsen said that because he had a preconceived idea of the spirit world, he adjusted quickly to his new condition. After crossing over, he said he found himself in a beautiful woodland setting with a climate reminiscent of a late summer's day. Animals roamed freely, and there were thousands of people residing in apartment-style homes. He described children attending schools, and vast cities but without the factories, noise and filth. Although the scenes sound similar to elements of earthly life, he insisted it was vastly different. Everything was more vibrant, more exciting, and so far removed from anything we experience on earth. "You see this is a real world but it's not a material world," he explained. "Here it's a world of absolute beauty and there's a joy of progress in everything, the feeling of elation that comes with the realization that all the time you're stepping forward."

He said he now saw the physical world as "a dark, dreary, foggy atmosphere, with terrible negative thought forces emanating from it driven by hate, negativity, and fear," and in hindsight he wondered how he got through life.

In *After Death: Letters from Julia,* Julia wrote after her passing: "I found myself free from my body. It was such a strange new feeling. I was standing close to the bedside on which my body was lying; I saw everything in the room just as before I closed my eyes."

She said she was met by friends, relatives—and an angel—who told her many things that at first startled her: "They said, for instance, that I should be able to go among all those whom I had left, and that I should feel no sense of separation, for the spirits of our friends are open to us on this side.

"Then I said, 'There is no death,' and they laughed merrily. 'Of course not,' they said, 'not to us who are "dead." Death is only a sense of deprivation and separation which the so-called living feel—an incident of limitation of "life." Death only exists for the "living," not for us.'"

The Eye of the Needle

In the New Testament, Jesus reportedly said to His disciples: "Truly I tell you, it is hard for someone who is rich to enter the kingdom of heaven. Again I tell you, it is easier for a camel to go through the eye of a needle than for someone who is rich to enter the kingdom of God" (Matt. 19:23–24).

Some scholars suggest "camel" in Matthew could be a mistranslation of a word meaning "rope." Whichever translation is correct, Jesus was indicating rich people have a hard time after they die. Why should that be? There are plenty of loving, altruistic, kind, rich people, so why would having money be an impediment after death? It could be to do with not sharing wealth in an unequal society, but it seems to be more than that.

Studies show that wealthier people are more anxious and worry about material possessions than their less well-off neighbors. It's understandable, if you don't have a yacht you're probably not going to spend time worrying about not having one. If you're driving an old car rather than a $500,000 Lamborghini, it's less likely to be stolen. If you're wearing a cheap watch rather than a gold Rolex, you probably won't be mugged for it. If you enjoy a high maintenance lifestyle that requires a lot of money, it's natural to think about money. The more stuff you have, the more you're likely to think about stuff. It's simple really.

We are told by communicators that five minutes after we die we are no different from the person we were five minutes before we took our last breath, and the more engrossed we are in our earth lives, our beliefs, possessions, addictions, family, and so forth, the more we are bound to them.

In the Vedic tradition the act of abandoning material possessions is more than a symbolic gesture of detachment from the material world. It's a transformative step to prepare for the journey ahead. The *Bhagavad Gita* states: "The wise man who has cast off all attachments, who is free from desires, who is content with whatever comes his way, he is indeed a brahmana" (Bhagavad Gita 2.55).

The idea of the eye of the needle (the narrow gate) also comes up in the Quran. It states: "Surely the gates of heaven shall not be opened for those who reject Our signs as false and turn away from them in arrogance; nor shall they enter Paradise until a camel passes through the eye of a needle" (Surah Al-A'raf 7:40). While the Quranic verse is not specifically about wealth, it expresses the same idea—that arrogance, often rooted in ignorance, and attachment to worldly affairs can be barriers to spiritual progress after death.

In Riddle's message to Padgett on December 16, 1914, he concurred:

"I see that material things are not of very much importance to a man even when he is on earth. You may do everything possible to accumulate and enjoy these things but in a moment you are without them, except as your earthly desires and cravings for them may cause you to believe even after you are here, that they are still with you. This is the one great thing that prevents spirits from progressing to higher things. I never cared much for these material things. Yet, I find that even the little desires that I had to possess them have held me from progressing to a plane where I am informed intellect rules supreme, and when great minds exchange thoughts of moment to both spirit and earth life."

It seems that it's not so much that you have a $500,000 Lamborghini in the garage—it's more that you have an attachment to it and that binds you to the earth plane. It could be a $2,000 pickup truck—it's the clinging to earthly things that seems to hinder progression after death.

Observations

On February 25, 1915, Salyards communicated to Padgett that he wanted to share his observations of people crossing over:

"I have noticed that the spirit, when it first comes into this life, is very often in a condition of darkness, not realizing where it is, or what its surroundings are. In many instances it requires quite a long time for the spirit to realize that it is not still of earth. ... I attribute the first mentioned condition to be due to the fact, that when on earth the mortal had no definite belief as to what the future life might be. In many instances [the mortal] believed that the soul went into the grave with the body, to await 'the great resurrection day.' Some of your religious denominations are preaching that doctrine now. The consequence will be, that all those who believe the doctrine will experience the condition of darkness, and the want of knowledge of the continuity of life that I have spoken of."

Salyards explained that some people understand immediately that they have died, and assume they are in heaven or the "place of the wicked." They are sometimes disappointed, "For while our spirit world may be a heaven, or hell to them, yet the heaven, or hell, that they expect to find is not here."

We know from historic records that Padgett's wife, Helen, passed away on February 12, 1914, and was buried at the Mount Olivet Cemetery, Fredrick, Maryland on February 15.

The first message from Helen that Padgett kept was on May 31, 1914, three months after her death, and she appeared to have become acclimatized to her conditions.

In a message on December 9, 1914, she shared her experience: "When I realized that the time had come for me to go, I did not fear to do so, but calmly waited and thought that all my sufferings would soon end. And when my spirit left the body I commenced to feel as if I was rising out of it and that I was going upward to the place that I had so often heard my father speak about."

Helen was met by Padgett's mother who assured her that she had nothing to fear. "She was so beautiful that I hardly realized that it was she," she wrote. "And when I commenced to see that I was no longer in my body, I asked her not to leave me but to take me with her to where she lived. She told me that I could not go there, but that God had prepared a place for me to go to, and that she would accompany me and show me the truth of my future existence. I went with her, and she took me to a place that was very beautiful and filled with spirits who had recently passed over. ..."

Helen was joined by Padgett's grandmother whom she described as so "beautiful and bright that I scarcely could look at her." She said at one point, she thought she was still with Padgett and could get back into her body. She tried to talk to him but he ignored her, because he couldn't see her. Then his parents reminded her again that she was no longer alive in the physical world.

"So you see," she continued, "I was so very fortunate in having your dear parents and grandmother welcome me when I passed over. If they had not received me I do not know to what condition of fear and distraction I might have been subjected. No spirit can learn the truth of the change, unless in some way helped by others. ..."

Helen had been brought up in the Methodist tradition. Her father Rev. George W. Heyde, was a minister for more than fifty-five years. He died on January 20, 1913. Her mother, Olivia Whitehill Heyde, died on June 16, 1905, so by the time Helen had passed, her father had been dead for a little over a year, and her mother, nine years.

Padgett asked if she had met them:

"I first saw my parents, after I commenced to believe that I was in the spirit world; and when I saw them they did not know me, but thought that I was still in the body and that they were still on earth, as they had not yet awakened to the fact that they were in the spirit world. They were very unhappy, and it took considerable talking to make them believe that they were spirits and not mortals.

"My father was more easily convinced than was my mother. My mother would not believe so soon, for she continued to think that she was with her acquaintances on earth, and that they were not treating her very courteously, for when she spoke to them, they would not answer."

Helen's easy passing seems to have been in part because Padgett's family were there to meet her, and she listened to them and followed their lead.

One of the questions Betty Greene and George Woods regularly asked communicators was, "What was your experience after passing over?" As with French and Padgett's communicators, they were told that a person's experience after death is as individual as their physical life, but there are commonalities. Some describe it as like waking up from a dream. It looks like the physical world but is far better than here. They don't experience time, space, and distance as we do. The lowest levels—the earth planes—are illusory, but like the physical world, real to the people inhabiting them. Beliefs, thoughts, and actions during physical life, reflect their environment. There is no permanent hell as the main Christian denominations teach but people experience hellish conditions of their own making.

During a Flint sitting on March 14, 1966, a communicator named David with a Scottish accent came through.[2] He explained that he was doing rescue work, helping people in the lower levels who refused to believe they were dead, or who couldn't accept that they weren't in heaven or hell, or were just confused as to what had happened to them.

"You get some people who, really, you think to yourself, *this man really is so stupid*, you know," he told Betty Greene. "And people with so-called brains or intelligence when on earth—highly cultured types too, some of them, that you would have thought would have been very quick to learn, very quick to take unto themselves new knowledge and experience, who'd be only too glad to be helped. Often, they prove, sometimes anyway—uh, very difficult to help."

"They've probably got a one-track mind," Greene replied.

"Aye. The religious ones are always the worst. I think their prejudice is so strong and they are so concerned with themselves and their salvation and they're ... they're so convinced that they're eventually going to be given a great reward. I think it's a great shock to them when they realize that the only reward they're going to have, is what they've had to work darn hard to get, and it can't be just had for the sake of saying, 'I believe in this' and there it is. You've got to work for it. There's nothing given away."

When Helen's father, George, died and once again found himself with Olivia, didn't he wonder where she had been for the past eight years? From our perspective, it's hard to imagine a married couple who died eight years apart, still thinking they were in the company of friends who were ignoring them. It's possible they were experiencing the "dream-like feeling" Barbie warned about in Chapter 6, until Helen convinced them they were no longer in the physical world. Maybe with the absence of time, that dream-like illusion could go on indefinitely. The Bible suggests that might be the case: "But do not forget this one thing, dear friends: With the Lord a day is like a thousand years, and a thousand years are like a day" (2 Peter 3:8).

Unlike George and Olivia, Olsen and Julia were having a lovely time. Olsen told Flint, Woods, and Greene that "people should consider themselves lucky the day they kick the bucket!"

21

PRAYER

Meet Me Halfway

A man, whom I'll call Joe, kneels by his bed every evening before going to sleep. Hands folded, looking upward, he utters the words, "Please God help me win the lottery, help me become rich." He does this night after night, year after year, decade after decade, but to no avail. Then one night there's a crack of thunder, light fills the room and a voice booms out, "Joe! Meet me halfway. Buy a ticket."

∞

I recently visited my grandson in London. His parents aren't particularly religious and both are open-minded. It was during Ramadan, and a few days earlier he'd been on a school trip to a local mosque. After returning home, he started to cry. His mother tried to comfort him and asked what was troubling him. "I'm worried about death," he said. "My friend prays five times a day. He told me if he doesn't pray, he'll go to hell."

It seems that even in cosmopolitan London the fear of hell is still being instilled in the young, with prayer being presented as the only escape route.

In an ever-increasing non-religious society, prayer can be a divisive or embarrassing topic to bring up. If someone is suffering from anxiety you might suggest they meditate or practice mindfulness, but if you suggest they pray you might get a strange look or a snigger.

In 2016, a nurse in the UK was fired from her job because she offered to pray for patients before their operations. During an interview she said, "I discuss my religion with the patient and how I have found Jesus Christ and how much peace I have, especially when patients come to me feeling really, really devastated." Her employer claimed they had received complaints about her and said, "We have a duty to our patients to ensure that when they are at their most vulnerable, they are not exposed to the unsolicited beliefs and/or views of others, religious or otherwise."[1]

When I volunteered for a suicide prevention charity, the rules were very strict: no self-disclosure, no advice given, and no promotion of religious or secular beliefs. When I read about the nurse, I felt sorry for her but the rules are understandable.

In 2001, I received a phone call to say my father was dying. I had only met him twice since I was three years old and I hesitated about going to see him because I felt conflicted. My stepfather had taken care of me for as long as I could remember and I felt I'd be betraying him in some way, which I was wrong about because, having discovered my father was dying, he had said to my mother that he felt I should have the opportunity to see him. What tipped the balance was my son who persuaded me to go because he wanted to know more about his grandfather's side of the family.

Having made the decision, I didn't arrange to visit him: I just drove to the hospital there and then. I hadn't seen him for many years and when I walked into the ward he looked visibly shaken, and for a moment, not wanting to cause him more distress, I wondered if I had made the right decision. My stepmother, Jennifer, greeted me warmly as she had in the past and I sat between them and we talked. He was clearly close to death. He reminded me of Jackie, mentioned elsewhere in this book, the cancer had sucked the life out of him and he looked like a shell of the man I remembered all those years ago. It was a strange meeting. We didn't know each other, yet there we were trying to cobble together a conversation that might well be the last we would have. I didn't know what to say and blurted out, "Are you prepared for what comes next?" I had never asked that question to someone on their deathbed before and I'm not quite sure why I said it, and he replied, "Well, Jennifer is Catholic and my friends are Jewish and they all say they are praying for me. I'll go with anyone who will take me!" We both laughed, his gallows humor brightening up an otherwise somber moment.

I saw him once more later that week but he was too weak to talk and died the next day. I'll never forget that conversation and I'm so grateful that I was able to spend that short time with him before he departed from this world. Like him, if someone prayed for me on my deathbed, even when I was an atheist, I would have appreciated the thought.

Populations around the world—whether it be indigenous tribes, Hindus, Jews, Muslims, or Christians—all have a process of connecting with the divine either by prayer, as in asking for something, silent prayer, or meditation, and billions of people take part in the practice daily. According to a 2014 Pew Research Center survey, 55 percent of Americans say they pray every day.

∞

On October 8, 1914, *The New York Times* reported: WASHINGTON.— Hugh Thomas Taggart:[2] a distinguished member of the Washington bar is dead at his home here. He was 70 years old and was born in Maryland.

> In 1869 he was admitted to the bar of the District of Columbia. He founded The Washington Law Reporter and was President of the company which published it. As Assistant District Attorney here, he prepared the Government's case for the prosecution of Charles J. Guiteau, the assassin of President Garfield. He served in the District Attorney's office for twenty-five years, part of the time as the head of the office. Mr. Taggart served also as President of the Bar Association of the District of Columbia. He is survived by a widow and nine children.

Two months later, on December 30, 1914, during a conversation between Padgett and his father, Padgett asked if he had seen Taggart. "I have seen him very recently," he replied, "and he is in the same condition as when I wrote you first about him. He does not seem to realize that he needs any assistance to help him to become happier or to progress to a better condition and it is difficult to convince him."

Padgett asked if he knew where Mackey, another friend who had passed away, was. "No, I do not," came the reply. "But I can find him if you desire that I shall. He might want to say something to you, but only through me, as you must not get into rapport with these strangers to our band, for it will do harm, and we must not run the risk." Finding people in the spirit world seems to take no time and during the same session his father wrote, "They (Mackey and Taggart) say that they are very glad that you have given them the opportunity to say a word. He (Mackey) says that he is much happier than when he first came over as he has commenced to see the things that are necessary to make him happier."

In a later message Mackey identified himself as Franklin H. Mackey,[3] who died in Washington, D.C. in 1904, aged sixty-one. Like Padgett, Mackey was an attorney in the same city during the same period.

Mackey said that after he died, he was in a condition of unrest and spiritual blindness. Despite having passed away ten years before, he said he was still in the earth plane, and described having had "to travel a very dark and dreadful road" in which he saw nothing but darkness and depravity. He had been surrounded by evil spirits who tried to convince everyone around them that there was no hope and that their suffering and unhappiness was permanent. Since then he had received a little light from someone who told him in order to escape his darkness, he only had to believe that God would help him open up his soul to better influences, and it would happen. It appeared to be working. "I am much more beautiful than Mr. Taggart," he said, "and more happy looking."

Padgett's father wrote and explained that Mackey was coming to the realization that the spirits around Padgett were so much brighter than him, and he was very motivated to get out of the almost continuous darkness and despair that plagued him.

Padgett asked his father if Mackey had seen Riddle. Mackey said he hadn't and wasn't aware he had died but would see if he could find him. Padgett must have suggested that Mackey connect with his band and pray for divine love, and that he would pray for him too. His father replied, "He says that for the sake of what you say, that if any of these spirits that you speak of, should come to him, he will listen to them even though he may not believe, that he cannot promise to believe."

Padgett asked if Taggart was still there. "Yes, Mr. Taggart has heard it all," the reply came. "He says that you certainly did put it up to Mackey to try the experiment, but that he is very doubtful if you will see any good results flow from it. He says that he will wait and see what effect it has on Mackey, and then he may be willing to consider the matter."

Taggart, still the skeptic, then wrote, "I guess Mackey is not such a big fool to try the experiment, and having confidence in you as a friend that has at heart my welfare, I will do the same as Mackey has promised to do. So you can pray for me too, and I will pray also, but of course I will not be able to have any belief that my prayers will be answered. So you see I am not only hardheaded, but hard hearted also. ..."

Padgett's father was impressed by his son's tenacity in convincing Mackey and Taggart to pray. "I believe that you have impressed them to such a degree that they will be lead [sic] to learn the truth," he wrote, and the conversation ended.

Being a part of the Washington legal and political fraternity at the end of the nineteenth and early twentieth century, Taggart and Mackey may well have frequented Harvey's restaurant in Washington, D.C.

Harvey's was established by George W. Harvey in 1858. Reportedly, "They entertained the political and literary leaders of the nation for sixty-six years and every president from Ulysses S. Grant to Franklin D. Roosevelt had dined in the building."

Harvey[4] died on May 5, 1909. His obituary in the *Evening Star* reported:—"Probably there was never a better known restaurant in the world than 'Harvey's oyster house' as conducted by Mr Harvey. During the Civil War its first success was achieved and its future assured ... Gallon upon gallon, bushel upon bushel of oysters went to feed the army in those days. ..."

Less than two weeks after the Taggart/Mackey communication, a message came through: "I am here, George W. Harvey: I lived in Washington and kept a restaurant on Pennsylvania Avenue and Tenth Street. I am in the spirit world and in the earth plane and in hell also. I am not happy for I am in darkness and despair."

Padgett asked Harvey if during his life he had prayed: "Yes, I did," he replied. "But that did not keep me from hell. The priests misled me and they are here too, damn them. Can you help me any? If you can, do so."

Harvey said that throughout his life he had been a Catholic who attended to his duties. In his will he even left some money for the priests to "pray him out of purgatory," but it hadn't worked. Having died and found himself very much alive he concluded there was no God to pray to.

Padgett asked if he had seen Taggart. Harvey said that he was there but thought he was in no better condition than he was. Taggart interjected saying he was now feeling the benefit of Padgett's prayers and his own. Harvey accused him of being misled by Padgett, just as he believed the priests had misled him during his life.

"Be a man who can keep his mind open to what he sees," said Taggart, "and the reasons therefore may come to you. Let us not become hardheaded in this matter. As you were so easy to believe on earth what your priests told you about purgatory and the hells and the necessity for you to pay for prayers to help you out of purgatory, why can't you try to believe a little when the same thing is told you without your having to pay for it?"

Nevertheless, Harvey was adamant there was no efficacy in prayer. "Taggart, what is the use of being fooled twice," he complained. "Once is enough for me. Priests are here with me, and suffering more than I am, and when I ask them why they don't pray themselves out of purgatory, they say, 'To hell with prayer.'"

Eventually, Taggart persuaded him to experiment by listening to the more evolved spirits and praying to God for divine love. "Well Taggart, there may be something in what you say," he conceded, "and I am willing to go with you, for as you say, if it does no good, it can do no harm. So let me hear again what I am to say and I will commence."

Helen had criticized her husband for letting the dark spirits write because it could hinder their important work, but after witnessing the conversation with Harvey, Mackey, and Taggart, she admitted, "You are too wonderful in your way of getting the attention of spirits who are in darkness to turn their thoughts to things that may help them. And I am so glad that you are helping these spirits, even though you did let Mr. Harvey write. But who knows, maybe such interferences are intended for some good purposes."

The following year on July 22, 1915, Mackey and Taggart both communicated:

"I have been much benefited by your advice," wrote Mackey, "and the help which your band has given me, and I am commencing to see the light and to know what the Love of the Father means to a poor benighted soul who has been in a state of torment. I will not write longer but say that I am so grateful and will never forget your kindness and sympathy. May God bless you and keep you in His care.

"Your old friend and brother lawyer that was—Franklin H. Mackey."

Then Taggart wrote, "When on earth, while I knew that you believed in Spiritualism, yet I never realized what your belief and experience meant to you, and what a great help it would be to me, when the time came for me to become a spirit. ...

"I pray and my faith is becoming stronger all the time. The great proof to me, aside from what I see in the condition of other spirits who claim to have this love, is my own change in soul happiness and in desire to progress to the higher spheres, which your band tells me exists, and that I may find my home there if I will only pray more to the Father and let my faith enlarge."

Meanwhile, Harvey, who had passed away five years before Taggart, still appeared to be trying to figure out why Taggart and Mackey were doing better than he was.

"Wait a while until I say something," he interjected at the end of Taggart's message. "I want to tell you that Mackey and Taggart have changed so much, that I wonder why they have and I have not. They tell me that it is because they have received the love of God in their souls, and faith in what the beautiful spirits of your band tell them. I hardly know what to think and I want to ask what you think is the cause. I am a doubting Thomas."

Presumably, Padgett suggested once again that prayer was the solution. "Well, I have heard what you said and I will try to do as you say. I will do so. And I want to express to you my gratitude for the interest you have taken in me. Your friend, George W. Harvey."

In a message on October 25, 1918, Jesus gave Padgett some advice on prayer:

"A long prayer, or even one formulated into words, is not necessary, as in order to have the longing it is not necessary that words should be used to give it form. The longing may be rapid as unformed thought, and as effective for the father to catch, as I may say. The longing is quicker than the thought, and the answer to the same will come with as much certainty and love as if you were to put the longing into the most exact form. Prayers of this kind ascend to the Father and are heard and answered, and, by a law of your relationship to the Father, affect the qualities of the brain in the way of preparing it for the union with the spiritual thoughts of the spirits who desire to write, as I have stated. Your thoughts of spiritual things or of the truths of the spirit world, as they have already been revealed to you, and especially those which pertain to the love and mercy of the Father, and to His will, in their passing and operating, also affect the qualities of the brain so as to produce the condition which is so necessary for our rapport. ..."

One passage in the Bible that resonates with me every time I repeat it in my mind is—"Be still and Know that I am God" (Ps. 46:10). If we can meditate on the breath or a mantra, why not on God?

Jesus in ACIM:

91 As you come closer to a brother, you *do* approach me and, as you withdraw from him, *I* become distant to you. Your giant step forward was to insist on a 'collaborative venture.' This does not go against the true spirit of meditation; it is inherent in it. Meditation is a collaborative venture with God. It *cannot* be undertaken successfully by those who disengage themselves from the Sonship because they are disengaging themselves from me. God will come to you only as you will give Him

to your brothers. Learn first of them, and you will be ready to hear God as you hear them. That is because the function of love is one (4.VII:91).

In the New Testament, Jesus said: "You have heard that it was said, 'Love your neighbor and hate your enemy.' But I tell you, love your enemies and pray for those who persecute you, that you may be children of your Father in heaven" (Matt. 5:44-45).

In ACIM, there are no *real* enemies. Each time we perceive an enemy, we reinforce the illusion of separation: "The ego is the symbol of separation, just as the Holy Spirit is the symbol of peace. What you perceive in others, you are strengthening in *yourself*" (5.V:41).

> 60 As long as perception lasts, prayer has a place. Since perception rests on lack, those who perceive have not totally accepted the Atonement and given themselves over to truth. Perception is a separated state, and a perceiver *does* need healing. Communion, not prayer, is the natural state of those who know. God and His miracles *are* inseparable. How beautiful indeed are the Thoughts of God who live in His light! Your worth is beyond perception because it is beyond doubt. Do not perceive yourself in different lights. *Know* yourself in the One Light where the miracle that is you is perfectly clear (3.VII:60).

One evening Padgett was in a discussion with a friend about the value of prayer relative to works. They had attended a church where the preacher had said that works brought great happiness to the world, whereas prayer was not so important. Padgett disagreed. He felt that prayer was more important. Unlike the preacher, Padgett was spending every evening helping deceased people transcend their states by advising them to pray, and appeared to be getting results. So, he was probably looking at life from a spirit world perspective rather than physical, which might explain his thinking.

John, who had been observing the conversation, came through and shared his opinion:

"Works are desirable, and in some cases necessary, but prayer is absolutely indispensable. So let you and your friend understand and never doubt, that without prayer the works of men would be unavailing to accomplish the great good which even now man performs for his brother.

"Pray, and works will follow. Work, and you may do good, but the soul does not benefit, for God is a God that answers prayer through the ministrations of His angels and through the influence of His Holy Spirit, which works on the interior or real part of man."

One person might pray every day and have a miserable existence, while another might live a fulfilling, long life without ever uttering a single prayer. Whether prayer is beneficial in the physical world is an open question, as the experience is subjective. But after death, reportedly, it becomes the currency needed for progress—and if we begin during physical life, we're told we build up spiritual capital to help us on our way.

If communication in the spirit world occurs by thought, as is reported, then a prayer to God for divine love is simply a loving thought. Perhaps the absence of loving thoughts can be likened to the absence of breath in the physical world: if we refuse to breathe, the body ceases to function. We are told, in the worlds beyond this one, life without prayer is a life disconnected from reality. The absence of loving thoughts—both given and received—might be like sitting in a darkened room without realizing there's a light switch. We remain in the dark until we flick the switch. Praying for love lets the light in.

Meister Eckhart, the thirteenth-century Christian mystic, said, "If the only prayer you ever say in your entire life is thank you, it will be enough." If someone gives us something, we say, "Thank you." If the Holy Spirit is the dispenser of divine love and we want to charge our souls, we are told we have to love and ask for love—forgive and ask for forgiveness. It's a reciprocal arrangement. In the spirit world, where it's the difference between stagnation and progress, that sounds like a good deal.

So, if you have never uttered a single prayer throughout your life, and you wake up one morning and you think you might be dead—if everything is dull and dreary and you're in darkness and suffering—try praying.

Like Joe, if we want to win the prize, we have to meet God halfway.

22

THE NUMBERED LEVELS

Multiple heavens are mentioned throughout the major religions and philosophies of the world. We might think of them as multidimensional, vibrational, interwoven worlds—the lower being denser, slower, and darker; the higher, more rarefied, faster, lighter, and purer.

The very first verse of the Bible reads: "In the beginning, God created the heavens and the earth" (Gen. 1:1). **Note:** *heavens,* plural.

In the Quran, a verse reads: "Allah is the One Who created seven heavens ⸢in layers⸣, and likewise for the earth" Surah At-Talaq (65:12).

In Hinduism, there's the concept of loka, meaning "world" or "plane." Plato, writing in *Republic,* spoke of the soul's journey after death, ascending or descending to different realms according to its inner nature. In Chinese Daoism, it's the celestial realms where immortals *(xian,* 仙) dwell. Japanese Shinto has *Takamagahara*—the home of the *kami,* or divine spirits.

Buddhism, like Christianity, has different denominations. But generally speaking, it teaches that there are Six Realms of Rebirth—planes of existence determined by one's karma—which could be compared to the "many mansions" Jesus referred to. In Pure Land Buddhism, the aspiration after death is to be reborn in *Jōdo*—a paradise-like realm. It is not part of the karmic cycle of the Six Realms; it is essentially a seventh—a place of refuge and spiritual progress, accessible through faith and devotion alone. Some compare it to the Third Heaven described by Paul in the Bible, though, because entry depends solely on faith and devotion, *Jōdo* sounds more like the seventh sphere described in the Padgett messages. It seems to be the final stop before achieving Nirvana, just as the seventh sphere is the gateway to the Kingdom of Heaven.

In the New Testament, Paul wrote, "I know a man In Christ who fourteen years ago was caught up to the third heaven. Whether it was in the body or out of the body I do not know—God knows" (2 Cor. 12:2). Some point out that Paul's statement sounds like an out-of-body experience. The term "Third Heaven" is not mentioned elsewhere in the Bible. So what is the Third Heaven?

2 Enoch, also known as The Book of the Secrets of Enoch,[1] is thought to be a Jewish text written in the first century CE—although the dating is debated. The first known copy of the manuscript was discovered in Russia in the nineteenth century. In the book, Enoch, the great-grandfather of Noah, is escorted by angels through multiple heavens and taught about the nature of the cosmos and the fate of humans after death. Although ten heavens are mentioned, prominence is placed on the second and third: "And those men took me and led me up to the second heaven. And they showed me darkness, greater than earthly darkness. And there I saw prisoners, bound and awaiting the great and boundless judgment. And these angels were dark-looking, more than earthly darkness, and they wept all the time" (2 Enoch 7:1-3).

> And those men took me thence, and led me up on to the third heaven, and placed me there; and I looked downwards, and saw the sweetness of Paradise. That place is beyond all the heavens, and exceedingly excellent. And I beheld all the trees of beautiful colors and their fruits were ripe and fragrant, with all kinds of food springing up with delightful fragrance. In the midst of them was the Tree of Life, in that place where the Lord takes rest when He goes into paradise (2 Enoch 8:1-3).

The Spiritualist concept of the "Summerland" is sometimes referred to as the third sphere, where souls reside after death. It is frequently depicted as a place of peace, rest, and reflection, where individuals review their lives and plan their next steps in their spiritual journey.

Robert Monroe,[2] a pioneer in out-of-body experience research, referred to states or phases of consciousness during physical life and after death as "focus levels," some of which can be reached while in an out-of-body state. Focus 1 is ordinary reality, where the mind is fully awake and active. In Focus 10, the physical body is deeply relaxed while the mind remains conscious, awake, and alert—"mind awake, body asleep." Focus 15 is described as a state of "no time," in which there's an awareness of separation from the physical body.

Focus 23 is the state immediately after death, often marked by confusion—people feel stuck, unaware they've died. Focus 24–26 are known as the Belief System Territories, populated by individuals with strong religious or cultural convictions that shape their postmortem experience. Focus 27 is a transitional space. It's described as the limit of human cognitive capacity, a place for rest, recovery from physical death, life review, and future planning—Monroe called it "The Park."

What these sources suggest is that the Third Heaven, sphere, Paradise, the Park, the Summerland all refer to the same state of consciousness. Like the physical world, it's not our ultimate reality. It's a way station for the rest of the journey, where one can rest in peace in a state of bliss and happiness.

Earth Planes

In the Padgett messages, the first sphere is not mentioned by name, but is described as the earth planes or hells.

On December 22, 1915, a communicator named John B. Comeys described the transition from the earth planes to the second sphere:

"These hells, as you may imagine, are very numerous," he wrote, "for the conditions of spirits are very varied, and each spirit has a place in which to live fitted to its condition.

"As the spirit becomes freed from some of these conditions, which as to them causes the law of attraction to work, he progresses to a higher and better place, and finds that his surroundings are not so dark and painful. And as this progression continues, such spirit will ultimately find himself in the planes of light and comparative happiness, where the evil recollections have to a large extent left him, and the good deeds which he did on earth then come to him and cause a happiness that makes him realize that he was not all bad, and that God has been good to him in relieving him from the sins and evil thoughts which bound him to the place from which he has progressed.

"But after all this, he has not gotten into any of the spheres which are above the earth planes, and he may have to remain there for a great many years before he enters the second sphere which is next in gradation to the earth plane. This latter plane is the most populous of all the spheres, for it has spirits coming to it in great numbers—in greater numbers than are progressing from it to higher spheres, and hence it has a greater variety of sub-planes than has any of the other spheres, and is filled with a greater variety and kind of spirits than are any of these higher spheres."

When asked if the celestial worlds could be reached during out-of-body states or dreams by those in the physical world, Ann Rollins replied, "I do not think these mortals who claim that they left their bodies and entered the celestial spheres, ever did so," she replied, "and I have grave doubt that they ever entered the spiritual spheres above the third."

In a message on June 4, 1915, Rollins elaborated on the different spheres:

"The second, the fourth and the sixth spheres are appropriated for those spirits who have more of the qualifications and desires for advancement in their mental and moral pursuits, or rather for the development of those qualities possessed by them which pertain more to the mental and moral natures.

"Of course, in their progress from the lowest to the respective higher spheres that I have mentioned, the spirit must pass through the intervening spheres; but they do not linger in them or seek to make them their homes, or stay in them for their development, because in these intervening spheres the qualities which these spirits are attempting to develop, are not given much attention, and these spirits would not be much benefitted by remaining in these spheres.

"But the fact of passing through these intervening spheres does not indicate (for the contrary is true) that these spirits in so passing, in any degree, receive any additional love or development of their soul qualities. So that a spirit in the third sphere, possessing the divine love, may have more soul development than one who lives in the sixth sphere who has not the divine love.

"And so in contrast to the second, fourth and sixth spheres, that I have named, the third, fifth and seventh spheres are the ones appropriated to and specially prepared for the spirits who are seeking the development of the divine love into their souls; and in these spheres, divine love is the great thing that is sought for and acquired. ...

"As I have said, beyond the sixth sphere, these merely mental or moral seekers cannot progress, unless they seek for the divine love, and in this sixth sphere the mind's happiness is reached."

In Chapter 14, Helen described the Buddha as a "perfect man" living in the sixth sphere—the highest of the mental and moral worlds.

Notwithstanding his former belief in reincarnation, it appears he needed no belief in God, the Holy Spirit, or Jesus to reach that level.

Many fundamentalist Christian theologians believe that anyone who dies without accepting Jesus Christ as their Savior—including historical figures such as the Buddha, who lived before Jesus's time—is in hell. The sixth sphere doesn't sound like hell.

Similarly, in Chapter 16, Lafayette also said he was in the sixth sphere, where he had a beautiful home, many friends, and much entertainment. Padgett had suggested he reach out to Washington, who was in a higher sphere where, with the benefit of divine love, greater progress was possible. The following year, on April 26, 1916, Lafayette reported that he had done just that—and Washington had been more than happy to see him:

"He [Washington] was so pleased at my inquiry that he actually took me in his arms and called me his boy as he had on earth, and with his face beaming with love and happiness, he told me what this Love meant and what it had done for him, and what happiness it had brought him, and how he was now progressing towards the Celestial Heavens of light and truth. ...

"Well, without taking up your time by rehearsing the steps of my progress, I am glad to tell you that I have this Love to some extent and that I am now an inhabitant of the third sphere and enjoying the associations of spirits who also have this Love and are striving to progress."

Padgett must have asked whether he was still paying attention to the war—"Yes, I am still interested in the war, but now I do not have any hatred for the Germans that I had before. I see that they are all brothers, and children of the Father, and that only the ambitions of some and the passions and hatred of others are prolonging the war. ...

"I will not write more tonight and, in closing, give you my love and sign myself with a new name, which is,

Your brother in Christ, Lafayette."

Divine Love and Revelation

Throughout the Padgett messages, divine love is frequently described as the currency needed to . Jesus repeatedly tells us that until divine love flows into the soul, it is not immortal. Moral goodness does not appear to affect the soul's development, but moral goodness must be present for the soul to develop. From this perspective, someone like the Buddha could be a perfectly moral human yet have no soul development—because he doesn't believe he is a soul—while someone less perfect with some soul development could be closer to becoming In Christ.

Lafayette said he had progressed from the sixth to the third—the Third Heaven—a way station towards the celestial worlds—because he now had "love to some extent."

Divine love is the essence of God, which is obtained by asking for it—by prayer. Not prayer to Jesus, because that's above his pay grade, but by praying to God. It doesn't happen in one go. Like breathing, it's a process—one breath won't do it.

In ACIM, "Revelation" seems to be the inflowing of divine love from God:

48 77 Revelation is literally unspeakable because it is an experience of unspeakable love. Awe should be reserved for revelation, to which it is perfectly and correctly applicable. It is not appropriate for miracles because a state of awe is worshipful. It implies that one of a lesser order stands before a greater one. This is the case only when a Soul stands before its Creator. Souls are perfect creations and experience awe only in the Presence of the Creator of perfection.

48 79 'No man cometh unto the Father but by me' is among the most misunderstood statements in the Bible. It does not mean that I am in any way separate or different from you except in time, which does not really exist at all. Actually, the quotation is more meaningful if it is considered on a vertical rather than a horizontal axis. Regarded along the vertical, man stands below me and I stand below God. In the process of 'rising up,' I am higher. This is because, without me, the distance between God and man would be too great for you to encompass (1.I:48).

49 The Holy Spirit is the highest communication medium. Miracles do not involve this type of communication because they are *temporary* communication devices. When man returns to his original form of communication with God, the need for miracles is over. The Holy Spirit mediates higher to lower communication, keeping the direct channel from God to man open for revelation. Revelation is not reciprocal. It is always *from* God to man. The miracle *is* reciprocal because it involves equality (1.I:48–49).

Rollins and other In Christ communicators who report being in the celestial heavens all describe themselves as being in receipt of divine love. Requesting this love is part of the atonement process of becoming In Christ. According to Jesus, it's possible to achieve this state during physical life, but by the early twentieth century, it wasn't widespread. Comeys' statement that the second sphere is the most populated—with more arriving than leaving—suggests that most of us have a long way to go.

23

IMMORTALITY

The Great Gift

Shortly after my accident, I was driving into London one day when my business partner called to discuss a problem at the office. "Don't worry about it," I said. "We're immortal beings." He burst out laughing. I'm sure he thought I'd lost my mind, and of course it didn't solve the problem at the office, but for me it was a feeling I now had that whatever happens, ultimately, everything is fine. We still laugh about it today. What I meant by "immortal" is a continuation of life after death, but according to Jesus in the Padgett messages, life after death isn't immortality.

When Jesus said, "I am the resurrection and the life," he didn't say I'll be resurrected when I die, or at some point in the future there will be a resurrection. He didn't say his physical body will be resurrected. He didn't say his spiritual body will be resurrected. What he said was: "I am the resurrection and the life." He is what we can become.

Jesus came to tell anyone who would listen that the soul has the potential to become divine and achieve immortality as he had. To be born again. Prior to his coming, no one had been given that opportunity since The Fall. With his arrival, this was the new deal, or rather a restoration of the old deal.

The Cain and Abel story in Genesis symbolizes The Fall. Cain and Abel, the sons of Adam and Eve, the first parents in that particular story, made offerings to God, but God accepted Abel's offerings while declining Cain's. Cain took umbrage and remonstrated with God. He envied his younger brother, he wanted more, more love, more attention, and he was filled with anger and greed. God advised him to get his emotions in order: to examine his inner life, rather than seeing himself as a victim and blaming others for his woes. But Cain didn't heed God's advice, instead he invited Abel into a field and killed him, thus, committing the first murder. Later, God asked him where his brother was. "I do not know, am I my brother's keeper?" He lied. God told him that as a result he would have to live with his error and become a restless wanderer of the earth. Cain found the whole thing too much to bear and said he would hide and wait for someone to kill him and put him out of his misery. God, not to be outwitted, responded by putting a mark on him meaning that if anyone killed him, they would suffer his penalty sevenfold.

God took away the human's divine potentiality, withholding the option of immortality, meaning that humans would be limited to the physical and spirit world. It was the start of The Fall and we've been killing each other ever since.

The good news brought by Jesus was that the restoration was now available to anyone living in a physical body or in the spirit world: every soul that has ever individualized. Everyone.

According to Jesus, existing for an indefinite time in the spirit world is not the same as immortality, because since a soul is created, in theory it can be destroyed. Its lifespan is indefinite, whereas immortality isn't subject to death. This is the real Resurrection. It's the Great Gift as Paul called it. But at some point, if and when the experiment ends, if that's what this is, and "heaven and earth shall pass away" (Matt. 24:35), what will happen to those who haven't accepted the gift? Is there a cutoff point?

The White Throne

A verse in the book of Revelation reads:

> Then I saw a great white throne and him who was seated on it. The earth and the heavens fled from his presence, and there was no place for them. And I saw the dead, great and small, standing before the throne, and books were opened. Another book was opened, which is the book of life. The dead were judged according to what they had done as recorded in the books. The sea gave up the dead that were in

it, and death and Hades gave up the dead that were in them, and each person was judged according to what they had done. Then death and Hades were thrown into the lake of fire. The lake of fire is the second death. Anyone whose name was not found written in the book of life was thrown into the lake of fire (Rev. 20:11–15).

On March 12, 1916, after Padgett had attended a church sermon, John wrote a message on Revelation:

"I was with you tonight and heard the sermon of the preacher on heaven and what it is and, as his text was founded on some expressions in a book of the Bible ascribed to me and which I did write, though not just as is contained in the Bible, I thought it meet (appropriate) that I should come and write you as to the truth of the sermon, and as to the value of the book as descriptive or suggestive of what heaven is and what its appearances are, and what the spirits of the redeemed are doing in what the preacher designated as service.

"Well, I first want to say that while I did write a book of the nature of the one in the Bible named Revelation, yet this one does not contain my writings to any great extent, nor are my ideas set forth or followed in this book of Revelation.

"As you may now know, in my time, and for a long time previous, the Jewish writers, because of the great troubles and persecutions their nation was undergoing, were accustomed to write books in the nature of the one contained in the Bible, and called Revelations, (sic) for the purpose of encouraging their people to believe that all the wrongs that they were suffering would be avenged by God, and their enemies made to suffer and become destroyed, and that in the end their nation would be rescued from its condition of servitude and sufferings and become the ruling nation of the earth; and these writings were accepted by the Jews as having the authority of divine inspiration and conveying to their nation the truths of God and the same promises of His intervening in their behalf.

"The writings were always ascribed to some prophet, seer, or man of God who had the special privilege of coming in contact with God or some of His angels through the mysterious and sacred means of visions.

"Of course, these writings were merely intended to encourage the Jews to establish their faith in God and in the belief that He would send them a Messiah who would have the power to redeem them from the punishments and thralldom that they were undergoing under the tyranny and strength of their heathen captors and persecutors.

"Always were these writings prophetic and held forth the promises for the future, without ever attempting to fix a time for their fulfillment, or the ending of the nation's woes and the coming of its deliverer, so that time went on and the promises were not fulfilled, hope continued to exist and the belief of the Jews was not lessened, and non-fulfillment was explained by the further belief that the time for the consummation of their eagerly wished for expectations had not yet arrived.

"That God was all knowing as well as all powerful and careful for their race and that He and He alone understood just when the proper and fitting time should arrive.

"This hope upon hope was a wonderful force in keeping up the beliefs and expectations of the Jews, and so effective was it that to this day they remain a nation or rather a race in belief and expectation of this coming Messiah.

"But, alas, as they did not recognize and accept him when he did appear, they will never again see his appearance, for he will never come as their Messiah as expected of old, but only as the great teacher and redeemer, not only of their race, but of all the peoples of the earth.

"He has already come as such a redeemer, and is working now to lead men to the true and only way to life and happiness and immortality.

"But never will any Messiah come to the Jews to establish them on earth as a great and chosen nation, as nearly all of them believe and still look for.

"Thus, as I say, many books or manuscripts were written by the claimed Jewish prophets holding forth to the Jews the results of visions claimed to have been experienced by these writers.

"But as the prophecies, in the sense that the Jews understood them, have never been fulfilled, neither will they be fulfilled in the future, and their value has no reality.

"This custom as I may call it, continued from these early times down to the time in which I lived and wrote, and my book of prophecy was written by me, not with the purpose of establishing the Jews as a nation on earth, or causing them to believe that their hopes or longings would be fulfilled, but for the purpose of encouraging the Christians to believe that notwithstanding their persecution and sufferings and martyrdom they would in the future life, when they should meet the Master and the saints, find joy and peace and heaven.

"But in my writings nothing was said about the wrath of God being visited upon the persecutors of the Christians or of their having to go into a hell of fire and brimstone, so that from that fact the happiness of the redeemed would be increased.

"My writings have been added to and all kinds of grotesque imagery interpolated so that the whole design and purpose of my writings were changed and destroyed and the present Book of Revelation is only a mere allegory of some one or more writers who were gifted with some knowledge of the Christian teachings and unusually oriented imaginations.

"This book is of no value, but on the contrary is doing much harm to the cause of the truth as taught by the Master; as we who are in the celestial heavens and have knowledge of things heavenly as well as things earthly know to be the fact.

"It should not be accepted as a truth of the revelation of truths, and not be believed in for any purpose.

"It has lead (*sic*) many good men and honest and earnest seekers after the truth astray, and caused them to believe and teach false doctrines that have resulted in much darkness and stagnation in the development of human souls in their longings for the truth.

"So, I say, let men entirely discard its teachings, and any and all lessons that the preachers or others, who think that they can understand its meaning, attempt to teach.

"The writings that I gave to my people, of the kind mentioned, have long ago served their purpose, and the writings called the revelations contain in it no truth that will help mankind to the Heavenly Kingdom or to their eternal happiness and at-onement with the Father.

"Let it die the death of a falsehood, born out of time."

"I also was interested in the struggle of the preacher to explain what heaven is, and, what his people who may consider themselves redeemed children of God, will find when they become inhabitants of that heaven.

"Well, he spoke truly when he said heaven is a place as well as a condition, for it is inconceivable that any condition of the spirit of a mortal could exist unless there be a place where that spirit could find a habitation. All space in the universe of God is a place, or contains places where things of existence must find localities. There is no such thing as a vacuum in God's economy, and all parts of space are fitted with something having substance, either material or spiritual, and wherever such substance is, there is a place for its abiding.

"Yes, heaven is a place, or a number of places, for the preacher is far from having the true conception of heaven when he supposes it is one large place, where all believers go after death, irrespective of their condition of soul and moral perfections. As I say, there are many heavens and many places, all as real and substantial as are the different stories and rooms in your home of earth. And the partitions, if I may so speak, between these different places are just as impassable for spirits that have not the proper qualifications to pass through as are the partition walls between the various rooms in your earth homes for you mortals to pass through. These places are distinctive, and the many mansions that the preacher referred to, are situated in many heavens or more correctly many spheres of the heavens.

"Strictly speaking, there are two heavens in God's spirit universe, namely, the heavens of the redeemed and transformed soul by the divine love called the celestial heavens, and the heavens of the restored perfect man, called the spiritual heavens, each and all of them being places of real perfection and substance.

"As one star differs from another star in glory, so these several heavens within heavens differ from one another in glory and appearance and in those things which help to make the mansions of their inhabitants beautiful and attractive and glorious.

"It would take too long for me to attempt to describe any of these heavens, for they each and all excel any conception that the mortal is capable of having; but I will say this, that there are no streets of gold or pearly gates, or suns or stars in any of them; only the light of God's love and mercy illuminates them."

∞

Scientists are looking ahead to a time when virtual reality will be indistinguishable from reality. We don't know whether it's decades or hundreds of years away, but with the advent of transhumanism, it's not hard to imagine a future where VR headsets for gamers are replaced by brain implants, bodies are fed intravenously, and waste is managed the same way.

Continuing the game analogy: imagine spending long periods in the game—perhaps years. To exit safely, you have to realize you're in a game. That might sound obvious, but denial is psychologically powerful. We can convince ourselves of just about anything. By the time the game is over, most players will have logged out and be relaxing at home. But some will be so immersed they refuse to believe there's anything beyond the game.

Eventually, the game ends—and whoever's in charge decides that's it. If you're not coming now, you're not coming. The plug gets pulled, and they're left comatose.

One apparent difference between Jesus in the Padgett messages and in *A Course in Miracles* is that, in the Padgett messages, he tells us we can achieve immortality—but not until divine love is flowing into our souls. Immortality is opt-in—it's a gift—not an obligation. According to ACIM, however, we are already immortal—but until the Atonement is complete, "revelation of the divine order is impossible." Like the gamers, if we haven't accepted that this isn't our ultimate reality, we remain stuck in the game—limited to the physical and spirit world— until we do.

In ACIM, the white throne has been put in storage, and all of us eventually accept the great gift. "Your resurrection is your reawakening," Jesus tells us: "10 I am the model for rebirth, but rebirth itself is merely the dawning on your minds of what is already in them" (6.II:10). Jesus appears to be saying that, because as souls we ultimately exist beyond time, there are no real questions and answers. We already know what we need to know—it just hasn't dawned on us yet.

The Kingdom

The Kingdom of Heaven is like a king who prepared a wedding banquet for his son. He sent his servants to those who had been invited to the banquet to tell them to come, but they refused to come.

Then he sent some more servants and said, 'Tell those who have been invited that I have prepared my dinner: My oxen and fattened cattle have been butchered, and everything is ready. Come to the wedding banquet.'

But they paid no attention and went off—one to his field, another to his business. The rest seized his servants, mistreated them, and killed them. The king was enraged. He sent his army and destroyed those murderers and burned their city.

Then he said to his servants, 'The wedding banquet is ready, but those I invited did not deserve to come. So go to the street corners and invite to the banquet anyone you find.' So the servants went out into the streets and gathered all the people they could find, the bad as well as the good, and the wedding hall was filled with guests.

But when the king came in to see the guests, he noticed a man there who was not wearing wedding clothes. He asked, 'How did you get in here without wedding clothes, friend?' The man was speechless.

Then the king told the attendants, 'Tie him hand and foot, and throw him outside, into the darkness, where there will be weeping and gnashing of teeth.'

For many are invited, but few are chosen (Matt. 22:1–14).

Luke also has a version of the banquet story (Luke 14:16–24), as does the Gospel of Thomas (saying 64), in which the king is referred to simply as the "man" or the "master." Intriguingly, neither Luke nor Thomas mention cattle being butchered, servants being killed, or the king becoming enraged and taking revenge by destroying the murderers and burning their cities—all of which seem at odds with Jesus's broader message that God is love.

Perfect Man or Divine Angel?

On May 15, 1917, in a message to Padgett, Jesus asked rhetorically:

"Then what is the way that leads to this celestial kingdom? The only way? For there is but one! The observance of the moral precepts and the cleansing of men's souls from sin by following these precepts, will not lead to this kingdom, for as it can be readily seen, the stream can rise no higher than its source, and the source of the souls of men in a merely purified state, is the condition of the perfect man—that condition in which he was before his fall—and, hence the results of the observance and living of the merely moral precepts and the exercise of the natural love in its pure state, is, that man will be restored to the condition of the perfect man—the created man in whom there is nothing of the divine. ...

"But this restored condition of man will be so perfect and so in harmony with God's will and His laws governing the highest and most perfect of His creatures, that man will be very happy. Yet, he will continue to be only the created being, having nothing more than the image of his Maker.

"So, I say, living in a harmony with the moral laws and the exercise of this natural love in its highest and purest state towards God and towards his fellow man, will not lead into the way to the celestial kingdom, but the greatest height of his attainment will be the kingdom on earth or that in the spirit heavens.

"And the distinct and differing nature of these kingdoms from that of the celestial heavens, will enable mankind to understand the difference between the missions of the great teachers and reformers who preceded me in their work among men, and the mission which I was selected to perform on earth. The former could not possibly have taught the way to the celestial kingdom, for until my coming, this divine love of which I write was not possible for man to obtain. The privilege was not, before that time, in existence after the first parents lost it, and there was no celestial kingdom in which men could find their eternal home. ...

"But the way thereto is simple and single and men were taught that way by me when I was on earth; and could have been taught that way during all the centuries since I left the human life; and I must say that some have been so taught and have found that way, but comparatively few, for the mortals who's ostensible and claimed mission and privilege were to teach that way. I mean the priests and preachers and churches have neglected to teach the same, but rather, though in earnestness and realizing their allegiance to God and their obligations to mankind, have taught merely the way which the observance of the moral precepts would lead men into.

"And all this, notwithstanding, that in the Bible, which most of those professing to be Christians believe contains my sayings and teachings, is set forth this way to the celestial kingdom. The words are few and the way is plain, and no mystery prevents men from comprehending the meaning thereof. When I said, 'Except a man be born again, he cannot enter into the kingdom of God,' I disclosed the only and true way to this kingdom. During my time on earth there were some who understood this great truth, and since that time, there have been some who not only understood this truth, but found the way and followed it until they reached the goal and are now inhabitants of this kingdom; but the vast majority of men—priests, teachers and people—have never understood, and have never sought to find the way. This great truth to their spiritual senses has been, as it were, a hidden thing; and as they read or even recite the same to their hearers it has no special significance, but is merely as one of the moral precepts, such as 'Love your neighbor as yourself,' and with not as much importance attached to it as to some of these moral instructions.

"And so, all down the ages since the great kingdom has been waiting for men, they, though in all sincerity and in love towards God, have sought for and to a greater or lesser extent, found only the kingdom of the perfect man, and have neglected to seek for and missed the kingdom of the divine angel. ...

"The man who will thus believe and pray will never be disappointed, and the way to the kingdom will be his as certainly as that the sun shines day by day upon the just and the unjust alike. No mediator is needed, nor are the prayers or ceremonies of priests or preachers, for God comes to man, himself, and hears his prayers and responds thereto by sending the Comforter, which is the Father's messenger for conveying into the souls of men this great divine love.

"I have thus explained the only way to the celestial kingdom of God and to the divine nature in love; and there is no other way whereby it is possible to reach this kingdom and the certain knowledge of immortality.

"So, I implore men to meditate on these great truths, and in meditating believe, and when believing, pray to the Father for the inflowing into their souls of this divine love, and in doing so they will experience belief, faith and possession and ownership of that which can never be taken from them—no, not in all eternity.

"And so it is with man to choose and fix his destiny. Will that destiny be the perfect man or the Divine Angel?"

My understanding of the banquet parable is: the king/master is God; the wedding is the celestial kingdom; Jesus is the Son; and we, the Sonship, are the guests. The wedding garment is divine love, and without it we can't enter the kingdom.

In ACIM, Jesus says:

49 I cannot unite your will with God's *for* you, but I can erase all misperceptions from your mind if you will bring it under my guidance. *Only* your misperceptions stand in your own way. Without them your choice is certain. Sane perception *induces* sane choosing. The Atonement was an act based on true perception. I cannot choose for you, but I can help you make your own right choice. 'Many are called, but few are chosen' should read, 'All are called, but few choose to listen. Therefore, they do not choose *right.*'

"50 The 'chosen ones' are merely those who choose right sooner. This is the real meaning of the celestial speed-up. Strong wills can do this *now*, and you *will* find rest for your souls. God knows you only in peace, and this is your reality (3.VI:49–50).

The belief in time and death stops us choosing. Accepting immortality ultimately eliminates both.

Christian theology places great importance on physical death as the cutoff point to decide whether one is saved or goes to hell. According to

Jesus and the communicators, this isn't the case. While physical death establishes our baseline for our journey through the spirit world, we are not consigned to a permanent heaven or hell at death. We all have the potential to progress indefinitely. The cutoff point, if there is one, is level six, the highest of the intellectual spheres. Beyond that state what's needed to achieve salvation/immortality is faith in God and an inflowing of divine love.

The introduction of ACIM begins: "This is A Course in Miracles. It is a required course. Only the time you take it is voluntary. Free will does not mean that you can establish the curriculum. It means only that you can elect what you want to take at a given time." We can choose when to complete the atonement as long as we complete it, and physical death isn't a prerequisite because there is no death.

The soul is a creation of God, just as a physical body is the creation of its parents. Whereas the essence of God, which we can receive in the form of divine love, is an *emanation* from God, rather than a *creation*.

> 36 The Soul is in a state of grace forever.
> Man's reality is only his Soul.
> Therefore, man is in a state of grace forever
> (1.I:36).

∞

The physical and spirit world is the world of the perfect man. The celestial heaven is the world of the immortal being—the Divine Angel. Jesus was the first—the first to be In Christ, what Paul called "Glorification." Until Jesus's arrival, the kingdom didn't exist, or at least had been shuttered since the separation. Jesus came to announce its creation. We are saved by Jesus in that he is our guide to immortality—to the kingdom—his kingdom, bequeathed by God.

EPILOGUE

The Protagonist

Imagine you are the protagonist in a movie. But you don't realize it's a movie. You think it's real life. Antagonists are everywhere. Some appear evil, some are loving, others are just characters or external events putting stumbling blocks in your way.

You do your best to navigate life. Sometimes you wonder what it's all about. Is there any point to it? Is it some kind of school? Are we just meat sacks here by accident, wandering around like zombies, neurons firing, pushing us in this direction or that?

The blue canvas: we stare at it and see only blue. Then a white dot appears—just a single white dot. Neurons fire. We can't help ourselves— we have to know. What is that white dot? We focus on it, and for a moment, the white dot is everything. It consumes us. But then, within it we see a black dot. What is that black dot? The white dot is no longer important. It never really was. It was just a distraction, like all the other dots—the dot we focus on being the most important: the only thing that matters. Events in our lives are just dots.

Then one day, in this level or another, we realize we are in a movie. We are the protagonists. All the other characters—our parents, partners, wives, husbands, children, friends, enemies, bosses, employees, presidents, kings, queens, prisoners, killers, victims, priests, co-workers—the pet cat, the dog, the mosquito you just tried to swat—are all starring in their own movie.

But now we know. It's a wakeup call. And nothing will ever be the same again. Now, the antagonists don't look so scary. They are just playing their part. It was all an illusion: a mental construct necessary to complete that particular scene.

No One's Dead

Every day we wake up at the magic show: the magician pulling rabbits out of a hat, card tricks of every description, people sawn in half, coins pushed through bottles, and levitating assistants. But now we've seen how the trick is done, the sleight of hand—the illusion no longer distracts us—its allure gone, never to return.

We no longer stare at dots.

That's what being in the world but not of the world is.

When you figure it out it's the most important moment of your life.

EPILOGUE

THE SPIRIT WORLD ISN'T SALVATION.

SO WHAT IS IT?

SALVATION IS TO TRANSCEND THE SPIRIT WORLD.
SALVATION = IMMORTALITY.

SALVATION COMES FROM GOD.
SALVATION IS THROUGH FAITH ALONE.

NO WORKS ARE REQUIRED.

BUT ...

WORKS COME BEFORE SALVATION.
WORKS ARE DOWN TO US.

WHERE IMMORTALITY TAKES US IS UNKNOWN.
BUT IT MIGHT BE FUN!

JESUS SAID:

"ALL ARE CALLED, BUT FEW CHOOSE TO LISTEN."
YOU HAVE BEEN CALLED.

CHOOSE RIGHT.

A BIT ABOUT ME

I was born in Chiswick, London, in 1956. I left school at fifteen, worked blue-collar jobs (proper work), and sold clothes in my teens and early twenties before stumbling into a three-decade career in the music business, where I co-founded two independent record companies. It was a fun time. As the song goes, "Even the bad times were good." The main attractions were music, sex, celebrity and money—in no particular order. Although I had no particular interest in celebrity. I was too much of an introvert for that.

The irrepressible, gonzo Journalist Hunter S. Thompson called the TV industry "A cruel and shallow money trench; a long plastic hallway where thieves and pimps run free, and good men die like dogs." He could've been talking about the music business—and many thought he was. I spent many years in the "long plastic hallway," and loved every minute of it.

That chapter closed after a fall resulted in a head injury.

I woke up with a whole new worldview. I suddenly started talking about death, telling anyone who asked that there is no death. Then a friend who had died sent a message via a medium to say everything was as it should be and that it had been his time to die. He was only thirty-three, and I have often wondered why he chose to die on my living room floor.

At a dinner party, one friend quietly suggested I shouldn't talk about the life after death stuff because it would scare the host. Another said it sounded as if I'd found God. I replied that I wasn't looking for God—but maybe he found me. I told another friend, "You know, this isn't home."

"You mean we're fucking aliens," he replied.

"No I don't mean that. I mean we're just passing through."

I stopped talking about it unless people asked.

But people kept asking.

"Why did you abandon your career?"

"Why don't you eat meat anymore?"

"Why don't you drink anymore?"

"Why did you give up shooting animals?"

After a while, I got bored trying to explain. The only real answer I had was that one day I banged my head, and after a while, I didn't want to do that stuff anymore.

I was in a different hallway.

Somehow, years later, I woke up one morning and I'd become a book publisher. My main motivation was the question: *Why don't more people know about this stuff?* I had also left my lucrative career, and needed to earn a living. The name "White Crow Books" came to me in a dream. The psychologist William James was the inspiration. He reasoned that in order to demonstrate a phenomenon exists, only one example is needed. He said, "If you wish to upset the law that all crows are black, you mustn't seek to show that no crows are; it is enough if you prove one single crow to be white."

White Crow Books is a one-man curiosity factory, forever in pursuit of the White Crow—the anomaly that challenges our understanding of reality.

I didn't intend to write this book. It was going to be a letter—a letter to Robert. The Robert in the book. I didn't plan to mention Jesus—he wasn't in my thoughts. I wanted to tell Robert I was past wondering whether there is life after death—that I was certain. I doubted his competition—though laudable—would come up with any novel insights beyond the ever-increasing evidence of communication from beyond. There were already countless accounts in existence for anyone who's curious, and no doubt his competition would give people plenty more to read about.

A Bit About Me

Then a man from Thailand emailed me, asking if I could help promote a book he'd published years earlier on the automatic writings of James E. Padgett. I was aware of Padgett but hadn't paid much attention to his writings. I felt it was all a bit too religious for me. I explained that White Crow was a publisher, and since his books were already published, I couldn't really help.

We arranged to have a chat anyway and the same day a commenter in France mentioned "Padgett" on the White Crow website. That was unusual. Being the moderator, I checked and found that it was the first time Padgett had been mentioned in the comments for seven years. Coincidence? A sign? Who knows. Whatever it was it nudged me toward writing a book about contemporary messages purporting to come from Jesus.

I'm not an obvious candidate to be spreading the Word on behalf of Jesus. Back in 2001, our record company released an album by the extreme metal band *Cradle of Filth*. That year, Tower Records in Glasgow were raided by police for selling Cradle's "JESUS is a C**T" t-shirts. The Lord Provost of Glasgow held a press conference outside the store and said, "I have written to the head of Tower Records to convey my disgust and to underline that material like this must not be put on sale again."

We had nothing to do with the t-shirts, but sold a lot of records on the back of the media exposure.

I have to admit, I wasn't a fan of Christianity. Despite the good people who follow Jesus, in my simple mind I kept imagining a story of a Mustached Man.

He orchestrates the deaths of millions of Jews, Roma, the disabled, and anyone else he deems inferior and unworthy of life. He converts to Evangelical Protestantism, sincerely repents, and becomes a pastor. In his later years, he does good work—helping the poor and the sick. He dies and goes to heaven.

Meanwhile, the devout Jews and other innocent people he murdered are in hell because they didn't accept Jesus as their Savior.

I could understand the Mustached Man being forgiven and saved, but it's the millions of Jews condemned to a permanent, eternal hell that I couldn't comprehend. It didn't seem very Christlike. It made no sense to me then—and still doesn't.

While I appreciate that this book might be upsetting for some Christians, it's not my intention to upset anyone. I imagine that people who believe Jesus is God don't want to hear about someone claiming to be Jesus who says, "I was not God and never claimed to be. The worship of me as a God is blasphemous, and I did not teach it. I am a son of God as you are."

In one of the messages to Padgett, Emanuel Swedenborg said, "So, my brother, turn your thought more to this work and, if necessary, sacrifice every worldly consideration to carry forward your work and make perfect your efforts to fulfill the great mission with which you have been blessed."

When I read that, I felt I had to put the messages out there, as others have done in the past.

Looking back, I've realized I've never really planned any of the important stuff that's happened in my life, and this book is no exception: children, family, partners, friends, work, God. They just sort of show up—like magic.

Please don't ask me about God. I mean no disrespect, but you know as much as I do—maybe more. There's not much I can say, other than it's about love. As I said earlier, I feel I know *God is* yet paradoxically recognize that God is *unknowable.*

At least that's how it seems to me.

To paraphrase Luther again: "We have to do two things alone: our own believing and our own dying." Even if he didn't say it, it's a truism if I ever heard one.

Thanks for your time.

BIBLIOGRAPHY

Alvarado, Carlos. *Charles Richet: A Nobel Prize Winning Scientist's Exploration of Psychic Phenomena.* Guildford: White Crow Books, 2019.

Anonymous. *The Silence of Dr. Lang.* London: Psychic Press Ltd, 1942.

Ballard, Stan A., and Roger Green, eds. *The Silver Birch Book of Questions & Answers.* London: The Silver Birch Press, 1972.

Beard, Paul. *Living On: How Consciousness Continues and Evolves After Death.* Brighton: White Crow Books, 2015.

Beard, Paul, and Marie Cherrie. *The Barbanell Report: A Journey into the Afterlife.* Guildford: White Crow Productions, 2024.

Bhagavad Gita. Translated by Eknath Easwaran. 2nd ed. Petaluma, CA: Nilgiri Press, 2007.

Bonaventure, Saint. *The Life of Saint Francis of Assisi.* Edited by Cardinal Henry Edward Manning. London: TAN Books, 2010.

Bradley, H. Dennis. *Wisdom of the Gods.* 2nd ed. Brighton, UK: White Crow Books, 2013.

Church of England. *Spiritualism: The 1939 Report to the Archbishop of Canterbury.* Edited by Michael Perry. London: Churches' Fellowship for Psychical and Spiritual Studies, 1999.

Cocks, Michael. *Afterlife Teaching from Stephen the Martyr.* Guildford: White Crow Books, 2011.

Crookes, William. *Notes on Séances with D.D. Home.* Proceedings of the Society for Psychical Research, 1889.

Danby, L.C. *The Certainty of Eternity: The Story of Australia's Greatest Medium.* Guildford: White Crow Books, 2014.

Darwin, Charles. *On the Origin of Species by Means of Natural Selection, or the Preservation of Favoured Races in the Struggle for Life.* London: John Murray, 1859.

Darwin, Charles. *The Descent of Man, and Selection in Relation to Sex.* London: John Murray, 1871.

Ehrman, Bart D. *How Jesus Became God: The Exaltation of a Jewish Preacher from Galilee.* New York: HarperOne, 2014.

Ehrman, Bart D. *Jesus Interrupted: Revealing the Hidden Contradictions in the Bible (And Why We Don't Know About Them).* New York: HarperOne, 2009.

Ehrman, Bart D. *Misquoting Jesus: The Story Behind Who Changed the Bible and Why.* San Francisco: HarperSanFrancisco, 2005.

Flint, Leslie. *Voices in the Dark: My Life as a Medium.* London: Macmillan Company, 1971.

Galton, Francis. *Hereditary Genius: An Inquiry Into Its Laws and Consequences.* London: Macmillan, 1869.

Guinness World Records. *Guinness World Records 2021.* London: Guinness World Records, 2020.

Haraldsson, Erlendur. *Towards the Unknown: Memoir of a Psychical Researcher.* Guildford: White Crow Books, 2021.

Hart, David Bentley. *The New Testament: A Translation.* 2nd ed. New Haven, CT: Yale University Press, 2023.

Heagerty, N. Riley. *The French Revelation: Voice to Voice Conversations with Spirits Through the Mediumship of Emily S. French.* Guildford: White Crow Books, 2015.

James I, King of England. *Daemonologie.* Edited by G. B. Harrison. London: John Lane; New York: E. P. Dutton & Company.

Josephus, Flavius. *Antiquities of the Jews.* London: T. Nelson and Sons, 1867.

Krippner, Stanley, Montague Ullman, and Alan Vaughan. *Dream Telepathy: Experiments in Nocturnal Extrasensory Perception.* New York: Macmillan, 1973.

Lodge, Oliver. Proofs of Life After Death. Boston: Small, Maynard & Co., 1902.

Lodge, Oliver, and Raymond Lodge. Raymond, or Life and Death. New York: George H. Doran Company, 1916.

Palmstierna, Baron Erik. Horizons of Immortality: A Quest for Reality. London: Constable & Co. Ltd., 1937.

Palmstierna, Baron Erik. The World's Crisis and Faiths. London: John Lane, 1942.

Richet, Charles. La Grande Espérance [The Great Hope]. Paris: Éditions Montaigne, 1933.

Robinson, Sugar Ray, and Dave Anderson. Sugar Ray. New York: Viking Press, 1969.

Schucman, Helen, and William T. Thetford, eds. A Course in Miracles: Original Edition. Omaha: Course in Miracles Society, 2012.

Seneca, Lucius Annaeus. Epistulae Morales ad Lucilium. Translated by Richard M. Gummere. London: Heinemann, 1917.

Smith, Charles H., ed. Alfred Russel Wallace: Writings on Evolution 1843-1912. Bristol: Thoemmes Continuum, 2004.

Stead, Estelle Wilson. My Father: Personal & Spiritual Reminiscences. London: W. Heinemann; New York: George H. Doran Company, 1913.

Stead, William Thomas. After Death: Letters from Julia. Guildford: White Crow Books, 2011.

Stone, Leslie R., ed. The True Gospel Revealed Anew by Jesus: Volume I. Washington, D.C.: Foundation Church of the New Birth, 1958.

Stone, Leslie R., ed. The True Gospel Revealed Anew by Jesus: Volume II. Washington, D.C.: Foundation Church of the New Birth, 1950.

Stone, Leslie R., ed. The True Gospel Revealed Anew by Jesus: Volume III. Washington, D.C.: Foundation Church of the New Birth, 1969.

Stone, Leslie R., ed. The True Gospel Revealed Anew by Jesus: Volume IV. Washington, D.C.: Foundation Church of the New Birth, 1972.

Swedenborg, Emanuel. Heaven and Hell. Abridged. Edited by Simon Parke. Guildford: White Crow Books, 2011.

Swaffer, Hannen. *Northcliffe's Return*. London: Hutchinson & Co., 1925.

Tabor, James. *Paul and Jesus: How the Apostle Transformed Christianity*. New York: Simon & Schuster, 2012.

REFERENCES

WELCOME TO LEVEL ZERO

1   https://www.bigelowinstitute.org/index.php/bics-afterlife-proof/
2   https://www.prb.org/articles/how-many-people-have-ever-lived-on-earth/

WHO'S CALLING?

1   https://en.wikipedia.org/wiki/SpaceX_Mars_colonization_program
2   https://www.arthurfindlaycollege.org
3   https://digitalcommons.ciis.edu/cgi/viewcontent.cgi?article=1802 &context=ijts-transpersonalstudies

WHY JESUS?

1   There are a number of online sources of the Padgett material. The Foundation of the New Birth has free PDFs of the *True Gospel Revealed Anew by Jesus* series of books. www.divinelove.org. Alan Ross's books and website www.jamesepadgett.com is also a good source.

2   The first commercial publisher of *ACIM* was The Foundation for Inner Peace. www.acim.org. The quotes in this book are from the

"Original edition" published by The Course in Miracles Society, in which the verse numbers are different from the FFIP version. https://cimsmiracles.com.

JESUS HERE, JESUS THERE

[1]   https://www.sca-aware.org/about-sudden-cardiac-arrest/latest-statistics

[2]   https://channelingerik.com/interview-with-jesus-christ/

[3]   https://www.getreligion.org/getreligion/2022/1/9/talking-to-jesus-this-is-big-new-york-times-news-when-a-hollywood-spiritualist-is-involved

[4]   https://en.wikipedia.org/wiki/Christ_myth_theory

UNUSUAL PEOPLE

[1]   https://www.theguardian.com/world/2009/dec/22/kim-peek-rain-man-dies

[2]   https://spiritist.us/chico-xavier/

[3]   https://www.encyclopedia.com/science/encyclopedias-almanacs-transcripts-and-maps/french-emily-s-1830-1912

[4]   https://www.attackingthedevil.co.uk

[5]   https://dbpedia.org/page/Julia_A._Ames

[6]   https://psi-encyclopedia.spr.ac.uk/articles/etta-wriedt

[7]   https://www.leslieflint.com

[8]   https://www.spiritualtruthfoundation.org/barbanell-silver-birch/

[9]   https://www.encyclopedia.com/science/encyclopedias-almanacs-transcripts-and-maps/swaffer-hannen-1879-1962

[10] https://www.britannica.com/biography/Alfred-Charles-William-Harmsworth-Viscount-Northcliffe-of-Saint-Peter

11 https://www.telegraph.co.uk/news/obituaries/1397313/Paul-Beard. html

12 https://www.spiritualtruthfoundation.org/barbanell-silver-birch/

PSYCHIC STIGMA

1 https://psi-encyclopedia.spr.ac.uk/articles/daniel-dunglas-home

2 https://www.theiet.org/membership/library-and-archives/the-iet-archives/biographies/sir-william-crookes-1832-1919

3 https://wallacefund.myspecies.info

4 https://collections.countway.harvard.edu/onview/exhibits/show/galtonschildren/sir-francis-galton

5 https://www.darwinproject.ac.uk/letter/?docId=letters/DCP-LETT-8373.xml

6 https://www.darwinproject.ac.uk/letter/?docId=letters/DCP-LETT-9247.xml

7 https://www.nobelprize.org/prizes/medicine/1913/richet/biographical/

8 http://oliverlodge.org

9 https://www.theguardian.com/stage/2020/oct/25/james-randi-obituary

10 https://www.victorzammit.com

11 https://petition.parliament.uk/archived/petitions/55698

THE ARCHBISHOP AND THE SPIRITUALISTS

1 http://iapsop.com/archive/materials/light/light_v60_n3105_jul_18_1940.pdf

2 https://www.churchesfellowship.co.uk/product-page/spiritualism-the-1939-report-to-the-archbishop-of-canterbury-1

3   https://digitalcollections.lib.umanitoba.ca/islandora/object/uofm%3A2981874

4   https://www.sagb.org.uk/seven-principles.htm

ESP

1   https://www.youtube.com/watch?v=gaRVzooavRI

2   https://todayinsci.com/L/Lavoisier_Antoine/LavoisierAntoine-Quotations.htm

3   https://en.wikipedia.org/wiki/Harold_Jeffreys

4   https://pmc.ncbi.nlm.nih.gov/articles/PMC6396695/

5   fhttps://www.youtube.com/watch?v=kvA9woJ8V8o

SPIRIT COMMUNICATION

1   https://www.leslieflint.com/cosmo-lang-may-1959

2   https://www.youtube.com/watch?v=edSffwll8_k

3   https://www.youtube.com/watch?v=JqTFpPlLiOY

4   https://www.rcpsych.ac.uk/docs/default-source/members/sigs/spirituality-spsig/resources/spirituality-special-interest-group-publications-dr-alan-sanderson-the-case-for-spirit-release.pdf?sfvrsn=c256ac87_2

5   https://en.wikipedia.org/wiki/Squizzy_Taylor

WHY PADGETT?

1   https://swedenborg.com

REFERENCES

RIDDLE

1 https://case.edu/ech/articles/r/riddle-albert-g
2 https://www.whitehousehistory.org/bios/james-garfield

BELIEF

1 https://www.state.gov/international-religious-freedom-reports
2 https://news.gallup.com/poll/248837/losing-religion-two-thirds-people-say.aspx
3 https://bulletin.hds.harvard.edu/turning-ghosts-into-ancestors-in-contemporary-urban-china/
4 https://aspace.lib.jmu.edu/agents/people/744
5 https://www.theguardian.com/science/2011/may/15/stephen-hawking-interview-there-is-no-heaven

THE BIBLE

1 https://www.bartehrman.com
2 https://www.nytimes.com/2005/09/10/us/r-w-funk-79-creator-of-jesus-seminar-dies.html
3 https://en.wikipedia.org/wiki/Jesus_Seminar
4 https://jamestabor.com
5 https://www.jewishvirtuallibrary.org/martin-luther-quot-the-jews-and-their-lies-quot
6 https://www.vatican.va/content/francesco/en/apost_letters/documents/papa-francesco-lettera-ap_20161120_misericordia-et-misera.html
7 https://en.wikipedia.org/wiki/Pelagianism

8 https://northamanglican.com/exposition-of-the-thirty-nine-articles-article-ix/

9 https://allianceforthepeaceofjerusalem.com/are-the-jewish-people-responsible-for-killing-jesus/

10 https://www.theguardian.com/books/2018/sep/14/yuval-noah-harari-the-new-threat-to-liberal-democracy

11 https://www.nytimes.com/2019/03/30/us/politics/pompeo-christian-policy.html

12 https://www.pewresearch.org/short-reads/2022/12/08/about-four-in-ten-u-s-adults-believe-humanity-is-living-in-the-end-times/

13 http://news.bbc.co.uk/1/hi/uk/699929.stm

PAST LIVES OR OTHER LIVES?

1 https://psi-encyclopedia.spr.ac.uk/articles/erlendur-haraldsson

2 https://med.virginia.edu/perceptual-studies/wp-content/uploads/sites/360/2015/11/Stevenson-s-Obit-Emily.pdf

SENECA AND THE CRUCIFIXION

1 https://www.the-paulmccartney-project.com/1966/03/john-lennon-is-quoted-saying-were-more-popular-than-jesus-now/

WAR

1 https://www.theguardian.com/world/2005/oct/07/iraq.usa

2 http://news.bbc.co.uk/1/hi/4772142.stm

3 https://thecatholicherald.com/pope-blames-west-for-the-rise-of-islamic-state-and-lawless-libya/

4 https://en.wikipedia.org/wiki/Religious_affiliations_of_presidents_of_the_United_States

REFERENCES

5   https://www.euronews.com/2022/09/27/ukraine-crisis-russia-patriarch

6   https://timesofindia.indiatimes.com/world/rest-of-world/putin-predicts-victory-in-ukraine-conflict-god-is-with-us/articleshow/116698969.cms

7   https://www.themoscowtimes.com/2020/02/05/is-russias-church-about-to-ban-priests-from-blessing-nukes-a69182

8   https://www.theguardian.com/uk-news/2019/may/02/cnd-stage-die-in-westminster-abbey-nuclear-weapons-thanksgiving

9   https://www.themoscowtimes.com/2018/10/19/aggressors-will-be-annihilated-we-will-go-to-heaven-as-martyrs-putin-says-a63235

10   https://www.presidency.ucsb.edu/documents/address-delivered-the-first-annual-assemblage-the-league-enforce-peace-american-principles

11   https://en.wikipedia.org/wiki/Civilization_(film)

12   https://www.thecrimson.com/article/1927/1/11/mahatma-gandhi-says-he-believes-in/

13   https://en.wikipedia.org/wiki/List_of_countries_by_intentional_homicide_rate

THE DIVINE RIGHT

1   https://en.wikipedia.org/wiki/Anti-Homosexuality_Act,_2023

2   https://www.eighteenthcenturypoetry.org/works/o4986-w0150.shtml

3   https://www.declassifieduk.org/britains-secret-role-in-the-brutal-us-war-in-vietnam/

SUICIDE

1   https://www.nytimes.com/1915/07/18/archives/rr-perry-kills-himself-washington-lawyer-follows-example-of-his-two.html

² https://en.wikipedia.org/wiki/Stilson_Hutchins

CROSSING OVER

¹ https://www.leslieflint.com/george-olsen/george-olsen

² https://www.leslieflint.com/david-scott-march-1966

PRAYER

¹ https://www.dailymail.co.uk/news/article-4021094/Nurse-sacked-offering-pray-patients-despite-call-equality-watchdog-end-persecution-Christians.html

² https://www.nytimes.com/1914/10/09/archives/hugh-thomas-taggart.html

³ https://lawlit.net/lp-2001/mackey.html

⁴ https://historicsites.dcpreservation.org/items/show/1286

THE NUMBERED LEVELS

¹ https://en.wikipedia.org/wiki/2_Enoch

INDEX

A

Abortion, 134, 136, 160. *See*
  miscarriage
A Case for Spirit, 100. *See*
  Sanderson, Alan
Acts (book of), 149, 186,
A Course in Miracles (ACIM,)
  history of, 34-35
Adrian VI, 212
Agnostic (agnosticism), 73, 129-130,
  171
Agrippina, Julia, 185,186
al-Danaf, Nazih, 177
Ambrose of Milan, St.
  on Jews, 153
Ames, Julia A., 54-57
  on hell, 174
  evidence for spirit
    communication, 56
  fear of spirit communication,
    107-109
  on the moment of death, 237
  MINERVA, 55-56
Analytical overlay (AOL), 93
Angel, 106, 108, 114, 141-142, 170,
  181, 237, 251, 254, 263, 269, 270
  definition of, 30

Anne of Denmark, 67
A.R., 57,58
Archbishop of Canterbury, 79, 81,
  83, 209
Archon, 45,46
Armstrong, Eliza, 53
Arthur Findlay College, 15
Atkinson, Justice, 83
Atheist (atheism), 8, 19, 22, 34, 35,
  58, 88, 126, 145, 196, 245
Atonement, 39,40, 160, 161, 175,
  188, 198, 207, 223,224, 250, 259,
  267, 270, 271
Attraction, law of, 106, 174, 200,
  215, 255
Augustine, St., 40, 158,160
  on the Bible, 159
Automatic writing, 29, 30, 33, 35,
  50, 55, 279

B

Bahati, David, Ugandan politician,
  209
Baptism. 153, 165-166. *See*
  christening
Barbanell, Maurice "Barbie", 61,
  174, 180, 230

on different realities, 61-63
ease of transition, 63
on meeting his deceased mother,
61
precognition (being in two
times), 64
reincarnation, 180-181
Bardo, 26
Beard, Paul, 60, 63, 65, 174,
on reincarnation, 180,181
Beatles, The, 189
Beaverbrook, Lord (William
Maxwell Aitken), 59
Belief, at the point of death, 130
Benedict XVI, 195
Berkowitz, David, 98, 99. *See* Son
of Sam
Beyer, Gabriel A., 114
Bhagavad Gita, 238
Bible, The, evidence for
inconsistency, 151
Biden, Joseph "Joe", 196
Big Jump, 59-60. *See* Silver Birch
Bigelow, Robert, 7
Biggs, Brandon, 92,94
Bishop of Colchester, 197
Bismarck, Otto von, 148
B.L., 15-19, 32
B.J., 14-15, 277
Blair, Anthony "Tony", 195
Blank sitting, 111
Bonaventure, St., 91
Book of Common Prayer, 128, 213
Book of Revelation, The, 106,
262,263, 265
Bradley, H. Dennis, 59
Brahman, 183
Buddha, Siddhartha Gautama, 182,
256,258
Buddhism, 157, 183, 253

Bush, George W., 195, 197

C

Caligula (Emperor), 185
Cain and Abel, 261
Campaign for Nuclear
Disarmament (CND), 197
Cardiologists, reporting NDEs, 38
Catherine of Aragon, 213
Catholic Church, 106, 147, 158, 196,
213
Celestial heavens, 44, 162,163, 182,
212, 257, 259, 265,266, 268
Chambers, Robert, 70-71
Cherrie, Marie, 60-61, 180
Christ
(In), 30, 52, 85, 138, 153, 162-163,
168, 199, 254, 258-259, 271
Christening, 22, 165. *See* baptism
Christian,
definition of, 128
Christian Fundamentalism, 145,
257
Church of England, 82,83, 95, 211,
213
Churches Fellowship for Psychical
and Spiritual Studies, 83
Civilization (film, 1916), 201, 203,
205
Claudius, 185-186
Clouds of witnesses, 212
Cocks, Michael, 39, 127-128, 160
College of Psychic Studies, 60
Comeys, John B., 255, 259
Compensation, law of, 221
Continental drift,
Jeffreys, Sir Harold, views on, 89
Continuity of existence, 109
Corinthians, (book of) 22, 161, 170,
254

INDEX

Crookes, Sir William, 70-76
  on fraud, 74
Cyrus the Great, 155

D

Daimon, 103
Daily Sketch, 59, 81
Damascus (the road to), 42,43
Daniel (Old Testament prophet),
  155, 202, 219-220
Darby, John Nelson, 168
Darkness. 9-10, 46, 97-98, 131.
  171-174, 212, 214-215, 228, 239,
  246-248, 265. See dark spirits
Darwin, Charles, 69, 71,73
Dawkins, Richard, 88, 157
David, 241-242. See Leslie Flint
"Death: A Political Essay." See
  Porteus, Beilby, 211
Death (physical)
    from a spirit perspective, 135, 237,
    205, 242.
Delphi (ancient Greek sanctuary),
  186
Demiurge, 45,46
Derek, 119-120
Derek (uncle), 19, 134
Deuteronomy, 153
Devil (the), 97-99, 104-106, 108,
  153
Direct-Voice, 51, 56-58, 76. See
  mediumship
Divine angel, 141, 268,271
Divine Love,
    meaning of, 251, 256-259
Divine right of kings, 213
Doyle, Arthur Conan, 75,
  on Jesus, 85
Doyle, James "Jimmy", 92
Drayton-Thomas, Charles, 57

Dreams,
  lucid, 173
  precognitive. 92-94. See
    premonition
  shared, 90-91
  telepathy, 90. See Vaughan, Alan
du Motier, Gilbert, Marquis de
  Lafayette, 199
Duncan, Helen, 77

E

Earth-bound, 96
Earth planes, 24, 47, 98, 131, 174,
  241, 255
Eastnor Castle, 54
Ebionites, 152,153
ectoplasm, 74-76
Ego, 109, 172, 222, 231, 236, 250
Ehrman, Bart D., 145-146, 153
Einstein, Albert, 40, 205
Elizabeth I (Queen of England), 68,
  213-216
Elameros, 188
Enoch (great grandfather of Noah),
  254
Enoch, 1, 105
Enoch, 2, 254
Entities, 8, 24, 96-98, 103-104
Ephesians, 46
Erroneous beliefs, 130,131, 148
Eugenics, 72
Evil spirits, 101, 104, 106, 108, 110,
  174, 246. See entities
Exodus, 151
Exorcism, 99,100
Extra sensory perception (ESP), 18,
  21, 87-94
Eye of a needle (the), 238
Ezekiel, 157-158

F

Faith alone (*sola fide*), 148, 153

Fall (the), "separation", 183, 261-262, 268, 271

Fallen angels. 103, 105-106. *See* watchers

Findlay, Arthur, 15, 81

Fisher, John Arbuthnot "Jacky", 53

Flint, Leslie, 57,58, 76, 95, 236, 241,242

Francis of Assisi, 91

Fraud, 7, 26, 51, 68, 74, 76,77, 159, 215

Free will, 116, 123, 157,158, 166,168, 200, 271

French, Emeline "Emily" Sofia, 51-52, 241

Funk, Robert W., 145,147

G

Gabriel (angel), 155

Gallio Annaeanus, Lucius Junius, 186

Galton, Francis, 72,74

Gandhi, Mahatma, 206

Garfield, James A., 123-124, 245

Gatty, Oliver, 84

Genesis, 137, 151, 253, 261

Gnostic (gnosis), 45-46

Gospel of Thomas, 45-47, 146, 171, 229, 268

Grayfeather, 52-53

Great gift, 161, 261-262, 267

Greene, Betty, 57, 95, 236-237, 241-242

Gregory the Great, 172

Guardian (newspaper), 131, 166

H

Hall, John (Very Revd.), Dean of Westminster Abbey, 197

Haraldsson, Erlendur, 177-179

Harari, Yuval Noah, 166-167

Harmsworth, Alfred. *See* Northcliffe, Lord, 59

Harper, Edith K.,
on Direct-Voice mediumship, 57
on Stead, William, 53

Hart, David Bentley, 46

Harvey, George W., 247,249

Hawking, Stephen,
on life after death, 131

Hell,
definition of, 172-174, 241, 257, 264
"Nature of Hell" (Evangelical Alliance Report), 172

Henry VIII, 213

Heretic (heresy), 41, 153, 158

Heyde, Revd. George W., 240

Heyde, Olivia Whitehill, 240

High spirit, 30, 115,118, 199

Hinduism, 157, 182, 253

Hitchens, Christopher,
on heaven, 88

Hitler, Adolf, on Martin Luther, 148

Home, Daniel Dunglas, 70-76

Homosexuality, 211

Hood, Helen "Miss E.", 54-56

Horne, Janet, 68

Hudson, Kate, General Secretary of the Campaign for Nuclear Disarmament (CND), 197

Hutchins, Stilson, 225, 228,229

INDEX

I

I.D., 20-21, 119
Ignatius of Antioch, 47
Immortal (immortality),
　meaning of, 117, 136, 161, 163,
　168, 171, 261-271
Ince, Thomas, 201. *See Civilization*
In Christ,
　meaning of, 30, 52, 161-163
Infidel, 130 *See* atheism
Inge, William Ralph, 148
Innocent I, 158
Iraq War (2003), 195-196, 211
Isiah, 97, 154
Islam,
　on judgment, 220
　Original Sin, 157
Islamic State, 196

J

Jackie, 21, 244
James VI & I
Jeffreys, Sir Harold,
　on continental drift, 89
Jesus,
　on attack and murder, 198, 207,
　216
　baptism, 166
　chosen ones, 270
　death wishes, 229
　divine angel, 141, 268-270
　divine love, 162-164, 204, 213,
　269-270
　disciples, 156
　dead soul, 205
　demons/devils, 106
　free will, 167
　God, 138
　Sonship, 152, 164, 165
　image of God, 141-142
　in Christ, meaning of, 162-163
　judgment/judgment day, 221-224,
　219
　meditation, 249
　Messiah, 156
　miracles, 40, 223
　Original Sin, 160
　prayer, 249, 250, 258
　purpose of physical life, 135
　reincarnation, 182
　salvation, 137, 156, 162, 171, 198,
　207, 222-223
　Satan, 106
　sonship, 164-165, 249,
　soul individualization
　(incarnation), 135, 136
　spirit influence, 104
　spirit possession, 104
　Trinity (the), 152
　vicarious atonement, 188-189
　war, 198, 203-205
　why he chose Padgett, 116-118
Jesus Seminar, 146-147. *See* Westar
　Institute
Job (Book of), 105
John Paul II, on Hell, 172
John (Gospel of), 21, 47, 151-152,
　164, 210
John, St.
　on Book of Revelation, 263-265
　Emanuel Swedenborg, 113
　end of the world, 168, 169. *See*
　Rapture (the)
　Jewish prophets, 264
　judgment (sowing and reaping),
　169
　Kingdom of Heaven (the), 266
　law of communication and
　rapport, 112
　prayer vs. works, 250

problems with communication, 113
Rapture (the), 168-169
two heavens, 266
warning about séances and false spirits, 107
warning for leaders about war, 198
Josephus, Titus Flavius, 43-44
Judaism (Jews), 43-44, 148, 152-153, 155-157, 186, 188, 198, 220, 245, 263-264, 279
Judas Iscariot, 188
Judgment, 1, 185-186, 195, 203, 217,224, 254
Judgment day, 217, 219, 221, 223
Julia's Bureau, 54-57

K

Kardec, Allan, 75
Karma, 157, 182, 253
Khaddage, Mrs., 177-178
Khaddage, Fuad Assad, 178
Khomeini, Ruhollah, 197
Kingdom of Heaven, 47, 150, 156, 166, 169, 175, 183, 187, 238, 254, 267
Kirill, Patriarch (Russian Orthodox Church), 196

L

Lambeth Palace, 79, 81,83
Lampert, Vincent,
on exorcism, 99
Lang, Cosmo Gordon
dangers of mediumship, 96-97
dangers of spirit possession, 96-97
influencing the living, 96-97
importance of prayer, 96-97
report on Spiritualism, 79-84

Lavoisier, Antoine,
on meteorites, 88
Left Behind, (novels and TV series) 168-169
Lennon, John, 189
Leonard, Gladys Osborne, 59
Leo X, 212
Leo XIII, 105
Levels. *See* spheres, planes, worlds, 199, 219, 222, 241, 253-259
Leviticus, 22, 210
Life between life, 179
Light (newspaper), 79, 85
Lincoln, Abraham, 120,121
Linnean Society (of London), 71
Living agent psi (LAP), 21
Locusta, "The Crayfish", 185
Lodge, Sir Oliver, 59, 75,76
LORD (in the Old Testament, a title used to refer to God). *See* Yahweh, 151
Lucid dreaming therapy (LDT), 173
Lucifer, 106
Lucilius, 186-187
Luke (Gospel of), 103, 146, 151, 154, 156, 175, 181, 268
Luke, St.
on the authenticity of the Bible, 149-150
belief at death, 130
Jesus as Messiah, 150
Original Sin, 159
reincarnation, 181-182
Lunatic, 97
Luther, Martin
Catholic laymen, 212
on communicating with mediums, 149
divine right, 212
erroneous beliefs, 148

Jews, 148
popes in the spirit world, 212
spiritual darkness, 148
Luvilla, Julia, 158

M

Mackey, Franklin H., 245-249
Maiden Tribute of Modern Babylon
(The)
Majority Report, 82
Many Mansions, 47, 128, 253, 266
Mark (Gospel of), 45, 151, 153-154
Mars, 13
Materialist (Materialism), 8, 38, 87-89, 129, 167
Matrix, The (film), 40,41
Matthew (Gospel of), 146, 154, 198, 238
Matthew, St., 39, 138, 146, 154, 191, 198, 238
Meditation, 245, 249
Medium (Mediumship), 7, 15, 51, 74, 76, 84, 89
Messiah, 43, 48, 150, 152, 154,156, 263-264
Meteorites,
    Lavoisier, Antoine's views on, 88, 89
MINERVA, 55,56. See Francis Willard
Miracle, 29, 34, 39,40, 42, 73, 104, 147, 160, 171, 175, 202, 223, 250, 258, 267, 271
Miscarriage, 134. See Abortion
Missing Time, 100, 232
Mitzvot (Divine Instructions/
    Commandments), 153
Morgan, Eugene, 33
Moscow Times, 196
Moss, George, 24

N

Nag Hammadi, 45,48
Narrow gate (the), 191, 238
NASA, 88
Near-death experience (NDE), 7, 23, 38, 182, 213
Nero, 44, 185,186
New age teachings, 183
New York Times, 146, 225, 245
Nirvana, 183, 254
Nobel Prize, 50, 75, 94
North Berwick witch trials (1590–1592), Scotland, 68
Northcliffe, Lord. See Harmsworth, Alfred "the Chief", 59-60
Nonlocal, 9

O

Oaten, Earnest W.,
    on seances and mediums, 83, 109
Oblivion, fear of, 127-128, 227
Olsen, George,
    on the physical world, 237
    life in the spirit world, 236-237, 242
Original Sin, 116, 157,160, 175
Out-of-body experience (OBE), 7, 38, 182, 202, 213, 254
Owen, Louise, 59

P

Pacifist (pacifism), 201-202, 205
Padgett, Helen,
    on arriving in the spirit world, 240
    on meeting her deceased parents, 240-241
Padgett, James E., 29-33, 35, 111, 116-117

Padgett, John (James's father), 109, 246
Palmstierna, Baron Erik, 79, 84-85
Past life, 177-178, 180-181. *See* Reincarnation
Paul, St, 22, 42-43, 94, 147, 150, 157, 160, 186, 254
  on the Bible, 161
  resurrection, 169-170
  great gift, 161
  vicarious atonement, 161
Paul VI, 105
Peak-in-Darien Experience, 38
Peek, Kim, 49
Pelagius
  on Original Sin, 158, 160
Pentecost, 157
Pentecostal, 126
Perfect Man, 131, 141-142, 256-266, 268, 271
Perry, Richard Ross,
  on spirits in darkness, 226
  on Stilson Hutchins, 228-229
  on suicide, 226-227
Planes, 47, 131, 174, 241, 253, 255-256. *See* Spheres, Levels
Planck, Max, 94
Plato, 45, 187, 253
Pliny the Younger,
  on Christians, 44
Pompeo, Michael, 168-169
Pope,
  Adrian VI, 212
  Benedict XVI, 195-196
  Francis, 160, 196
  Gregory I (Gregory the Great), 172
  Innocent I, 158
  John Paul II, 172
  Leo X, 212

Leo XIII, 105
Paul VI, 105
Possession, 68, 99-100, 103-107. *See* Spirit Attachment
Post-Traumatic Stress Disorder (PTSD), 173
Poverty,
  the nature of, in the spirit world, 10, 39, 47, 185, 200, 206, 229
Prayer,
  as currency, 251, 257
  for divine love, 258
  to progress after death, 97, 112
  in relation to immortality, 161
Pru, 100
Psalms, 249
Psi, 21, 89
Psychic force, 70, 75
Psychic News (newspaper), 60, 81-83
Psychic phone lines, 109
Psychic Press, 81
Psychic stigma, 67-77
Putin, Vladimir, 196-197
Premonition, 64, 90, 92-94, 103
Prophecy, 93, 154-155, 264

Q

Quaker, 264
Quran, 42, 220, 238, 253

R

Randall, Edward C., 51,52, 80
Randi, James,
  on million-dollar challenge, 77
Rapport, 24, 107, 112, 116, 245, 249
Rapture (the), 168-169
Red light, 76
Reincarnation, 39, 84, 128, 177,178, 180,183, 257
Remote Viewing, 7, 89

INDEX

Reports on Biblical Figures
Communicating, 38-39, 42
Resurrection, 169-171
Richet, Charles,
on fraud, 76
ectoplasm, 75
Riddle, Albert Gallatin, 34, 109-110,
119-123, 226-227
on Jesus, 122
on material possessions, 239
Robertson, Marion Gordon "Pat", 146
Rollins, Ann,
on baptism, 165
spheres, 256
out-of-body experiences, 256
Robinson, Sugar Ray,
premonition, 92
Romans (Book of), 157-158, 161
Royal Society (The), 72, 74
Russian Invasion of Ukraine (2022),
196
Russian Orthodox Church, 196. See
Kirill

S

Sanderson, Alan, 100
Salyards, Joseph, 34, 109-110, 124,
130
observations of people arriving in
the spirit world, 239
Samuel (Old Testament prophet),
on the Crucifixion, 188
Sanhedrin, 43, 188
Satan, the nature of, 105-106
Satanic Bible, 99
Savant, 49
Schucman, Helen, 29, 34,35, 38,
41,42, 114
Séance, 31-32, 51, 57-60, 70-74, 76,
80, 83, 107, 109, 228, 236

danger of, 96-97, 107-108
Seneca, Lucius Annaeus the
Younger, 185,187, 189
Serial killer, 98, 210
Skeptic (skepticism), 22, 51, 58, 73,
83, 178, 211-212
Shakespeare, William.
(Hamlet), 127
Smith, Frederick Edwin, 1st Earl
of Birkett (also known as Lord
Birkett), 57
Silver Birch, 60, 180, 208, 230. See
Big Jump.
on Jesus (the Nazarene), 60
on suicide, 230
reincarnation, 180
Silver Beetles, The, 189. See The
Beatles
Smith, Rev. Samuel, 114
Society for Psychical Research,
83,84
Socrate, 103, 187s
Somerset, Lady Henry, 54,55
Son of Sam. See Berkowitz, David,
98
Soul
dead, 139, 205
definition, 142
individualization (incarnation),
135
Sphere(s), 30, 47, 52, 117, 123-124,
163, 169, 172, 174, 182. See Levels,
Planes, Worlds.
celestial spheres, 30, 47, 169, 199,
256
first sphere, 255
second sphere, 30, 255-256, 259
third sphere, 123, 229, 254, 256-
257. See Third Heaven
fourth sphere, 256

fifth sphere, 256
sixth sphere, 163, 182, 200, 256-258
seventh sphere, 52, 253-254, 256,
Spirit,
attachment, 99-100, 181. *See* Possession
dark, 173, 236, 248
definition of, 142
team (band), 107, 109-110, 123-124, 148, 215, 236, 245-246, 248-249
world, 138-139, 141-142, 152, 163, 171, 180, 182-183, 187, 199, 203-205, 212-216, 221, 239-241, 249-251, 262, 271
spiritually dead, 98, 137
Spiritualism, 58, 73, 79-85, 96, 248
seven principles of, 85
Spiritism, 84
Jesus, according to, 85
Spirit Release Therapy (SRT), 100
Spiritualists' National Union, 15
Stead, William Thomas, 52-57, 107
on God, 53
on Julia's Bureau, 54
Stead, William (Jr.) "Willie", 56
"Stead Act", 53
Stephen, The Martyr, 39
Stevenson, Ian, 178
Stone, Leslie R., 32-33
Stuart, Judge Dean,
on French, 51
Suicide, 109, 186, 217, 225, 227, 229, 231, 244
Sunday People (newspaper), 59
Surveys, on religion
2001 World Values Survey, 126
2019 Harvard Divinity Bulletin, 126
2022 Gallup Survey, 126
2022 Levada Center Survey, 126
Swaffer, Hannan, 59-60
Swedenborg, Emanuel, 29, 113, 157, 280
on hell, 173, 174
on his failings, 115
reincarnation, 181
Synchronicities, 23, 128

T

Table tipping
Tabor, James T., 147
Tacitus,
on Christians, 44
Taft, William Howard, 53
Taggart, Hugh Thomas, 245-249
Temperance Union, 54, 56
Thessalonians, 168,
Thetford, William, 34
Third Heaven, 123, 229, 254, 256-257. *See* spheres
Thirty-Nine Articles of Religion, 158, 213
Thomas (Gospel of), 45-47, 146, 171, 229, 268
Time (the nature of), 60, 63-65, 172, 173, 255,258
Titanic (RMS), 53
Torah, 44, 151, 153
Trinity (the), 116, 151-152
True Gospel Revealed Anew by Jesus (series), history of, 33
Trump, Donald J., 93,94, 197
Two Worlds (newsletter), 83

U

UFO, 90-91
Unconscious medium, 97
Underhill, Evelyn, 80

INDEX

Underhill, Francis, 80-81

V

Vatican (the), 195-196
Vaughan, Alan,
  on dream telepathy, 90-91
Vicarious Atonement, 160-161, 175
Virtual reality (VR), 9, 266
Vonnegut, Jr., Kurt, 90

W

War, 60, 79, 84, 195-208, 211, 216,
  219, 257
  war hawk, 106, 169
Wedding Banquet (parable), 267-
  268, 270
Wallace, Alfred Russel, 71,72
Walsh, Stan, 38, 102
Washington, George, 120, 199-201,
  257
Washington Post, 229
Watchers, 105. *See* Fallen Angels
Welby, Justin, Archbishop of
  Canterbury (2013–2024), 209
Wells, H. G. (Herbert George), 59
Wesley, Rev. John, 114
Westar Institute, 146. *See* Jesus
  Seminar
White Throne Judgment, 262
Wide Gate (The), 191, 193
Wilhelm II, Kaiser (1888–1918)
Willard, Francis, 54, 56
Williams, Samuel, 173
Wilson, Estelle Stead, 55
Wilson, Woodrow, 201, 203
Witch, 68
Witchcraft Act,
  1542, 67
  1604, 68
  1735, 68

Woods, George, 57, 95-96, 236, 241,
  242
Worlds, 9-10, 63, 96, 126, 142, 251,
  253, 256, 258. *See* Levels, Planes,
  Spheres
Wriedt, Etta, 56-57

X

Xavier, Francisco Cândido "Chico",
  50
  on Jesus, 50
Xenoglossy, 39

Y

Yahweh, 151, 210. *See* LORD

Z

Zammit, Victor & Wendy, 77

www.ingramcontent.com/pod-product-compliance
Lightning Source LLC
Chambersburg PA
CBHW021135090426
42740CB00008B/794